THE HOPI CHILD

THE UNIVERSITY OF VIRGINIA INSTITUTE FOR RESEARCH IN THE SOCIAL SCIENCES

John Lloyd Newcomb, B.A., C.E., D.Sc., LL.D.
President of the University

Wilson Gee, M.A., Ph.D., D.Sc., LL.D.
Director of the Institute

The Hopi Child

BY

WAYNE DENNIS

SCIENCE EDITIONS ®

John Wiley & Sons, Inc., New York

PREFACE

UPON REACHING a decision to conduct a study of the child in an American Indian culture, we cast about for a suitable group upon which to direct our attention. We wished to select a society which had maintained to the greatest degree its aboriginal condition. Upon good advice our search soon became centered upon the Southwest as an area in which primitive groups still live in a fashion quite similar to that of their pre-Columbian ancestors. The following pages will show to what extent the primitive customs are, and to what extent they are not, preserved in the modern life of the pueblos. We have not regretted our general choice of Pueblo culture, nor our selection of the Hopi from among the various Pueblo tribes.

Our observations were made during the summer months of 1937 and 1938. During these periods we (Mrs. Dennis, our daughter Mary, and myself) lived in a native house in New Oraibi. In consequence, a great deal of our observational data refer to behavior seen in this village, which is the most Americanized of the Hopi towns. The facts will show that this Americanization is not pronounced.

By working with informants, we obtained much information concerning Hotavila also. Since Hotavila is probably the most conservative of the Hopi pueblos, we did not find it feasible to live there. We were fortunate, however, to find admirable informants who were residents of Hotavila, but with whom we could work in privacy outside of the village.

Our information comes primarily from the two villages just mentioned. In addition, some data were secured relative to Mishongnovi and Shungopavi. We have, of course, consulted the writings of others upon all of the Hopi groups.

In presenting an account of the behavioral development of the child in an Indian pueblo, we shall divide our material into two main divisions. Our first task will be to picture the world which

v

surrounds the individual who is born into Hopi society. Later we shall try to show how the Hopi child behaves as he faces his cultural milieu. This is an arbitrary and practical division, since environment and response interact at every point. Child-rearing practices and child behavior bear an intimate relationship. It is scarcely possible to describe the methods of treating the child without mentioning the behavior with which they are designed to cope, nor is it easy to deal with responses apart from the situations in which they develop. For these reasons we shall avoid making our division of topics too rigid.

In such a report the anthropological description of child care is inevitably more complete than is the psychological account of child behavior. It is relatively easy to describe the general pattern of child care in a society, but to investigate the behavior which issues from the pattern is an endless task. If three generations of child psychologists have not yet completely described the behavior of the child of our Occidental civilization, it will not be expected that we can give a thorough account of the Hopi child within the period which has been at our disposal. Our work is admittedly unfinished, nor could it be otherwise. We hope that it will be preparatory to further researches. Incomplete as it is, we believe it best to present it as it now stands, because of the need of such data at the present time.

In the conduct of this study we have received aid from many sources. To the Social Science Research Council we are indebted for the opportunity of a year's study in social anthropology which was indispensable to the investigation, and for the opportunity of spending two summers in the field. To Drs. Leslie Spier, Clark Wissler, and the late Edward Sapir we owe much for background, and for counsel and advice. The Institute for Research in the Social Sciences at the University of Virginia provided freedom from teaching for part of the period during which the present manuscript was in preparation, and furnished valuable clerical assistance. Mrs. Dennis shared in all of the field work, much of which would have been impossible without her assistance, since most of the material had to be gathered through women informants who would not readily have given it to an isolated male investigator. We wish to express gratitude to these informants. They, like all Pueblo informants, prefer not to be thanked by name. Numerous favors were received at the hands of several members of the Indian Service; these too prefer not to be mentioned as sources of information. For critical reading of various portions of the manuscript in various phases of preparation, we express our appreciation to Mrs. Dennis, Dr. R. T. Sollenberger, Dr. Verne F. Ray, and Dr. R. W. Russell. Finally, for a reading of the entire manuscript, with the resulting suggestions, we are indebted to Dr. J. F. Dashiell.

WAYNE DENNIS

UNIVERSITY OF VIRGINIA

CONTENTS

An appendix has been added to this edition and follows the Bibliography.

ILLUSTRATIONS

PART I

THE WORLD
OF THE
HOPI CHILD

CHAPTER I

THE GENERAL SETTING

GEOGRAPHICAL SETTING

IN northern Arizona, east of the Grand Canyon, lies a high plateau which slopes gradually southward. About ninety miles south of the Arizona-Utah boundary the even declination of this land mass is broken by long irregular tongues of stone which have resisted erosion. To the north they become a part of the higher plateau of which we have spoken. Southward, relatively unbroken dry plains stretch from the base of these cliffs to the Little Colorado River and to the San Francisco Mountains near Flagstaff.

For centuries the Hopi Indians, who are one group of descendants of the pre-historic cliff dwellers, have lived at the southern termination of these rocky mesas. Their custom of living in permanent villages and of depending upon agriculture for a livelihood goes back to the time of their far distant ancestors. Corn, their chief crop, they plant near the washes that carry away the surface water which occasionally falls upon the arid plateau. Water for themselves the Hopi obtain from springs which occur at the foot of, or part way up the sides of the mesas. The geographical features of the country are such that only at the sites chosen by the Hopi can water sufficient to supply a small village be found. The Navaho, who live in the still more waterless region surrounding the Hopi mesas, manage to survive by living in small family units rather than in larger communities and by moving about when pasture and water fail.

Before the Navaho became numerous the Hopi seldom were subject to attack and consequently built their villages at the base of the cliffs near the springs and near their fields. The increasing troublesomeness of the Navaho finally caused the Hopi to move to the positions on top of the mesas, which were easily defended, although these locations made the work of the community much more difficult. Due to the protection of the United States, the Hopi have been free

3

of danger from the Navaho for fifty years, yet the majority of the inhabitants still live in the old picturesque sites [1] which resemble those often chosen for medieval fortresses.

The mesas which are now inhabited are three, although during the early Spanish period one pueblo, Awotobi, was located on still another mesa. The mesas have been named in the order in which they were approached by American explorers, so that the easternmost is called First Mesa, the next, Middle or Second Mesa, and the most western, the chief concern of this study, is Third Mesa.

That the Hopi Reservation is placed approximately in the center of the great desert region which has been set aside for the use of the Navaho has helped the Hopi preserve their privacy and their cultural integrity. The chief influences to which primitive groups are ordinarily subjected at the present time come not from other tribes but from the white man. Even today the Hopi have but little contact with any white persons except government employees. The nearest American settlement and the nearest railroad are sixty miles from the Hopi villages. The reservation can be entered only by means of unsurfaced roads which do not recommend themselves to the timid driver.

THE PEOPLE

The Pueblo Indians are short of stature. Hrdlička, who has presented measurements of 105 men and 34 women, found the former to range between 4 ft. 10 in. and 5 ft. 9 in. and the latter between 4 ft. 8 in. and 5 ft. 3 in., with average statures of 5 ft. 4½ in. and 4 ft. 11½ in. respectively. The children are correspondingly below white standards at all ages.

The general appearance of the Hopi is shown by the various Plates in this and later chapters.

The total population of the three mesas is roughly 3000, and this has been the approximate number of inhabitants throughout the major part of the historic period. While the number often has been temporarily decreased by famine and by disease, it seems never to have greatly exceeded 3000 in times of prosperity.

[1] The number of villages depends upon whether or not recent outgrowths of the old villages are counted as separate towns. In reaching the total of eleven, we have included the following towns : on First Mesa, Walpi, Sichumovi and Hano; on Second Mesa, Mishongnovi, Shipaulovi and Shungopovi; on Third Mesa, Old Oraibi, New Oraibi, Hotavila, Bacobi and Moenkopi.

Historical Setting [2]

In 1540 when Coronado explored the territory which is now New Mexico and Arizona he heard of Indian villages far to the north of those which he himself was visiting, and dispatched two of his subordinates, Tobar and Padilla, to inspect these northern towns. This order by Coronado led to the first contact between white men and the Indian groups which have variously been called Tusayan, Moki and Hopi, but which are now known by the latter name.

Tobar and Padilla remained several days among the Hopi and gained considerable information from them. It was from the Hopi that the Spaniards first learned of the existence of the Grand Canyon. With respect to the Hopi themselves, the white visitors found that these people lived much as did the town or Pueblo Indians which they had seen to the south. The Hopi towns varied in size from villages of a few hundred persons to one of perhaps three thousand inhabitants. The houses were of roughly dressed stone, which was sometimes plastered with adobe. They did not stand apart but were joined together into large structures which in some cases reached the height of four stories.

Most of the towns stood at the foot of or part way up the sides of the mesas. Oraibi, however, was on top of a mesa, as nearly all of the towns are at present. This village is notable for the fact that it is the only Hopi pueblo inhabited in 1540 which is still occupied today. Archaeologists have determined that Oraibi was built as early as 1290, and perhaps earlier, and that by virtue of this fact, it is the oldest continuously inhabited town in the United States.

The Spaniards found that the Hopi, like the other Pueblo peoples, were primarily farmers. The staple crop was corn. Beans and squash were also grown, and use was made of many wild plants. Hunting was engaged in, but it did not furnish a major portion of the food. The only domesticated animals, aside from dogs, were turkeys and captive eagles, both of these species being kept for their feathers rather than for their meat. Cotton was raised, and beautiful fabrics were woven from it.

[2] Most of the historical material here cited is to be found in the *Handbook of American Indians*, pp. 560–562. Other facts are from an article by F. H. Cushing, J. W. Fewkes and E. C. Parsons in the *Amer. Anthrop.*, 1922, 24, 253–298. A third source is the special report on American Indians which was a part of the 1890 census.

The Spaniards, as was their custom, claimed the newly discovered territory in the name of the Spanish crown. In 1598, Onate, who had been appointed governor of the territory, visited the Hopi, and caused the Hopi to admit their vassalage to Spain and to swear allegiance to the King.

Certain advantages soon accrued to the Hopi from their contacts with the Spaniards and chief among these was the introduction of certain domestic animals and of fruit trees. Although horses were brought into the region, they never became very important to the Hopi, as these townspeople, unlike many American tribes, moved about relatively little. On the other hand the sheep and the goats which the Spaniards introduced soon came to furnish a dependable supply of meat to replace the diminishing game. The Hopi learned to weave the wool into blankets and dresses. The peach trees which the Spaniards brought are today one of the most valued possessions in a country where native fruits are scarce.

The Spaniards, however, were more interested in the introduction of their religion than they were in the improvement of agriculture. In 1629 a mission was established at Awotobi, and soon thereafter missions were built on the other mesas as well. These activities were not specific to the Hopi, as missions were constructed in nearly all other pueblos, usually by the forced labor of the unwilling converts. Christianity would have affected the Hopi but little if it had meant merely the addition of new supernaturals and new rituals, for the Hopi are tolerant in these respects. But the priests attempted to put an end to the Hopi ceremonies. We shall have occasion later to see how important are these ceremonies to the pueblo dwellers.

In 1680 the pueblos plotted a joint action against the white residents. The missions were destroyed, and many Spaniards were killed, although a portion of them escaped. The Hopi joined in this action against the conquerors, and entirely rid themselves of the priests who were the only Spanish residents among the Hopi. We may say, parenthetically, that joint action is not traditional among the pueblos of the Southwest, and neither before nor since has there been a cooperative movement toward a common purpose among so many of these communities.

Spain was far away and her military forces were needed in many lands. It was twelve years after the revolt that soldiers came to

PLATE I

A HOPI PRIEST MAKING A KACHINA DOLL.

avenge the death of their countrymen, and to make a complete re-
conquest under the leadership of De Vargas. Missions were again
established, and in many of the Southwestern pueblos they still
stand. Among the Hopi, the Awotobi mission was reestablished in
1700, but soon thereafter Awotobi was abandoned, and it has never
been reoccupied. It is difficult to reconstruct an event in the history
of an illiterate people after an interval of more than two hundred
years, so we cannot say with certainty why Awotobi ceased to be
an inhabited town. The Hopi say that it was partially destroyed
and many of its people killed by the other villages because the
Awotobi people were wicked. It is altogether possible that its abandonment was forced because the Awotobi residents were becoming
friendly with the new priests. At any rate, it is clear that this
incident marked the end of Catholic missions among the Hopi, and
the virtual end of Spanish influence with this tribe. From the beginning the Hopi were on the periphery of the sphere of Spanish
conquest in the Southwest, and they were never as subject to Spanish domination as the more southern and eastern pueblos. In no
sense were they profitable to their conquerors, nor was the work
of the missionaries markedly successful. It is not surprising therefore to find that the Spanish governors paid but little attention to
the Hopi after 1700, nor is it surprising to find that the Hopi,
apart from making good use of European animals and European
plants, showed but little effect of 160 years of desultory but compulsory contact with the successors of the conquistadores.

If the Hopi were henceforward neglected by the Spaniards, they
were, as if for counterbalance, increasingly annoyed by the Utes
and the Navaho. These tribes raided the Hopi fields and carried
away livestock from the corrals. At times, they attacked the villages themselves. The mounting troublesomeness of the Navaho,
who were relative newcomers to the region, led the Hopi to move
to more easily defended sites on the top of the mesas, but this did
not protect their fields or their livestock. As late as 1819 the Hopi
asked the Spaniards, who still were the nominal rulers of the country, to protect them from the Navaho, but no aid was sent by the
authorities. It is doubtful whether all of the soldiers in the Southwest at that time could have succeeded in stopping the Navaho
raids.

When, following the Mexican War of 1846, the Southwest be-

came a part of the United States, the Navaho were still the chief
enemies of the Hopi. The first Indian agent to the new area did
not dare to travel from Zuni to the Hopi villages because of these
marauders and raiders. But if the agent could not get to the Hopi,
the Hopi managed somehow to send a delegation through the territory of the hostile tribe to the distant governmental seat at Santa
Fe. The representatives of the Hopi came to inquire concerning
the intentions of their new masters, and to complain bitterly of
the depredations of the Navaho.

The Americans themselves soon had reason to object to the
activities of the Navaho, and in 1864 Kit Carson finally managed
to trap a large part of them in Canyon De Chelly. He defeated and
captured them, and marched them 300 miles to a disastrous intern-
ment of five years at Fort Sumner, New Mexico. At the end of
this period, the Navaho promised that if they were permitted to
return to their lands they would never raid again—a promise
which has been kept with remarkable faithfulness, and which is as
binding upon the Navaho of today as it was to the leaders, now
dead, who made the promise. Thus one of the chief benefits that
came to the Hopi as a result of American sovereignty in the Southwest was the Hopi's new security from spoilation by the Navaho.

For many years relations between the Hopi and the Indian
Service were slight. There were contacts, of course, but in the main
these consisted of visits by the Indian agents which resulted in reports to Washington but which did not influence the status of the
Hopi. Since the Hopi had depended upon game only in a minor
way, and since flocks of sheep had largely compensated for the
decrease in game, the Indian Bureau did not have to issue rations
to the Hopi as it did to the Plains Indians. The Hopi continued
to live much as they had lived for seven centuries or more. Since
no gold or silver was discovered on their reservation, and since
their land was too much like a desert for any white man to want
it, the Hopi were affected practically not at all by the "building
of the West." In the remainder of this volume, we shall show that
even today the Hopi live a life that is essentially the life of their ancestors and not the life of the Americans who surround their desert
reservation.

THIRD MESA

For centuries Third Mesa had the distinction of being a mesa with only one town, Oraibi, and yet it was the most populous of all Hopi towns. Because it was the most western, the most remote from American cities, and the most distant from the Agency in Keams Canyon, it was for a long while but little subject to American influence, and for this reason, and perhaps from tradition as well, it was the most conservative of all of the villages. Today the unity of Third Mesa has disappeared. It has not one village but four (five, if Moenkopi be counted). On it stands the most conservative village among the Hopi, Hotavila; the village which is probably the most Americanized, New Oraibi; and the village which is most nearly a ruin, Old Oraibi, mother of Bacobi and Moenkopi as well as those just mentioned.

This division can best be understood by following its development. About 1893 the government agents began to encourage the Oraibi people to move off of their high mesa, so as to be nearer their fields and in proximity to locations where wells could be dug. This encouragement took the form of offering free building materials and occasional government jobs to anyone who would settle at the foot of the mesa. A few families did move to the site selected, which is about one mile distant from the old village. This offshoot of Old Oraibi is called New Oraibi. It has steadily grown until today it is more populous than Old Oraibi itself. The new high school which serves all of the Hopi villages is located at New Oraibi. A government physician and an agricultural adviser have their homes there. The new town has a post-office and three trading posts or general stores, whereas Old Oraibi has none.

The movement to New Oraibi has been slow and has not caused any open dissension. This was not the case with the divisions of opinion which led to the founding of Hotavila and Bacobi.

In the years shortly after 1900 the village chief at Oraibi was friendly to the whites, and was in favor of sending the children to school. (The first school for Hopi children was opened in Keams Canyon in 1887.) The chief in no sense advocated the giving up of Hopi ways of life, but rather, he was in favor of cooperating with the government instead of stubbornly resisting all suggestions. The conservative element took the contrary view. This situation led to several years of dissension in the village, to bickering and quarreling and even to a slight amount of open strife, and to an inability of the factions to cooperate in carrying out the all-important ceremonies. Finally, on September 28, 1906, the conservatives withdrew from Oraibi and founded a new village at a spot called Hotavila. We cannot follow in detail the history of this village. One of their first acts was to refuse to yield their children to the school authorities. This led to a visit by the U. S. troops and to the imprisonment of most of the men for several months. The women of the village were thus forced to live through a cold winter in temporary shelters, providing themselves with fuel.

After the first bitter experience, Hotavila found that it must send its children to school. (Attendance is not as compulsory today as it was in 1906.) In other respects, Hotavila has compromised but little with the white man. It has persistently refused to have water piped into the village, although water is pumped to the school a quarter of a mile distant. Instead, the women of the village carry all the water which is needed from a spring below the level of the town.

Bacobi was formed by another dissension in 1910. It is located on top of the mesa about five miles from Old Oraibi, and one mile from Hotavila. Moenkopi, located on the Little Colorado River, forty miles west of Third Mesa, has grown slowly and steadily because the river provides water for irrigation, an agricultural advantage not possessed by any other Hopi town.

Of the villages of Third Mesa, three are on top of the mesa—Old Oraibi, Hotavila, and Bacobi. Living on top of the mesa is not as uneconomical to the people of Hotavila and of Bacobi as it is for those of Old Oraibi and for the inhabitants of First and Second Mesas. In the latter villages nearly all of the fields border the arroyos far below the mesas and are sometimes as much as seven miles from their respective towns but at Hotavila and at Bacobi many of the fields are on top of the mesa, near the villages. A final advantage of Hotavila and of Bacobi is that by being on top of the mesa they are near to their source of firewood, for piñon and cedar do not grow at lower altitudes.

Old Oraibi today is an inhabited ruin. Because of the loss of population, occasioned by the settlement of New Oraibi, Hotavila, Bacobi, and Moenkopi many of the houses of Old Oraibi are unoccupied

PLATE II

HOTAVILA: *The village lies on top of the mesa and blends with the rock from which it is built. Below the town are the terraced gardens and a corn field. A peach orchard grows in the sand dunes.*

and are gradually disintegrating. The population of Old Oraibi is small, being only about 125 today.

It will require further chapters to develop a description of the culture of the Third Mesa. We shall first describe Hotavila. While it is the most conservative village, it is the town of which the anthropologists have written least. In describing Hotavila we can achieve a double purpose, that of picturing in a general way the older Hopi culture and that of adding to the anthropological literature an account of Hotavila in particular. Against this background, we shall later sketch some of the differences between Hotavila and certain other towns.

CHAPTER II

HOTAVILA CULTURE [1]

Economic Life

A T Hotavila the line which determines the ownership of property and the division of labor lies between the house and the field. It is the man who owns fields [2] and tills them, while the woman possesses the house and its contents and has the task of feeding the members of her household.

Earlier we have indicated that the cultivation of aboriginal varieties of maize and beans is the main economic activity. This work is done by the men. Women are seldom seen in the fields,[3] except at harvest time, when the entire family may join in the harvesting. The women, however, cultivate the small terraced and irrigated gardens which lie just below the Hotavila spring. Another outdoor

---

[1] There is practically no material on Hotavila in print; therefore there are very few references to other authors in the pages which follow. However, the customs of Hotavila are almost identical with the former practices of Old Oraibi, and those in turn are very similar to the ways of other Hopi villages. We have not attempted to call attention at all points to the similarities and the differences between Hotavila and other towns, but we have appended a full bibliography of anthropological writings on the Hopi. The references there cited contain a wealth of comparative material.

[2] Here is an interesting contrast between Hotavila custom and the custom of Old Oraibi. In Old Oraibi, and among the Hopi generally, the fields belong to the clan and are apportioned among clan members, whereas at Hotavila the fields belong to specific individuals and not to a clan. The contrast is striking because the Hotavila situation is in the direction of current trends among the Hopi, whereas Hotavila prides itself on honoring the old ways. We believe the contradiction can be solved in the following way, although we failed to question informants on this point. According to old practice, clan ownership was traditional in regard to fields which had been used for centuries. But if a man "made" a field, that is, cleared it, it belonged to him, although it probably reverted to his clan at his death. Since Hotavila is a new village, there are no traditional fields. All of the fields have been "made," in most cases by men who are still living and still are tilling them.

[3] Widows occasionally cultivate small plots, but more often their male relatives do this work for them.

12

occupation of the women is that of carrying the household water supply from this spring.

While the crops which are in the fields belong to the husband, once the harvest is stored in the house it becomes a part of the household property and is under the control of the wife.[4] Since the equivalent of one or more yearly crops is often kept in reserve against an always possible drought, this means that the wife is in no sense dependent day-by-day upon a husband, although she could not manage to live independently over a period of many years.

The men and boys shepherd the flocks of sheep and goats, whereas among the neighboring Navaho this work is performed chiefly by women. The Hopi men also bring in the firewood, although it is sometimes chopped by the women after it has been hauled to the village.

The husband does the heavy construction work in the building of Hopi houses, but the woman, in native thought, pays the man for building the house by feeding him while it is being constructed and hence owns it when it is completed. Upon her death, the house is inherited by one of her daughters. A house never becomes the property of a man unless he builds it before he marries, in which event it is said to be his. This probably happened very seldom in the past but it is occasionally done today.

A woman who owns a house plasters it on the inside, and sometimes on the outside, by the use of a special clay found nearby.

A house may be of only one room and rarely has more than three rooms. Hotavila houses are joined together, as in former days,[5] but rooms are seldom built on the roofs, so that Hotavila does not have the terraced appearance of Old Oraibi.

A home is occupied by a woman and her husband and children. If the children are mature, the husband of a daughter who does not yet have a house of her own may be living temporarily with the family. Many homes also contain an aged father or mother of the house owner.

The life of the Hopi woman is laborious chiefly because of the

---

[4] The economic life of Second Mesa has been dealt with by C. D. Forde in *J. Roy. Anthrop. Inst.*, 1931, 61, 357–405.

[5] See Victor Mindeleff, "A Study of Pueblo Architecture," *8th Ann. Rep., Bur. Amer. Ethnol.*, 1891, pp. 3–228.

elaborate attention which is paid to cooking. The Hopi cook has learned how to prepare corn in a surprising variety of palatable forms, many of which do not fit into our categories of corn puddings and breads and cakes. One of the most unique is "piki," which looks like folded tissue paper, and which has the flavor of fresh corn flakes.

All corn dishes, except boiled corn, hominy, and parched corn, require that the grain be ground. This is done by rubbing it between a large grinding stone, known as a "metate," which is placed on the floor and a movable stone which is held in the hand. Three such metates, graded from a coarse to a fine grain of stone, are placed side by side in a bin. Grinding is done by kneeling at this bin.

A part of the day of each woman must be spent at grinding. Thus far this work has not been lightened by the use of machine grinders. At Hotavila it is probably a matter of principle not to try such things, but both hand mills and motor-driven mills have been tried at New Oraibi with but little success. American corn meal is a coarse affair, fit for making corn sticks or spoon bread, but not suitable for Hopi dishes. Some of the meal ground by hand by the Hopi women has the consistency of corn starch rather than of commercial corn meal. Because no machines are available to the Hopi for making such fine meal, grinding must continue to be the biggest single item in the women's round of work.

Clothing is supplied by the men. Formerly it was made not in the home, but in the kiva, that underground chamber used by the men as a sort of combination chapel, lodge-room, assembly-hall and clubhouse. Clothing which is hand-made is still made by the men. But nowadays much clothing is purchased ready-made, or American cloth is purchased and made into clothing. In this case, the man purchases the cloth but the sewing is often the work of the woman. Most men today wear ready-made shirts and trousers. Sometimes they buy cotton cloth which is made into outfits which resemble pajamas. For everyday use the older costume for men has been abandoned, although ceremonial costumes are still woven by hand. Many men make the characteristic high-topped sandal or shoe, although the buckskin can no longer be captured on the hunt but must be purchased.

The older women wear a heavy woolen dress or "manta" woven

by the men. Such dresses will wear for years, and they are in demand among the Eastern Pueblo peoples who have ceased to weave them, so that the Hopi men, during the winter season, make more dresses than are required for local use and sell or trade them. The standard price of such a dress is $20. The girls and the younger women wear dresses made from American cotton cloth.

The men weave for sale as well as for use, blankets, kilts and belts, but the volume of such weaving is not great. Farming is of first importance, and a Hopi man will weave only when there are no crops to be tended.

The arts of Hotavila women, aside from cooking, are two: the making of pottery which is chiefly utilitarian, and basketry. Hotavila pots are undecorated and have little or no sale. The pottery for which the Hopi are well-known is made only on First Mesa. Third Mesa, however, is distinguished for its basketry, having a unique type of plaque, woven from native plants.[6] The materials are dyed with vegetable dyes before they are woven, and the plaques are figured with multicolored designs. These plaques have ceremonial uses, and are used to decorate the homes. In addition, some of them are sold.

Hopi life is not easy, nor is it unbearably severe. The Hopi works persistently but without ostentation. While he must work hard, he works with as little effort as is possible, often rising before daybreak in order to work in the fields before the heat of the day. He shows foresight in taking care of his needs, and is frugal in his use of foods, the fear of long droughts being ever present. Droughts which have decimated the population have occurred within the past century.

The stereotype of a lazy Indian is one which could scarcely find its realization among the Hopi. The lazy man would be ridiculed, and would soon go hungry. There is no place in Hopi society which does not involve continuous work. Ceremonial leaders do more work, not less, than the men who are not leaders, for ceremonial burdens are borne in addition to secular labors. Even medicine men, while they do not do much farming, must collect their herbs and charms and perform their services at the expenditure of considerable time and energy.

[6] Walter Hough, "Hopi Indian Collection in the U. S. National Museum," *Proc. U. S. Nat. Mus.*, 1919, 54, 235–296.

Retirement is impossible at any age. One cannot, in Hopi society, pile up credits which will support one, nor can one save materials on which to live for long. Some of the "rich" may have enough corn to last for four or five years, but that is always to be treated as a reserve store, never as something which in the future will provide leisure. The aged who have sons and daughters who could provide for them continue to work as long as they are able to do anything whatsoever.

There are no sharp class differences of an economic nature, yet the village is aware of everybody's status in regard to economic goods. Some families are so poor that they have scarcely enough corn to eat, have little or no mutton and have inferior clothing. At the other end of the economic scale are those whose fields, orchards and flocks are large. From the sale of wool, such a person may be able to buy much jewelry, and even, at the very top of the scale, an automobile. Of the seventy-odd households in Hotavila, five married couples were described by our informants as being very poor. In addition, two women whose husbands have deserted them must be described as very poor. The native storekeeper, who is the only merchant in Hotavila, is considered the wealthiest man in the village. A successful medicine man is next in order. Only four families possess automobiles, and none of these vehicles has great value. There are two radios in the village, one of these being in the village store.

MARRIAGE

Marriage is something to be arranged between a young man and a young woman after a courtship, but while the young people take the initiative in finding mates they usually attempt to get the approval of their respective families. An interchange of gifts and of services between the families is a traditional part of the marriage custom. We cannot enter into a detailed description of the marriage customs, as to do so would require space beyond that which would be justified in the present connection. Two of the major obligations consist in the wife's grinding a large amount of meal for the husband's family, and of the husband's male relatives weaving an elaborate white cotton wedding garment for the bride. These reciprocal obligations are completed not before the wedding but months afterward. The bridal couple start living together when, by a smaller exchange of gifts, the marriage is symbolically contracted.

For a short time after the marriage, the bride and groom live with the husband's family. Then they take up their residence with the wife's parents, and remain with them until the newly married pair build a house of their own.

Most marriages among the Hopi involve persons both of whom come from the same village. If the husband and wife are not members of the same community, it is traditional that they reside in the village of the wife, but nowadays matrilocal residence is not always observed.

Marriage is not possible between members of a matrilineal clan. A Coyote woman cannot marry a Coyote man because theoretically they have the same ancestors and are related, although no one at the present time may be able to name any ancestors common to the two. Marriage is also impossible between linked or associated clans, which will be described later. One should not marry a person who belongs to one's father's clan, because here, too, a theoretical relationship exists. The taboo against marrying into the father's clan is less strict, however, than that against marrying a person of the same clan. The latter taboo has never been broken at Hotavila. Polygamy is not practiced by the Hopi.

A husband and wife may separate at any time without seeking permission from anyone. Either the husband or the wife may initiate the separation. If the wife should desire her husband to leave her she simply tells him to do so, or if she should reach this decision during his absence, she places his personal effects outside the door. The man then goes to the home of his mother or, if she is not living, to the home of one of his sisters. During temporary rifts in the family, he may sleep in the kiva. If the husband wishes to part from his wife, he has only to leave.

Such separations may be either temporary or permanent. In the case of permanent separations either party is free to take another spouse at any time, but a previously married man chooses in remarriage a woman who has also been married one or more times. A later marriage is much simpler than a first marriage as in later marriages no wedding garments are made, and there is consequently no elaborate exchange of gifts. Divorces with subsequent remarriages are relatively common among the Hopi.

In event of separation, the children remain with the mother. Their father has no further responsibility for them, but a later husband of the woman is responsible for their support so long as he lives with their mother. The mother's relatives feel somewhat responsible for them until the mother remarries.

Celibacy is very rare. A person finds it practically impossible to keep house and to take care of fields at the same time, so that a single man or woman can scarcely fit into the economic scheme. Such a person can, and sometimes does, find a place in the household of some relative, but an arrangement of this sort is seldom permanent.

Girls are expected to be chaste before marriage, and fidelity is expected of women during marriage. This conduct does exist and does bring a good name. On the other hand these virtues are not possessed by all women, nor does the lack of them lead to any formal penalties or to life-long disgrace. A "bad" girl will be scolded by her parents and ostracized by her former playmates, but after she is married she may slowly be accepted once more.

Chastity or the lack of it makes no difference in the reputation of the Hopi man. When a man and woman are together, it is expected that their behavior will be determined by the woman, and she receives the sole blame for any misconduct. A man will respect a girl who wishes to be chaste.

The extra-marital affairs which occur are the occasion of a great deal of squabbling among the women. The men, however, feel that it is undignified to quarrel over a woman, and a man says nothing and does nothing to a man whom he knows to be his wife's lover. He may remonstrate with his wife, he may leave her, he may be greatly angered or grieved, but he says nothing to others.

There is nothing in Hopi society which is entirely comparable to the institution of prostitution, but there are, in most villages, women whom nearly any man may visit, and it is traditional that any man who visits such a woman makes her a present. It is said to be bad luck if a present is not made; the feeling does not seem to be one of payment for privileges, although in some cases the woman's motive may be largely economic. Our Hotavila informants told us of three such women in Hotavila in 1938; they have no distinctive native name. One is a married woman, with seven children, to whom men come when her husband is away. She is not especially poor. She was married at twelve years of age and is now thirty-two. Her oldest daughter, aged sixteen, is becoming promiscuous with boys, but is not as yet included in the same category as her mother by our informant. The other two cases are instances of women who have been married but whose husbands have left them. Both are described as very stupid. Both have children. One accepts only men who pay her, chiefly widowers, whereas the other accepts not only men but also boys who leave no gifts.

SOCIAL ORGANIZATION

The closest ties of a Hopi are with the members of his immediate family—his parents, his brothers and sisters. But he has a host of relatives, all of whom usually live in his own village and whom he sees almost daily. The sisters of his mother are called "mothers," although the young child knows which is his "true" mother. The brothers of his father are likewise called "fathers," and all children of his mothers and fathers are called brothers and sisters, so that he is surrounded by a large number of relatives who, nominally at least, are very close to him.

The mother's mother is of course his grandmother, as is his father's mother, but in addition all sisters of these grandmothers are also called grandmother. Grandfathers are similarly numerous. Eggan [7] has presented the Hopi kinship system in detail.

Between the individual and any relative exist a number of mutual obligations which tend to bind them together. There is, first of all, the fact that they address each other in terms of relationship, and, secondly, that they exchange services on such occasions as planting, harvesting, hunting, housebuilding, marriage, at the birth of children, and in event of death. These relationships have been described in detail for Old Oraibi by Eggan, and for Second Mesa by Beaglehole.[8] We shall have occasion later to see how they influence the life of the Hotavila child.

Beyond the family is a wider group, the clan. The child's clan is the clan of his mother; that is, clan membership is inherited in the female line. A child does not belong to the clan of his father,

[7] F. R. Eggan, "The Kinship System of the Hopi Indians," Univ. of Chic. Lib., 1936.

[8] E. Beaglehole, "Notes on Hopi Economic Life," *Yale Univ. Publ. Anthrop.* 1937, 15, 1–88.

but he is said to be a "child" of that clan, and considers himself to be to some extent affiliated with it.

All clan members consider themselves to be related, and they have a number of obligations to each other. There are numerous occasions when one would call upon a clan member for aid or for services before asking the cooperation of others. In addition, the clans each have their special history or mythology, not shared by other people, which gives the members a further common bond. Lastly each clan has a number of ceremonial duties, certain functions in the ceremonial life, and certain ceremonial positions which belong to the clan by inheritance.

The final complication to this system is the fact that certain *clans* are considered to be related to each other, and thus form what are usually called phratries,[9] but the Hopi have neither a general nor a specific name for these related clans. They simply say that such and such clans "go together." Members of related clans may not intermarry. They may be called multiple-clans, as the constituents form one group and are not differentiated socially in any way.

The multiple-clans of Hotavila are listed below:

1. Spider-Bear Clan
2. Warrior-Fire-Coyote Clan
3. Corn-Rain-Water Clan
4. Reed-Greasewood-Horn Clan
5. Sun-Moon-Eagle Clan
6. Kachina-Parrot-Rabbit Clan
7. Badger-Butterfly Clan
8. Sand-Snake-Lizard Clan

The clans are listed above in the order of their supposed arrival at Oraibi, which is identical with their general importance in the ceremonial system. In order to give some idea of the place of clans in the ceremonial life, some of the functions of the clans of Hotavila are described. The account is not exhaustive.

1. The Bear Clan is supposed to furnish the village chief and also the head of the Soyal Society,[10] but practically all Bear people remained at Oraibi, so that they are not important at Hotavila. Hotavila has no Soyal Society.

[9] See R. H. Lowie, "Hopi Kinship," and "Notes on Hopi Clans," *Anthrop. Papers, Amer. Mus. Nat. Hist.*, 1929, 30, 309–360 and 361–388.
[10] See G. A. Dorsey and H. R. Voth, "The Oraibi Soyal Ceremony," *Anthrop. Series, Field Mus. Nat. Hist.*, 1901, 3, No. 1, 1–59.

2. The chief of the Warrior Society must be a Warrior clansman although anyone may become a member of the Society regardless of clan. The Warrior chief or priest is the village chief of Hotavila, who is chairman of the council of the chiefs.

3. The chief of the Corn and Water people is next in rank to the village chief, although he is not the head of any society. The Water people have several functions relative to the water which is used during the ceremonies.

4. The Horn Clan owns the Horn altar and names the chief of the Horn Society.

5. The chief of the Sun Clan notes the time for various ceremonies by watching the point on the horizon at which the sun rises, and notifies the village chief of the proper time for ceremonies. In the absence of the Sun chief, the Eagle chief would substitute for him. At present, the Eagle chief is the head of the Singers Society, but we failed to inquire whether this is traditional.

6. The Kachina Clan takes care of kachina masks, helps dress the kachinas, carries water for them and otherwise aids them during the masked dances.

7. The Badgers have the duty of sprinkling corn meal upon the dancers. Furthermore, a Badger officiates as chief of the Powamu ceremony, the child's initiation ceremony.

8. The Sand Clan has no society or ceremonial headships, but it has the duty of supplying the sand which is necessary for certain ceremonies, particularly those which involve sand paintings. The Snake Clan provides the chief of the Snake Society, which performs the most widely publicized of Hopi ceremonies.[11] It should be noted that from the Hopi point of view, this is the least important ceremonial.

While the ceremonial leaderships or priesthoods nominally belong to certain clans, each really belongs to a certain *lineage* within the clan. When a man who holds an office dies, the office goes to his next youngest brother. Should he have no brother, the office would be inherited by the son of one of his sisters, who, because of matrilineal descent would belong to the clan of the priest. The position would not go to the priest's son, for that form of succession would carry the office into a different clan. If no near relative were avail-

---

[11] H. R. Voth, "The Oraibi Summer Snake Ceremony," *Anthrop. Series, Field Mus. Nat. Hist.*, 1903, 3, No. 4, 271–358.

able within the clan, the office would still remain within the clan even if it were to go to a clansman who could not trace blood relationship to the preceding official.

The succession in priesthoods is not inflexible, for some allowance is made for individual desires and for personal fitness. These ceremonial leaders hold positions of great responsibility. No one is forced to take the position if he feels that he should not, or if he does not desire it, although he might be urged to do so. Someone who is stupid, or who is too lazy to perform the arduous tasks, would be passed over in the succession. Similarly, one who is quarrelsome with neighbors or who is having difficulties with his wife, would be disqualified for the succession, for a ceremonial leader must be of untroubled mind.

The ceremonial positions entail duties rather than rewards. They bring no economic returns whatsoever, and while they bring respect, they bring no authority or power.

These positions are the only positions which in any way give a Hopi a social rôle different from that played by his fellows. Aside from ceremonial office and society membership, there is no differentiation of social rôles among the Hopi. At Hotavila there is no election of civil officers. Although a secular village council has been fostered in other villages by the Indian Bureau, Hotavila has thus far refused to introduce a formal mode of self-government. There are no courts, no policemen, no fines and no penalties, except those imposed by the Indian Bureau. There is no native machinery for settling disagreements, whether concerning property rights or personal injury.[12] The town council is entirely a religious council, which, in order to maintain its purity of mind, should not meddle in quarrels. The native system of government is, in effect, a practical form of anarchy.

Disagreements, arguments, injustices, troubles of all kinds, do arise, and the community is often upset by them; the troubles manage to get themselves settled without overt injury to anyone. The chief reason for this is the strong anti-violence tradition. The Hopi defended themselves vigorously when the Navaho attacked, but they practically never engaged in aggressive warfare. A Hopi will fight if he is forced to do so, and will fight savagely, but rarely

[12] H. S. Colton, "A Brief Survey of Hopi Common Law," *Mus. Notes of Mus. No. Ariz.*, 1934, 7, 21–24.

can he be induced to strike the first blow. In his opinion individual combat is not manly; it is childish, and is strongly disapproved.

The second factor which makes social life possible in a society without formal penalties and without systematic means of settling disputes is the impossibility of escaping public opinion. The Hopi cannot make a living except in his village, even today. In former days, the difficulty of finding a refuge elsewhere was even greater. The Hopi must stay at home and face the consequence of his conduct, and the consequence of misconduct is the maddening, insistent clamor of a small town, where gossip is rife, and little incidents are long remembered. One's neighbors in Hotavila are not merely one's neighbors, but one's entire world. The disapproval of one's neighbors means to the Hopi the disapproval of nearly everyone he knows or can ever hope to know. There is no wider world to which one can look for approval. There is no hope of escape from the immediate environment. One hesitates before incurring a social ostracism of such immensity.

CEREMONIAL LIFE

The Hopi are as assiduous in seeking the good-will of the gods as they are in caring for their crops.[13] This is to be expected, since both activities function to the same end. Without the good-will of the supernaturals favorable weather does not come, and without that, life is impossible. It is therefore absolutely essential that the cosmic forces be controlled, and this is done by means of a long series of observances. There is not a month without a ceremony, and each ceremony engages the attention of the entire community for at least one day. A long period of application is required from those persons who participate in it.

Each ceremony has two aspects. There is the private or esoteric part which is performed by the ceremonial leaders and their helpers. In connection with nearly every ceremony there is something to be done by the appropriate ceremonial leaders on each of nine days. These performances, which were described in detail by Voth just before the division of Old Oraibi, involve the preparation and placement of carefully constructed prayer sticks and prayer feath-

[13] The monographs by Voth which are cited in the bibliography deal with the ceremonies of Old Oraibi, most of which have been transferred to Hotavila.

ers, the erection of altars and the careful arrangement of ancient
ceremonial paraphernalia about the altars, the singing of songs and
the recitation of chants before the altars. Those persons who participate must purify themselves in certain ways before the beginning of the ceremony, and must de-charm themselves at the end.

The public part of each ceremony takes place on the last of
the nine ceremonial days. It is seen by the entire populace of the
village, and often by visitors from neighboring villages and by
white visitors as well. In spring, summer, and fall these public performances are held during the day in a central part of the village.
In winter, they are held at night in one of the "kivas," ceremonial
chambers in which many of the religious observances take place.

We have no analogue of these performances among ourselves,
but both Americans and Hopi agree in giving them in English the
name of "dance." Dancing is certainly a part of the performances,
but it is not a sort of terpsichorean display which the word suggests to us. The dances are not social dances. In the majority of
the ceremonies only men take part; in a few the dancing is done
solely by women.

The dancers are arranged in a long line. As the dance progresses
the line may move single-file from one side of the plaza to another, and in the act of dancing the direction in which the dancers
are facing may be changed, but the linear arrangement is almost
always maintained.

The steps of the dance are restrained, and while they are more
complicated than they seem, it is not unfair to say that the principal
element is a rhythmic stamping of the right foot. This is done in
perfect unison, often by as many as forty performers. Since the
rhythm varies from time to time, it is no easy task to memorize the
steps of a dance.

Singing by the performers accompanies the dance. A dance lasts
for an entire day or through most of a night, although rest intervals are interspersed throughout the programs. New songs [14] and
new dances are composed for each ceremony, and these must be
learned to automaticity by every performer. This fact gives an indication of the amount of time and effort which the participants

[14] For the nature of Hopi music, see B. I. Gilman, "Hopi Songs," *J. Amer.
Ethnol. & Arch.*, 1908, 5.

in such a ceremony must expend in preparation. This preparation takes place at night in the kivas.

Each ceremony is performed by one of the ceremonial societies. Of these, at Hotavila, there are six for men and three for women. Each adult man is expected to join one of four societies, the Warrior Society, the Horn Society, the Singers Society, or the Wuwucim Society. In addition, all members of the Snake Clan are members of the Snake Society, and all members of the Antelope Clan are members of the Antelope Society, the two ceremonial groups which perform the famed Snake Dance.

Participation in the work of these societies is a religious and social duty which is expected of every man, although it is not expected that every society member will dance at every performance given by the society. Participation in the religious observances brings no special favor to the participants. The ceremonies are carried out in order that the whole community may benefit. Failure to do one's ceremonial duties properly would bring ill-fortune to the entire community.

We return now to the nature of the public dances. They may be divided into two sorts according to the dress of the dancers. In fall and winter the faces of the dancers are not covered, and while special costumes are worn, the dancers are easily recognizable and they make no attempt to conceal their identity. These dances are called unmasked dances. In spring and summer, however, masks are worn by the dancers, and these performances are called masked dances, or, because the masks represent the gods or "kachinas" they are called kachina dances.

The gods are said to have bodies like men, but their heads are quite different. The supernatural who is being portrayed is recognized by the markings and the decoration of his head, which is depicted by means of a skillfully made mask worn by the dancer. The uninitiated children are told, and they believe, that the masked dancers are the real gods who in spring and summer leave their winter home, the San Francisco Peaks, which are near Flagstaff, Arizona, and come to dance before the Hopi. The adults hold that long ago such was really the case, but that now the Hopi impersonate the dances which the gods formerly performed on their visits to the mesas.

The multiplicity of the gods [15] affords infinite variety to the ceremonial program. While the time, and the general nature, of a ceremony is fixed, the society which performs it may choose among the several kinds of kachinas which are appropriate for a certain dance. There is therefore much interest in noting the appearance of unusual, or of favorate kachinas.

The ostensible purpose of the ceremonies is religious, but an account of the ceremonies would not be adequate unless it called attention to the fact that the ceremonies furnish satisfaction to a very wide range of human interests. If the Hopi universe were limited to the events of the work-a-day world, it would be drab indeed. To the Hopi the ceremonies furnish all the other parts of life. This fact makes understandable the many-sidedness of Hopi ceremonials, and their extensive place in the Hopi calendar.

The dances are the only social occasions among the Hopi. At no other time do the people of a village gather in one body. At no other time does everybody forsake work and devote a whole day to visiting, to feasting, to music and to the watching of performances which are esthetic and dramatic as well as religious. The importance of the element of variety and of relief from monotony should not be overlooked. Among the Hopi there are no holidays, no Sundays, no feast days—only dance days. The ceremonies furnish the chief recreation and the main occasion for sociability in a life which otherwise would be characterized chiefly by effort and by a quite rugged individualism.

In connection with the ceremonies a creative person can indulge his interest in the composition of songs and the invention of dance steps. There are few other avenues of creative esthetic activity open to the Hopi.

We should not fail to mention the element of comedy. In many of the dances, usually in the intervals when the dancers are resting, clowns appear and delight the crowd with their fun. Clowns have appeared in pueblo ceremonies for a very long time and are not imitations of Spanish or American clowns. The American finds the clowns of the Hopi as amusing as his own. The Hopi, who remain silent and unexpressive during the dances, become animated when the clowns come on the scene, and laugh loudly at their

[15] J. W. Fewkes, "Hopi Katcinas Drawn by Native Artists," *21st Ann. Rep., Bur. Amer. Ethnol.,* 1903, 21, 3–126.

pranks. The strength of the appeal of the clowns is shown by the fact that the dances at which clowns are expected draw many more visitors from other Hopi villages than do the dances which lack this attraction. At the present time Hotavila has the very best troupe of Hopi clowns. They are often asked to perform at dances held in other villages.

Since the ceremonies still play such a prominent part among the Hopi at the present time, it is apparent that the native religion has not been replaced by Christianity. At Hotavila there is only one Christian, a blind woman who is helped by missionaries. A crippled boy from Hotavila lives with a missionary at Bacobi. There are no missionaries at Hotavila, and it is doubtful that they could get permission from the inhabitants to locate there. There are missionaries in or near other villages, but their efforts to convert the Hopi have not met with marked success. The absence of a specific rain-bringing ritual is a tremendous handicap to Christian workers among the Hopi. Christianity fails to offer the one thing which the Hopi need most of all—an increase in rainfall.

HOPI IDEALS

The Hopi have a word which can best be translated as "the good life." This means to the Hopi a condition in which he has peace of mind and only good thoughts—free from anxiety and worry and hatred. This may be said to be his "summum bonum." It does not involve the achievement of prestige, of position, of distinction, or of power. It is not that the Hopi wants the reputation of enjoying a good life, he wants the good life itself. It is not an excited or rapturous or highly emotional condition, but is defined largely in negative terms as the absence of evil.

The Hopi wants economic well-being, but it is not easy to separate this from the desire for the good life. Hopi existence is so near to the danger of death from thirst and starvation that scarcity of water and of food is the most prominent evil. Whether the Hopi would pile up economic goods far beyond what he himself could consume, either from the desire for prestige, or for the sheer joy of amassing or through a compulsive industriousness, is a question which cannot be answered until the Hopi fields are irrigated so as to make possible a greater accumulation of goods.

The Hopi wants white man's goods, particularly foods, automobiles and radios, but no Hopi has yet acquired these goods to an extent which would be considered immoderate in a small farmer. In American standards no Hopi is rich or even well-to-do.

We have been speaking of what a man desires for himself. What does the citizen of Hotavila approve of in others? According to our informants, the Hopi approves most highly of a man who is good-natured and industrious and who causes no trouble. To be approved of, a man should do his duties by his clan and his ceremonial group. The Hopi also thinks favorably of people who are well-to-do, which means, according to our informants, people who have a three- or four-year store of corn and beans and plenty of livestock. Food is more important in this regard than is the character of one's house or automobile. Even the ceremonial leaders would not be well thought of if they did not do their farming well. In this respect, as in regard to religious duties, the priests should set a good example. A lazy man is scorned. A lazy man, it should be noted, is not a man who does nothing, for that is impossible. A lazy man is the sort of fellow who in summer time goes down into the cool kiva *to weave* when he should be out in his fields.

The good man and the good woman have the same characteristics, and what men admire in men they also admire in the opposite sex. Young boys may look for wives who are pretty, but the wiser men look for women who are industrious and of a good disposition. They avoid women who are cross, greedy, gossipy and quarrelsome.

CHAPTER III

HOTAVILA CHILD CARE

Childbirth and the Care of the Newborn [1]

VERY little is done by way of preparation for the birth of the child. The wardrobe of the newborn is scanty, and since it consists only of blankets, cloths and rags, it is at hand beforetimes. The cradleboard may be constructed either before or after the birth of the child.

The family of the expectant mother is responsible for her care during labor and delivery, and for most of the subsequent day, while the family of her husband assists her for the ensuing twenty days.

The infant is born in the house of his mother. Nowadays a government hospital is available free of charge at Keams Canyon, and government representatives attempt to encourage hospitalization. Thus far their efforts have met with but little success. No women from Hotavila, and very few from New Oraibi, are taken to the hospital unless the woman has been in labor for many days and is near death, nor is a doctor called to the home until then.

In a general way the Hopi lack confidence in government doctors. But in connection with childbirth a further factor prevents the use of the hospital facilities. The rules of the hospital forbid the shading of the windows of the room in which lies the parturient woman and her newborn infant, a matter which the Hopi consider to be very important since they believe light to be injurious at this time. Further, the hospital foods are not prepared in accordance with the Hopi ideas of the dietary requirements of the woman in confinement. Thus it comes about that American medicine has influenced scarcely at all the old practices in regard to childbirth,

---

[1] Oraibi birth practices are described by H. R. Voth in "Oraibi Natal Customs and Ceremonies," *Anthrop. Series, Field Mus. Nat. Hist.*, 1905, 6, No. 2, 47–61.

and the customs at Hotavila are the same as those observed by Voth at Old Oraibi between 1900 and 1905.

At childbirth the woman's mother and father are present and sometimes her husband also is in the room. Children may remain in the house almost to the moment that the child is born. No medicine man is called unless trouble develops. During strong labor pains the woman assumes a kneeling position on the floor, with both hands on the floor, and the head somewhat raised. The infant is born on a sheepskin. As soon as the infant is born, the mother takes a recumbent position. Sand is heated by the woman's mother, and the parturient woman lies on the floor on a bed of hot sand during the first day. The bed is kept hot by constant reheating of the sand. The sand not only provides heat but it serves to collect the after discharges, which are taken outside and deposited in a place traditionally used for this purpose. The mother during the first day drinks only warm water in which juniper has been boiled, and she drinks this twice daily during the first twenty days. For twenty days she must not eat salt, nor fresh fruits and vegetables, as these are believed to have a bad effect upon the breast milk.

If the mother is a primipara, she must remain indoors for twenty days. If she is a multipara, she need stay in only four days. Whatever her period of seclusion, she should not sleep with her husband until twenty days after the expiration of this period.

During the twenty days following the birth of the baby, a woman of the father's family—usually his mother or a sister—takes care of the infant and mother. The paternal relative remains with the mother day and night, prepares the food, carries the water, and bathes both infant and mother. The mother is given a bath by her attendant every five days, the last of these being given on the twentieth day. The naming ceremony also occurs on this day. After its conclusion the care of the infant is assumed by the mother herself.

Let us turn now to the care of the infant. As soon as he is born, blankets are placed before the door and before the windows, because light is harmful to the infant during this period. The newborn infant is not placed on the bed of hot sand but is wrapped in cloths. As soon as the busy attendant has an opportunity, the child is "cleaned" as follows: First, ashes are applied to the baby. Formerly a type of volcanic ashes, which are found a few miles from

Third Mesa, were used but now ashes secured by burning sage are used instead. Following the application of the ashes, the baby is bathed in yucca suds and warm water, the suds being made by shaking a piece of pounded yucca root in a basin of water. In bathing the baby, his shoulders are put in the basin, the legs being elevated and protruding from the vessel. After the bath, ashes are again applied and are not removed.

The infant is then wrapped as follows: He is placed on a blanket. A piece of cotton cloth is placed over his chest and passed between the chest and the arms so that the arms will not be brought against bare flesh. Rags are placed under the buttocks and between the legs. Nowadays diapers are sometimes used in place of the rags. Then one side of the blanket is brought over one arm of the infant and passed between the chest and the arm of the opposite side and tucked under the infant's body. The other side of the blanket is passed over both arms, which are extended along the body of the infant, and it too is tucked under the infant. Thus wrapped, the infant is placed upon the cradleboard.

The old cradles were of two styles, shown in Plate III. These woven cradles have now been largely replaced by a board cradle because the latter is more easily constructed. The cradle is made by the father's mother, who also supplies the blankets and cloths for the newborn.

During the first twenty days an ear of white corn is placed on either side of the infant when he is on the cradleboard. These ears must be perfect specimens. The father, when husking, watches for such ears and puts them aside for future use. It is said that one of the ears represents the mother, the other the baby. The corn is ·saved for planting during the subsequent spring.

The baby is bound to the cradle during the first day. This is done by lacing strings (formerly buckskin thongs) through holes provided at the side of the cradle, or by tying strips of cloth around both child and cradle. The ties are passed over the legs also, so that they can be flexed only slightly. The purpose of this binding is to ensure that the child will be straight and of good carriage.

A small pad of folded cloth is placed under the head to ease the discomfort of the hard board. A roll of cloth is placed under the neck to keep the child from becoming short-necked or "bull-necked."

The child is taken off the cradle only for changing the soiled cloths and for bathing. He is put to the breast and nursed while on the board. When he has gone to sleep, the board is placed on the floor or on a bed. At night, the cradleboard rests beside the mother. When the infant is asleep, a cloth is placed over the face-guard, for the purpose of excluding the light, preventing drafts from striking the face and keeping flies from the child.

The day which marks the end of the darkening of the house is also the day of the naming ceremony. Since Voth [2] has described this practice in some detail, it will be reviewed only briefly here.

Before daybreak the mother and the sisters of the child's father come to the house and each woman bathes the baby and gives it a name. (Voth's statement on Page 54 that these women are maternal relatives is an error, and contradicts his later statements in the same publication.) The child may receive as many as eight or ten names and an equal number of baths. Just at daybreak the child's maternal grandmother, accompanied by the child's mother, carries the infant toward the rising sun. When a certain point is reached, prayers are said, the child's names are repeated, and an offering of ceremonial corn meal is sprinkled toward the sun. The women then return to the house, where a breakfast has been prepared for the paternal relatives by the woman's mother. After breakfast, the mother-in-law receives a large tray of "piki," a favorite native form of wafer or bread, for her services during the preceding twenty days. The blankets which have kept out the sunlight are now removed from the door and windows. Other people in the village may be invited to a second breakfast to mark the occasion.

It may be remarked that the members of the mother's family, by their usage, determine which of the names just given by the paternal relatives will "stick." The remainder of the names fall into disuse and are forgotten.

Infant Care

The forms of child care which characterize the first day of life continue throughout most of the first year. The baby is bathed each morning as described, although the use of ashes and of yucca is discontinued when the vernix caseosa has disappeared.

[2] H. R. Voth in "Oraibi Natal Customs and Ceremonies," *Anthrop. Series, Field Mus. Nat. Hist.*, 1905, 6, No. 2, 47–61.

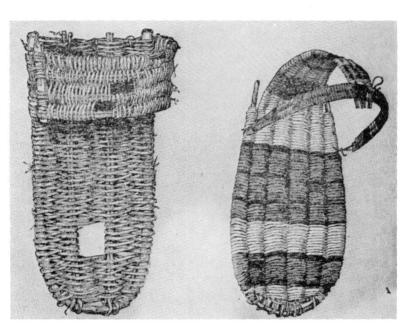

PLATE III
OLD HOPI CRADLES (*from Mason, 1887*).

Formerly the rags which were the primitive antecedent of diapers were dried in the sun and rubbed clean with fresh dry sand, although periodically they were washed. At present soap and water are used as the cleaning agents, and, as was noted earlier, modern diapers are used by some mothers. However, no other element of American baby clothes has yet come into use. Aside from rags or a diaper, the child within the blankets is naked.

If the anogenital region becomes sore, mutton tallow, chicken grease or bone marrow is applied to the affected parts. A fine corn meal powder, as fine as corn starch, is also used.

The cradleboard is employed very assiduously for the first three months, the child being taken off the board only for cleaning and bathing, acts which combined do not occupy more than an hour daily. After three months the straightness of the child is assured and the mother may discard the cradleboard whenever she pleases. Actually, its use is seldom discontinued before the child is six months of age and it rarely is employed beyond the first year of life. The duration of the cradle usage depends in part upon the restlessness of the child and in part upon his motor development. If a child becomes restless on the board, he is freed earlier than would otherwise be the case. If he walks precociously he is taken from the board at an early age, for the board is seldom used after the child begins to walk.

The child is nursed whenever he expresses a desire for the breast. This means that the intervals between feedings are short. In addition to serving the function of feeding, the breast is used to pacify the infant if he is crying from some reason other than hunger.

The infant is tied to the board before he is nursed. If he does not go to sleep while nursing, he may be shaken on the mother's knees, or she may sing to him, or both things may be done at the same time. The mother has a gourd rattle which she may shake to distract the crying child and to induce sleep. If the child cries persistently, either parent may walk the floor with him.

In case of illness, the mother calls a medicine man who treats the child or who advises the mother as to the proper course of action. The treatment often consists of the singing of curing songs by the medicine man, the sprinkling of corn meal, etc. The medicine man makes use of some herbs, and for dysentery he prescribes the eating of a white clay found not far from Hotavila. In case of colic, the snake priest sings over the baby, for the Snake Society deals with all diseases which involve swelling of the abdomen.

A mother should not attempt to treat the sick baby herself, although a few mothers do so. If the mother is dissatisfied with the treatment of the medicine man first called, she should not go to a second practitioner until four days have elapsed, but here, as elsewhere, practice does not conform to theory, and an anxious mother may call several medicine men in rapid succession. In severe cases the parents may promise that if he recovers the child will be given, as a member, to one of the societies. As a last resort, they may call the government nurse or the government doctor.

Infant mortality is quite high, but we are not qualified to determine the chief causes of illness among Hopi children. Many white people, including some nurses, feel that a great deal of illness is due to digestive disturbances which are traced to the custom of permitting children to eat whatever they please. During the summer, as opportunity arises, the child gorges himself with fruits which are often in an unripe condition. Green corn and green melons are eaten in large quantities. Green chili also is eaten by children.

Supplementary feeding starts whenever the infant shows a desire for something which is in the hands of others—often at three months of age—and when this occurs the infant is given part of the food which is being consumed by the adult. This may be a piece of stewed jerky or it may be a cup of coffee. It is thought to be very unkind to refuse to give a child something to eat if he asks for it.

There are a number of observances whose concern is the well-being of the child. The infant must not be placed on his abdomen before he can get himself into this position, for to do so will hurt the child. The child must not be tossed in the air in play until he is eight or ten months of age. He should be tickled only a little because much tickling will keep him from going to sleep. He is not taken out of doors until he is about four months of age, or if he is taken out earlier, he is covered in protection from the strong sun. To put one's hand across a child's mouth will keep him from talking properly.

Babies are petted and fondled, they are placed on the lap, and are carried about. It is believed that the child should not be left alone, as this would expose him to danger from witches. In consequence, the child is always in the presence of someone.

The care of the child during the early months is provided by the child's mother. Thereafter an older sister of the child, if there be one, takes over his care to a greater and greater degree. She watches over him, carries him about, and takes him out of the house for a part of the day. In carrying the baby, the older child places him on her back and then puts around him a shawl, the ends of which she holds securely in her hands. The baby should not be carried until he is three or four months of age. Before this age, he is not considered strong enough to be carried and so remains at home.

After six months of age he is often placed on his back on the floor in order that he may exercise himself. When he is old enough, he is led by the hand to encourage walking. He is expected to walk shortly after he is one year old. If he should be late in starting to walk, his legs may be rubbed early in the morning and he may be bathed in cold water.

The first words are expected soon after he is a year of age. Efforts are made to teach the child to speak, and a baby vocabulary is provided. The baby word [3] for father is "tata"; for mother it is "yaya." "Mama" is a native term but it does not mean mother to the Hopi child, but instead it refers to something to eat, including the breast. To nurse, as opposed to eating, has the further name "yoyo." "Vava" is the word for brother and "gaga" the name for sister. The adult forms are, of course, much more difficult. Our informants believed that most babies pronounce "tata" as their first word and that "mama" is the next addition to their vocabulary.

The nails of the baby may be cut at any time but his hair must not be cut until the time of the new moon which precedes the Bean Dance, a ceremony which occurs in February. Bangs are worn and a small amount of hair remains over each temple. Over the remainder of the head the hair is closely cut but becomes long in the course of the year. This is the only occasion on which a child's hair should be cut, although the bangs which would other-

---

[3] Since our interest at this point is only in the fact that baby words are used, we have not tried to render them in accurate phonetic form. The sounds approximate those which the spellings will suggest to the American reader.

wise fall over the eyes may be trimmed at other times. In the case of an infant whose hair is cut for the first time, the hair which is removed is spun into a piece of yarn string which is worn about the baby's neck until it falls off. Our informants knew no reason for this custom.

WEANING

Very few babies are weaned before the end of the first year. Some children nurse even to the age of seven and eight years, but these are rare cases. The most common time for weaning is during the second year. Our informants stated that only a few babies nurse for more than two years, because in most cases the mother is again pregnant within two years of the birth of the preceding child. A child is usually weaned at the beginning of the next pregnancy, but this rule is not invariable. Some mothers have been known to nurse the older infant even after the birth of a new sibling. There is a belief, however, that an infant which is nursed during a pregnancy is likely to die.

To wean a baby the mother may put powdered red chili on the breast. Another means, sometimes used as a supplement to the first, is to turn the child over to one of his grandmothers for several days.

TOILET TRAINING

No toilet training is attempted until the child is able to walk, and to understand some words. He is then told to go outside when he needs to defecate and urinate. To the beginner, this means literally just outside the door, although older children go to a corner of the plaza, and adults go outside of the village. If the child fails to go out of doors at the proper time, he is spanked.

At a slightly later age he is supposed to tell his mother when he needs to eliminate during the night, but he is not expected to avoid all bedwetting until he is two years of age.

Persistent cases of nocturnal enuresis are rare but they do occur. If a girl wets the bed when she is six or seven years of age, she is made to wash her own bedclothes. For boys who are enuretic at that age, there is a more drastic treatment. In the past two years it has been employed at Hotavila only once.

The boy's parents do not themselves undertake the treatment, but ask one of the boy's maternal uncles to do so. For several days the uncle comes to the boy's bed about daybreak and feels the bedding. If the bed is dry, the uncle departs without awakening the boy. When the bed is found to be wet, he puts the boy on his back with only a blanket around the naked body of the youngster. If the enuretic is sleeping with other boys, they accompany the uncle and nephew on their trip, all with a serious mien, as this is not a prank but a treatment. The other boys also wear only a blanket.

The procession goes to the house of a woman of the Corn-Water Clan, who has been notified in advance, and at whose home other women of the Corn-Water Clan are gathered. The boys sing a song which is used only on such occasions. The women then throw cold water on each boy—on the innocent as well as on the guilty. The other boys, who have known all along what is coming, as the enuretic may also have known, receive the treatment voluntarily in order to help cure the one who is afflicted. The blankets are removed during the administration of the cold water. There is no ridicule, no fun-making, no laughter. At the conclusion, the boys return to their homes.

The treatment is repeated if the boy is again found to be wet. It is customary to give this treatment only during the cold months as it is said to be more effective at that time.

EATING AND SLEEPING

The child may come home to eat whenever he pleases, and may eat anything that is available. He need not eat when the other members of the family are eating, and need not come home at any particular time. No one waits for him or scolds him for remaining away. In general, however, he does eat with the family when the meals are served, but in addition he pieces between meals. A child may be seen with a piece of food at any hour.

As soon as the child can walk, he may go to bed whenever he wishes. The younger children usually become sleepy before the parents retire; the older children often go to bed at the same time as do the parents. A girl sleeps in her parents' house, but may

occasionally visit a girl chum for the night. In summer, boys often
sleep out of doors, either on the roof or near the building. In
winter, they sleep in a storage room, which may be some distance
from the house, or in a kiva. A number of boys usually sleep together.

Children of six years or older are roused at the same time that
the parents get up. A child should not sleep late in the morning;
to do so is a sign of laziness.

OBEDIENCE

The child owes obedience to his mother and father, to his mother's
brothers, and to some extent to his father's brothers who are called
"fathers." Grandparents should be respected, but they are not dis-
ciplinarians and do not enforce obedience. Young children are almost
continuously under the care of older sisters, but the older sibling
cannot take punishment into her own hands in order to obtain
obedience to her commands. The younger child usually obeys the
older child, but in cases in which this does not occur, the older
sibling must appeal to the parents. Other people in the village may
not command the child, nor threaten, nor punish the child, but they
are free to reprove him for wrong-doing and to report his misbehavior to his parents.

CHILDHOOD PROHIBITIONS

The Hopi child is free from many of the frustrations which are
continually imposed upon the modern city child. The primitive
child, generally, lives in a much simpler material culture, where
valuable objects are more rare and not so easily damaged as are
our own. He is surrounded by a minimum of breakable property,
and in consequence there is no occasion to tell him not to spill
things on the floor, not to pull books off the shelves, not to touch
the telephone or the radio, not to climb on chairs or on stairs, not
to put his hands on the windows, and not to pull the table cloth.
He escapes a thousand and one other demands which are made
upon the child in the American home. Among the Hopi, the property which the child might damage, such as ceremonial garments
and masks, "best" clothing and jewelry, are kept either out of sight

or out of reach. The child may touch everything which he sees. There is a striking absence in the Hopi home of the constant admonishment of the child not to handle or touch this and that.

If we may, for a moment, carry our discussion outside of Hotavila, we will be able to show how firm is the attitude that the child has a right to manipulate his environment by showing that this attitude survives in Hopi homes in which there is a considerable amount of American furniture. We spent part of one day in a Hopi home in Upper Moenkopi where the inhabitants live, to a large extent, "white man's way." The home had wooden floors, it had much furniture, and on the walls were snapshots and tinted photographs of members of the family. There were books and magazines and a dining table, for Moenkopi with its irrigated fields is the most prosperous of all Hopi villages.

In the home was a boy one year of age who was able to pull to standing and who could walk while holding on. He was practicing these arts by grasping the kitchen stove, which happened not to be hot at the moment, but which obviously was heated at other times. The mother admitted that this worried her, but she did not know what to do about it. A few moments later the child pulled all of the magazines off of a table. Another Hopi woman called the mother's attention to this fact but nothing was done about it.

We have wished to emphasize the respects in which the situation of the Hopi child differs from that of many American children. It would be erroneous, however, if we were to conclude that the Hopi child is subject to no prohibitions at all, and we must proceed to describe the things which he is supposed to avoid.

The very young child at Hotavila is warned about the edge of the cliff, which borders one side of the town, and which at some places is a sheer precipice of one hundred feet, with a very steep slope below the initial drop. He is warned not to go near a fire. The cliff and the fire provide the two greatest physical dangers to the child. He is also warned to keep away from the hatchways which descend into the kivas.

He should not fight nor tease nor injure anyone, but these things are not effectively prevented from happening, as we shall see later.

Other people's possessions should be left strictly alone. Stealing is strongly condemned, and the child is early required to respect property rights. However, our informants named several families which, it is alleged, actually encourage their children to pilfer. These families are, of course, held in low opinion by the remainder of the community. It is important that the child in no way injure the gardens, the fields of beans and corn and the fruit trees.

To talk back to adults is considered bad. However, there are no word taboos, no bad words except an impolite name for Navaho.

A child may not enter a house if the inhabitants are away, although he may come in if someone is there. It is very impolite to watch people when they are eating, but at other times it is pardonable for the child to stop outside of a house to see what is going on within.

Only a few kinds of play are taboo. The child must not play at being sick, as this might bring on sickness. He must not imitate the Snake Dance nor sing Snake Dance songs, as this would cause swelling of the abdomen, but other dances and other songs may be imitated. Youngsters must not play with yucca, for this belongs to the kachinas, and similarly, prayer sticks must not be meddled with. In imitative play, masks may not be used, as masks are for the kachinas and for the "koyemshi," the "mudheads" or clowns with grotesque knobbed heads.

One of the strongest prohibitions which is placed upon the older child, who has been initiated, and who consequently knows that the kachinas who appear in the dances are only men, is that he shall not reveal this secret to the uninitiated.

Childhood Duties

Until he is six years of age, the boy has practically no duties to perform, being free to play about the village all day long. But at about this age he begins to accompany his father to the fields and helps with the light work there. He guards his father's cornfields against prairie dogs and his father's orchards against birds. He also begins to help his father's brothers, who will weave his wife's wedding garments for him when he marries. He accompanies his father, or some relative, in taking care of the sheep and cattle. He runs errands and chops a little wood. When the fruit is ripe he helps to pick it and to carry it, and he also helps with the harvesting of the fields. As he grows older, his work gradually approaches that of the mature man.

If there are no girls in the family, a boy may be required to help take care of the younger children. A boy is seldom seen with a baby or with a sister, but he more often takes around with him his younger brother.

In addition to work, there are other duties which also fall upon a boy. One of these, which is not insisted upon by all parents in Hotavila but the practice of which is enforced by some, is that of causing the boy to get up before sunrise, run naked to a distant spring, bathe, and run back. He should get back before sunrise so that women will not see him. In order to warn the women not to appear, he sometimes wears a cowbell on the trip. The purpose of this early morning performance is to make him strong and healthy. Whether the boy bathes each morning or not, he is expected to rise early, which means at or shortly after sunrise. Some men also go to bathe each morning, but they go to the near spring, not to the far one, and they walk rather than run.

The girl's work is a miniature of the tasks done by her mother. One of the girl's chief tasks is to take care of the youngest, or next to the youngest child. If the girl is playing, she should return home about the time the baby wakens, and she is responsible for him until he again goes to sleep, unless relieved by someone else. However, she may play while she is looking after the younger sibling, and she often takes her charge to a place where some of her playmates are gathered.

The girl is responsible for helping with the housework. If there are two or more girls, only one is needed to care for the baby, and the younger one is usually chosen for this task. The older girls help in carrying water, in sweeping the floor, in tending the gardens, in shelling corn and in cooking. The girl also begins to grind when about eight years of age and her task in this regard gradually increases.

She is sent on errands to the store or to carry messages or to borrow from neighbors.

Beyond the age of twelve the girl no longer plays freely throughout the village, but is expected to stay at home. The feeling that the older girl should always stay at home is in part prompted by modesty and propriety, but it also results in her contributing a great deal to the work of the household.

Good and Bad Behavior

Good behavior in a Hotavila child is defined largely in terms of observing the prohibitions and in performing the duties which have just been described, and bad behavior conversely consists in the failure to conform to these expectations. A good child is one who is "not naughty." But we may mention a few matters which come under the present heading and which were not treated in the preceding sections.

It is said that a child, like an adult, should be industrious, not lazy. This does not mean that he should be continuously busy, and certainly not that he should be hyperactive. It means only that he should do the work which is assigned to him. Beyond that requirement, his time is his own. He is not disapproved of for sitting and daydreaming, if his tasks have been accomplished, but he should finish his chores before doing anything else.

Being relatively quiet rather than boisterous and noisy seems to be encouraged by Hopi parents. A child should not talk too much, and he should not be given to ridiculing others.

A consideration of the expectations of Hopi parents reveals that the desire to have their child excell all others is not possessed by them, or, if it is, it is not expressed. The child is supposed to do what is right, as is everybody else. He is not urged to be better than all other children. He is not encouraged to outdo his companions, although he may be told that he should do as well as they.

In spite of the opposition to American schools thirty-five years ago, today many Hotavila parents want their children to go to school and to learn to speak English and to learn some sort of trade. This attitude is a practical one, as it is motivated by the feeling that the reservation may some day be opened to the white man, as other reservations have been opened, and that the members of the younger generation may have to shift for themselves in a world of white man's ways. There is the further consideration that at the present time a speaking knowledge of English, and the possession of a manual skill, are important in getting an occasional government job or a position in an American city. The behavior of the child in school is therefore judged in terms of these practical standards rather than in terms of grades.

Conduct in school is thought to be the teacher's problem, although Hotavila parents prefer that the teacher be strict and make the child behave.

One of the points on which Hopi and white standards of behavior differ most pronouncedly is in regard to the morality of social dancing. Social dancing is not a Hopi custom, nor does embracing in public or any public exhibition of intimacy ever occur. The native theory is that even in courtship the boy and girl should not be close enough to touch each other. Therefore the Hopi look upon social dances, which the young want to engage in and which the schools sometimes arrange as a school activity, as disgraceful and sinful.

Means of Social Control

If we inquire by what means the Hopi seek to maintain good behavior in their children, we can divide the topic into two parts: positive methods and negative methods. By positive means of social control we mean the methods whereby good behavior is rewarded, or by which it is encouraged by making it satisfying. By negative methods, we refer to methods of punishing or penalizing bad behavior.

In our account the negative methods of the Hopi will receive more space than will the positive ones. We do not believe that this represents the true balance between these two means of control. Hopi children do not seem to be punished often, nor do we gather that they are in continual fear of punishment. On the other hand they do not expect praise for doing what is required of them. It would seem that in the majority of instances the child accepts Hopi standards as he accepts sun and sky and stars. He does not consider that things should be otherwise, and does not always need reward or punishment to induce him to accept his rôle as a Hopi child.

There is a predominance of *formalized* methods of punishment over formalized methods of reward. We believe this is because reward is informal and personal and is bestowed by the parent, whereas many punishments are organized as the action of a wider group.

Punishment

The most common punishment is that of scolding. We asked our informants what would be done in the case of each of many kinds of misbehavior. The most common reply was "scold them." Children are scolded for lying, for quarreling, for disrespect for old people, for breaking things, and, we suspect, for all minor forms of mischief.

Ridicule and teasing are also employed. If children are quarreling they may be told that they sound like dogs, and must go outside with the dogs. If a child sucks his thumb, he is told that he is nursing. If he eats greedily, he is compared to a pig.

Threatening to withhold favors is also utilized as a means of making the child conform to the parents' wishes. The most common form of intimidation is to suggest that the kachinas will not bring gifts. Seldom if ever are gifts entirely withheld, but the gift may not be forthcoming until the very last dance of the day. Previous to the last dance, the child will have believed that he is going to receive nothing, and will have promised faithfully to reform.

During the winter, dances are held in the kivas, and all children are anxious to see these entertaining performances. At this period, bad behavior may bring a warning from the parent that the child will not be taken to see the next dance. In some cases this threat is actually carried out.

A traditional means of frightening children which formerly was common to all the villages, is the summoning of bugaboo kachinas of dreadful appearance, who carry ropes and axes and saws and who bear on their backs baskets in which they are said to carry away children. In Hopi terms, the leader of these is "Soyoko." In some villages, she may be called whenever any parent desires. When she and her companions appear they go from house to house, demanding the children, and citing all of the bad behavior of the young. The parents of the children play the rôle of defenders of their loved ones, holding the door against Soyoko, and finally inducing the monsters to leave by getting them to accept other food instead of young and tender, though wayward, human flesh. The children are badly scared, and their love for their parents is even greater than before—a very clever psychological device.

Children in Hotavila are still threatened with Soyoko, but in fact Soyoko, in the rôle of disciplinarian, has not visited the village for eight years. The discontinuance of the appearances of Soyoko at Hotavila is an interesting instance of Hopi notions of cause and effect. Because the last man to play the part of Soyoko at Hotavila became very ill soon after he had frightened the children, no one at present is willing to frighten the children in this manner. Soyoko appears in the winter dances but not as a punisher of children. At other villages, however, Soyoko continues to play the rôle of children's bugaboo.

As punishment for divulging the true character of the masked dancers, whipper kachinas, not Soyoko, are supposed to come and whip the guilty party. On Second Mesa this actually occurs. Our Mishongnovi informant gave a graphic account of a chastisement by whipper kachinas which she herself saw. On Third Mesa it is a theory which has not been realized in practice for some time.

Corporal punishment has been used, by some families at least, for as long as the oldest living inhabitants can remember. The notion that Pueblo children are not punished has no basis in fact, so far as Third Mesa is concerned. Corporal punishment takes the form of whipping with withes or with a strap or of spanking. A child is never slapped, nor is he stood in a corner, or locked in a room at Hotavila.

The whipping, if of a minor character, may be done by the mother. The father whips less often but his punishment is more severe. He is likely to punish when he himself has been annoyed by the child's conduct rather than at the request of the child's mother. If the mother thinks that the child deserves a serious punishment, she asks one of her brothers to perform the chastisement. The father would usually be unwilling to do so. There is the feeling that serious offenses should be handled by the child's own clan.

A further feature of punishment by a maternal uncle is the fact that he oftens deals it out to an entire set of brothers. He may know full well that only one boy has done wrong, but nevertheless all are whipped.

About four years ago some of H's sons developed the habit of chasing and hanging onto automobiles which came through Hotavila. One day H's brother strapped them with his belt, even though not all had been guilty. Some of H's sister's boys were whipped also. H said she felt sorry for them but it had to be done. They were whipped according to size, the small ones being struck very lightly.

Whipping is occasioned by laziness, by stealing, by disobedience, by stubbornness and by hurting other children. Our informants gave laziness as the chief cause of punishment. H gave as examples some of the punishments she suffered as a child. Her mother once asked her to bring a meal sifter from her aunt's home. H refused, and her mother whipped her with a strap of leather. Her mother also whipped her for running off to play and failing to take care of her younger sister.

Whipping is never employed with children as old as fifteen years. No child is whipped at night, as that would cause the child to die.

Another disciplinary action consists in pouring cold water on the child or rolling him in the snow. The pouring of cold water as a punishment is distinguished from the use of water as a treatment of enuresis by the fact that when water is used as a punishment the child is not carried on the back, he is not necessarily naked, and the pouring is not done by the Corn-Water people. Either of the parents or one of the uncles may punish the child with cold water or with snow. These substances may be used for any offense, but with young children they are used particularly in the case of tantrums.

A form of punishment which is thought of as very severe and which is used in Hotavila not more than once every two or three years consists in holding the child over a green cedar smudge.[4] This punishment is always administered by a maternal uncle, never by the parents themselves. A very pungent smudge is made from green cedar, the leaves as well as small twigs being used. The child—the treatment may be applied to either a boy or a girl—is held upside down over the smudge, with a blanket hanging downward from his shoulders so as to collect dense smoke about his head. The child is held far enough above the fire so that there is no danger of burning, but the fumes are stifling.

[4] This type of punishment is also utilized by the Havasupai. (Leslie Spier, "Havasupai Ethnography," *Anthrop. Papers, Amer. Mus. Nat. Hist.*, Vol. 2, Part 3, 1928.)

This treatment is used for severe cases of fighting, quarreling, and teasing and also for being impertinent to one's mother. H's brother applied it to four of H's sister's children about ten years ago. Not all of the children had been naughty, but he did it to all of them "to give them a lesson." It is used chiefly for children between four and ten years of age. The smudge is said to be resorted to only when all other methods have failed.

The punishment is fitted to the child in the sense that a penalty is selected to which the child is particularly susceptible. A child who dislikes to be ridiculed may be punished in that fashion, whereas one who dislikes cold water may find his parents and uncles disposed to make use of this form of disciplinary action. The punitive methods are suited to the season also, water being more often used in winter than in summer.

REWARDS

The parent occasionally praises the child for doing well, or shows approval by smile or tone of voice, or gives the child a friendly pat. There is strong affection between parents and children and knowledge of approval and disapproval is undoubtedly in itself a very powerful means of social control.

Of rewards of a public and formal character, the most prominent is the giving of gifts to the children by the masked dancers. The gifts are understood as a mark of favor and approval from those omniscient beings, the kachinas. Interpretation of the gifts may be guided by the comments of the parents. The mother may say to her son, "You have helped your father in the fields, so the kachinas brought you a nice bow and arrow," or to her daughter, "They gave you a kachina doll because you have taken care of your little brother." While the child thinks that the gifts come from the gods themselves, each present is made by a relative for a specific child and is thus particularized to the situation and to the wishes of the child. The reader will recognize in the gift-dispensing kachinas all the socializing possibilities of Santa Claus. "If you are a good boy, Santa will bring what you want" becomes in Hopiland, "If you are a good boy the kachinas will bring you nice gifts." The kachinas have an advantage over Santa in that they come intermittently from February to August. The appeal to Santa is good only during the fall months, whereas the kachinas influence behavior for more than half of the year.

A formal reward is received for helping in the care of the eagles which are captured and reared for their feathers. The eagles must be fed fresh meat, and small animals are caught for them. The boy is encouraged to catch mice and young rabbits and prairie dogs for the eagles. After the Niman Kachina Dance, when the eagles are killed and plucked, the boy receives one feather for each animal he has brought to the eagle. The fluffy feathers he proudly wears in his hair; others he may use in making arrows.

PLAY

Thus far we have dealt with the duties and the taboos which are placed upon Hopi children and the methods by which they are enforced. In doing this we have not intended to give these things a place of undue prominence. The Hopi child does have duties to perform, and it is proper that we should describe them first, since in Hopi opinion work should be finished before play is begun. Work should be completed early in the day, but when it is done children are free to amuse themselves. Evening is especially a time of play, and on moonlight nights play may continue long after sunset.

In play, the child has the run of the village. That is, it is not demanded that the child play in his own yard. There is, in fact, scarcely such a thing as a front or back yard in connection with any Hopi house, nor is there any place in the village where it is expected that all children will play. No shelters are constructed for the benefit of children, nor are sand boxes or ropes or other apparatus provided. There are spots in the village which are chosen more often for play than are other locations; however, play does not remain in one place but moves about from this locality to that. Except on cold days, all play takes place out of doors.

There are roughly three kinds of play groups. One of these consists of the young girls with their charges. These girls are usually under twelve years of age, because, as we have seen, older girls must stay at home. One finds, therefore, play groups of nurse-maids, made up of girls below twelve years of age, with one-, two-

and three-year-olds who are in their care. There are many little circles of this sort to be seen at almost any time of day.

A second kind of play group consists of the boys who no longer need to be supervised by their older sisters but who are not old enough to do much work in the fields or in the orchards. In age, they range roughly from four to eight years. Because their duties are light, they may play most of the day.

A third class of playmates is made up of the older boys. Two things tend to mark them off from the younger boys. One is the work in the fields which is such that their play occurs chiefly in the late afternoon and in the evening. This naturally tends to separate them from the younger boys. An additional point is that the older boys have been initiated, which gives them a superior status. Initiated boys seldom play with those who have not yet been whipped by the kachinas.

The division of the play groups is not always as sharp as we have sketched it above. The amount of work done in the fields varies from boy to boy and does not divide boys sharply into the two classes of workers and non-workers. The line of initiation is sometimes crossed in play. The sex division is fairly definite; boys and girls seldom play together, if we except the very young boys who are in the care of their older sisters.

Unorganized Games

In this section we wish to describe some of the forms of play which are traditional among Hotavila children, but which do not fall into the category of games having fixed procedures and rules. The latter will be considered in the section on organized games which follows.

It has been noticed that much of the play of the child in all societies copies the patterns of the adults whom the child admires and wants to be like. The Hopi child furnishes no exception.

Much of the play of the Hopi girl centers about the activities of the home, with which she is so familiar. Playhouses are constructed by two kinds of procedures. The first sort of playhouse is made by simply drawing lines on the ground, or by placing sticks on the ground which indicate the walls of the rooms. These are very useful houses, as makeshift furniture can be placed in them, and play can proceed without any hindrance from the make-believe walls. A second form of dwelling is harder to construct but it looks more like a real house. The walls are built of wet mud, and are well-modeled. In order to construct the adobe roof, the entire house is filled with dry sand, and the wet earthen roof is applied on top of this. In a few minutes, the dry sand can be taken out through the windows and doors, and a very real-looking Hopi house is ready for use.

Both types of buildings are made only on a small scale. The child sits outside and manipulates the contents of the house; the dwelling, even one of the outline variety, is not made large enough for the child to get inside of the structure.

For dolls, sticks may be used, and clothing may be tied to the sticks. An interesting traditional form of doll is made by letting the different parts of the forefoot of a sheep or calf impersonate different human characters. These are shown in Plate IV. The markings on the girl-doll are supposed to resemble the whorls into which Hopi maidens formerly arranged their hair. The grandmother figure is said to be bent because she has worked so long at the grinding bin.

Playhouses are equipped by searching the village for scraps of appropriate materials. A fragment of mirror makes a mirror, a piece of linoleum a rug, a small can a stove, an empty spool a sewing machine, etc. A house of this character is often built and furnished jointly by a group of girls playing together. It may occupy them for an entire day, or perhaps longer, but it is not a permanent thing. Interest eventually turns to something else, and the site soon resembles those villages which were deserted centuries ago by the ancestors of the children.

Make-believe gardens and fields and orchards are built about these houses by sticking twigs and leaves into the ground. Theoretically this is men's work but since boys and girls do not play together the girls make the fields themselves.

Girls also play at pottery-making, shaping small pots and actually firing them out of doors. This sometimes accompanies the pottery-making of a mature woman, but as the shaping and firing of pottery is only an occasional activity at Hotavila, the girls frequently perform the sham pot-making by themselves.

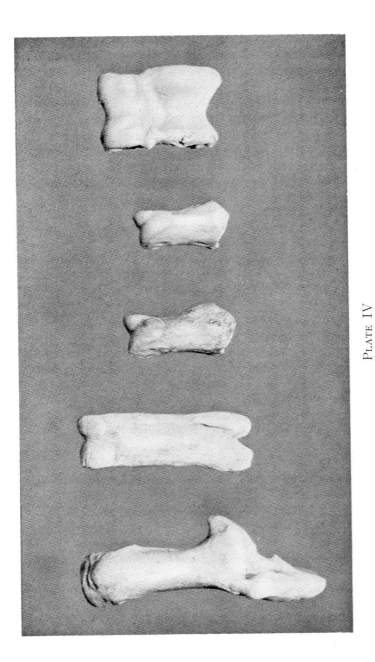

PLATE IV

TRADITIONAL BONE DOLLS: *From left to right, the bones represent a father, a mother, two children, and a grandmother.*

Using play metates for the grinding of grain or the powdering of pigments is another feminine game. The grain is often sand or small pieces of sandstone.

The girls do not play much with dolls like those of our own children. We have already described the temporary dolls of stick and bone. No attachment is shown to them; they are discarded at the end of the play period. The girls prize the carved and painted and ornamented figurines which are given to them by the masked dancers, but these dolls are not meant for play. They are hung on the walls and are seldom taken down. If a Hopi girl possesses an American doll, she is likely to treat it in the same manner. She may bring it out on special occasions, but it is too precious to be subjected to the vicissitudes of everyday life.

The boys in their play imitate the work of their fathers and uncles. Imitation corrals are built, in which peach seeds serve as sheep. Play fields are likewise constructed. True to the pattern set by the men, the boys' activities have little or nothing to do with the work of the home. Although men build houses, they do not own them. We have never seen boys constructing houses in play.

Playing horse is a favorite activity which exists in many forms. One boy may play the part of the horse, holding a rope in his mouth, while another boy seizes the reins and drives. Or a boy may hold a tin can in either hand, thus making hoofs, and run about on all fours impersonating a horse. Of course, there is the time-honored and probably universal style of equine dramatization in which the horse is represented by a stick which the boy straddles and rides, always at high speed. While being ridden, the horse is beaten by a whip derived from a weed or a twig.

Rabbit hunting is another subject for dramatization. The rôle of the rabbit may be played by a tin can, and at it are thrown sticks, just as men throw sticks in the real rabbit hunts.

Play with bows and arrows can scarcely be put down as imitative play at the present time, as the adults seldom make use of these implements. The use of bows and arrows in play occurs most markedly on the days following the kachina dances in which the dancers present them to the young boys.

Not only are the everyday activities of the adults imitated, but the ceremonial patterns also are copied in miniature and in fragmentary form by the children. Girls play at the Butterfly Dance, the Basket Dance and at other women's dances, whereas the boys imitate the steps of the men's performances. Both boys and girls sing snatches of the kachina songs. Boys often obtain an old pail or dishpan and play at beating the drum. Children may even imitate Soyoko. We have mentioned earlier that children must not array themselves in masks as do the kachina dancers, nor may they imitate the Snake Dance.

Girls often put on mud-fights as do certain women following a marriage. Boys do not engage in such throwing of mud, as it is a woman's activity.

Much play occurs which does not take adult life as its model. Playing at seesaw on a log placed across a large stone is an example, as is swinging in a swing formerly made of thong but now constructed of commercial rope. These are old pastimes, enjoyed by the grandparents of the youngsters of today. So, too, are the throwing of snowballs and the holding of snow battles, games engaged in by both sexes. However, the making of snow men and the building of snow houses are innovations introduced by American teachers.

A new game among the boys is the rolling of old automobile tires and the rolling of hoops. These may be rolled by one boy alone, or by several. Boys may simply roll tires as they go about, or they may race with them. There are many possibilities with this toy. The tires (or hoops) may be taken up a long slope and rolled down the incline. Here the tires may race unaided by their owners. They may be directed at each other, to see which hoop will remain erect after the impact.

Pets are kept by both boys and girls. Dogs are pets of the boys, while the cats belong to the girls. In summer time both boys and girls may catch young birds, rabbits and prairie dogs and keep them for pets. These wild animals do not survive long, usually because of the treatment to which they are subjected by the children. The mortality rate among kittens and pups also must be very high, as the play of the child seems to leave the well-being of the animal entirely out of account. The eagles which are kept are not pets but are respected birds, protected and well-fed to provide feathers essential to the ceremonies.

ORGANIZED GAMES

Seasonal Games. Many of the organized games are played only at appropriate seasons while others may be played at any time. The seasonal games will be described first.

Shinny. At the Bean Dance in February the boys are given shinny balls and shinny clubs, and shinny is engaged in during the following month. The ball is about three inches in diameter. It was formerly made of buckskin and stuffed with native cotton, but now it is ordinarily made of canvas and filled with wool. The larger boys are provided with larger balls and clubs than are the small boys. The club is shaped like our own shinny club and may be made of a branch of any hard wood, often being of cedar.

The big boys and the little boys play separately and the big boys use a larger course than do the younger ones.

Sides are formed by leaders who choose alternately from among the boys who wish to play. The first choice is decided by applying the familiar hand-over-hand technique to the shinny club.

Goals are marked off at either end of the course. With the big boys the goals are usually marked by lines on the ground while the small boys dig at either end of the course a hole which is called the "ball house."

To start the play the ball is placed in a hole in the middle of the course and covered with dirt. The teams take turns striking at the ball until it comes out. The game starts. When a goal is made, the teams exchange goals. There is no agreed stopping point, and the game sometimes goes on by moonlight. There are no forfeits and no prizes, except that the losing side sometimes gives up its ball.

Girls do not receive shinny equipment at the Bean Dance, but they do sometimes play the game. They do not play with the boys, nor do they play after dark.

Top Game. Tops are played with in March and at no other time of the year. Tops make a humming noise which sounds like the wind, and hence will bring wind. It is all right to cause wind in the early spring before any crops are planted, but at a later period wind storms are very destructive of young plants. Furthermore, early spring winds often bring rain, whereas at other times of the year high winds tend to prevent rain.

Tops are for children from about four to eight years of age. They are whittled from wood by the child's father or older brother. The boys' tops are decorated, whereas the girls' are plain.

The tops are spun by winding a string about the top and pulling the string. The string is attached to a stick. After the tops are started they are whipped by this string to keep them going. Children may run races by whipping their tops ahead of them, a game which requires a great deal of skill.

Somewhat older boys occasionally play a top game in which there are two teams. Each player, by whipping his top, attempts to make it jump suddenly so as to touch a player of the opposite side. A player so touched is "out"; or, according to another set of rules, he must join the side of the player who tagged him.

Bull-roarers, sticks which are whirled by a string or thong, may be played with only in the early spring period. Parents are very strict about this, as it is felt that the bull-roarer is certain to bring winds which at other times of the year would be very harmful.

Stick Throwing Game. This is a game for older boys, ten or more years of age. Traditionally, it is played in the late spring, although it may be played at other times of the year.

The sticks or clubs which are used are found or made by the boys themselves. They are straight pieces of wood about the size of the boy's forearm. They are not like the throwing stick used in hunting. Rules vary as to the number of sticks which each player shall have, sometimes two and sometimes three being used. There is, in addition, a target stick.

The boys line up and one boy throws the target stick. He may throw it as far as he can, thus testing whether the other boys can throw sticks as far as he, but usually he prefers to throw it so that it goes out of sight behind some obstacle. The other boys then throw their sticks, attempting to hit the target stick. If the target stick cannot be seen, the players are forbidden to move so as to see it, but when a player has thrown his sticks he may move as he pleases, he may tell where the stick is, and he may coach the other members of his team in their throwing. There is no order of throwing; each boy may throw whenever he pleases.

The team which owns the stick that falls nearest the target gains one point. If the stick touches the target, two points are counted. However, if both teams touch the target, or if the two nearest sticks are equidistant from the target, no points are counted.

The team which first gains four points provisionally wins, or, rather, is eligible for a final test to determine whether it can win. For if it wins the next point it wins the game, but if it fails on the final point, both teams start again at zero, with no game won!

Rabbit Hunting. Perhaps rabbit hunting should not be included under games, because it has economic aspects as well as its sporting phases. The hunt serves to provide meat, and also to destroy animals which, if too numerous, would endanger the crops. Nevertheless, rabbit hunting is never looked upon as work. It is a sport in which young men are anxious to engage.

If a young man decides that he wants to start a rabbit hunt, he goes to an old man who helps him make the proper prayer feathers. After these are deposited, he takes some corn meal to the town crier and asks him to make the announcement. The boy's request to the crier must be in the same words that the latter traditionally uses on this occasion. After sundown the crier will announce from his usual position the following:

"Boys, young men, men and old men. Give me your attention. I wish to announce that tomorrow we are going on a hunting party for game, including jackrabbits, cottontails, deer, antelope, mountain sheep, wild cats, coyotes, foxes and any other animals which are edible. Early tomorrow morning when we rise and as soon as the women build fires and cook breakfast and we eat breakfast we will leave by the ———— trail. We will gather at ————. When every one of us has gathered there, then we shall start toward ————. When we have killed game more than our number, then we shall go toward ———— killing as much game as we can as we go, and when we have reached ————, then we shall turn toward ———— and follow this course toward home. We will stop hunting at ————. This is the announcement I was asked to make, so I have made the announcement. All of you think about the hunt this evening and keep it in mind as you go to bed, so that you may dream favorably."

Although it is understood that only cottontails are to be found nowadays, it will be noticed that the names of former game animals are retained in the announcement.

The reference to dreaming is explained as follows: Certain dreams bring good luck in hunting, therefore the prospective hunters should think about the hunt in order to cause such dreams. There is probably also a suggestion of the pueblo belief that concentration on an end aids in bringing it to reality.[5]

A single [6] village, or any number of villages, may participate in a rabbit hunt. If the leader wishes other villages to join with his people, he must carry meal to the town crier of each village and ask him to make the same announcement which was issued in the leader's own town. Through conversation everyone soon knows who is responsible for calling the hunt, and the good or bad luck of the hunt will be attributed in part to him. If it rains during the hunt, he gains credit for it.

The leader must rise earlier than the others on the morning of the hunt, go to the appointed place of meeting, build a fire and put in it an offering of corn meal and of certain grasses which are liked by animals. This is necessary to render the animals willing to be captured by the hunters.

Any boy or man who pleases may go on the hunt, but since it is an all day trip and an arduous one young boys do not join. The majority of the hunters go on horseback, the remainder are on foot. Most of them carry only rabbit sticks, but a few take guns. Guns are dangerous in group hunting, hence not every person who owns a gun carries it. Each man takes his own lunch.

When a hunter reaches the sacrificial fire, he puts grass onto the fire and draws his throwing stick through the smoke of the burning grass.

After the hunters have collected, and the offerings have been made, the style of hunt is decided upon. It is the leader's privilege to decide, but in reality he asks the advice of a number of older men and decides in accordance with the opinion of the majority. The leader is usually a young man, nearly always unmarried.

In one style of hunting, the hunters move forward continuously

---

[5] Elsie Clews Parsons, *Pueblo Indian Religion,* Univ. Chicago Press, 1939, Vol. I, p. 437.

[6] For Second Mesa practices, see E. Beaglehole, "Hopi Hunting and Hunting Ritual," *Yale U. Publ. Anthrop.,* 1936, 4, 1–26.

in a straight line, the men and boys being deployed in such a manner as to leave a space of several yards between adjoining members of the line.

A second form of hunt consists in repeatedly forming a circle and closing in on the game within the circle. In this case the leader chooses an assistant. After consultation, the two men start moving in opposite directions, and gradually curve so as to meet each other at a predetermined point to complete the circle. The other hunters follow the two leaders at appropriate distances, keeping about five yards apart. The circle may be as much as a mile in diameter, the size depending upon the number of hunters.

When the circle is completed, the leaders stand still and the other hunters gradually move toward the leaders, taking game as they come. The men who form the circle are on foot. The men who are on horseback remain outside the circle and chase whatever game escapes the hunters who form the circle.

When one circular plot of territory has been covered in this fashion, the leaders move on to form a new circle. In starting a new circle, however, each leader takes the side of the circle opposite to that which he marked out just previously.

A rabbit belongs to him who kills it. The leader gets no extra share.

If the catch is to be given to the boys' aunts, the announcement is made somewhat differently, but otherwise the hunt is conducted in the manner described above.

If girls are to take part in the hunt, this too is indicated in the announcement. The girls who may go are the unmarried girls, roughly above ten years of age. They make somiviki, a special dish, which provides the lunch of the entire group. The feminine members of the party do not carry sticks and do not hunt. They dress in their best for the occasion, and wear red and white robes. When a boy kills a rabbit, he calls. The girls run toward him; the first one to reach the rabbit becomes the owner of it.

The favorite hunting season is from June to August, when young rabbits are plentiful and when they are dangerous to the corn. A village may hold from three to twelve hunts within this period. In addition, there is a hunt in December which is connected with the ceremonies of that season. The individual hunter, moreover, may take game at any time.

Girls' Grinding Party. In August, before the Niman Kachina Dance, a group of six or eight girls who are fourteen years of age or older may engage in a grinding party. They grind together in the home of one of the girls and they sleep in the same home. During the party each grinding stone must be busy from sunrise to sunset, except for a period for eating lunch. If a girl stops for a while, her mother takes her place at the metate.

During the first three days the girl grinds for a different relative each day. The relative for whom the grinding is being done supplies the corn which is to be ground, and provides food for the girl for that day. At the close of the day the girl takes the corn meal to its owner and gets grain for the following day from another relative.

On the fourth day each girl grinds for her own home; her mother supplies and cooks her food.

On the fifth day, the girls practice the making of piki. Only one piki stone is heated, the girls taking turns at using it. On the evening of the fifth day, the girls take a walk together and the party disbands.

At the Niman Kachina Dance much food is needed for the dancers and for visitors, so that much corn must be ground. This "party" seems to be a way of performing the work in a more sociable, if more formal, manner.

A Snake Game. This game may be played by boys or by girls but the two sexes do not play together. It is played more often by the boys and is usually thought of as a masculine game. The appropriate time is the late summer and fall, because the participants sing for food, and autumn is the period in which food is most plentiful. Like many Hopi games, it takes place in the evening.

Someone who is a favorite or is a leader may start the game. Any boy may join, but boys under six years seldom do so. Behind the leader the boys will form in line in order of size. The one who started the game is at the head of the line, regardless of his size, but immediately behind him follows the largest boy, the smallest boy being last. Each boy grasps the boy in front of him by the waist or by the belt. The boys are then guided by the leader along a crooked course, as a snake goes. As they proceed, they sing a song which is used only in this game. In accordance with the song, the tempo of the step varies from fast to slow, or the direction of travel may be reversed. The players are privileged to go anywhere, even through homes. When they tire of this they go from house to house singing for gifts of melons and fruits. After food is given, a song of thanks is sung, and they proceed to another house. When they have enough, they go somewhere outside the village, divide the food equally, and have a feast.

Archery. This game is played in summer or fall, because the hoop which serves as a target ordinarily is made of green corn leaves or of corn husks, although occasionally it is constructed of young willow or of sage. It must not be played until after the Niman Kachina Dance, when bows and arrows are given as presents. A hoop is made of one of the materials mentioned above and is wound round and round with yucca or with string. The hoop is six to eight inches in diameter, and is about one inch thick. The aim is to hit the rim of this hoop while it is in motion. The game is played by a number of boys, ten to twenty of them, who are divided into two sides. The boys range in age from six to fifteen years.

Two boys who take the initiative in starting the game become the leaders. They choose sides by taking alternate choices. In order to determine which side shall shoot first, one of the leaders tosses an arrow to the other. If he catches it at the tip, his side gets the privilege of beginning the shooting. If he seizes the arrow elsewhere, the two leaders grasp the arrow alternately hand over hand, starting from the point at which it was caught. The boy who grasps the tip wins for his side the right to the first trial at marksmanship.

The boys who are to shoot form a line and the leader of the opposite side rolls the hoop past them. He throws it so that it rolls rapidly. The first boy shoots at it. If he misses, the hoop is rolled again and the second boy tries to hit it. In order to count as a hit, the arrow must stick in the rim. If every boy in the line misses, it then becomes the right of the other team to shoot.

However, when a hit is made, each boy of the opposite side in turn takes the exact position of the boy who let go the accurate arrow and tries to hit the hoop which is now lying still, perhaps some distance from where it was originally struck. The arrows which miss become temporarily the property of the other side, the first going to the leader, the next to the second in line, etc. The temporary winners of these arrows must hit the motionless hoop with them in order to keep them. If a temporary winner does not hit the hoop with the arrow, he must return it to its owner. (Each boy's arrows are distinctively marked.) When the end of this shooting is reached, the teams exchange positions and the game proceeds. This alternation may go on as long as the boys wish to play. The game may last from mid-afternoon until dark. The only event which brings the game to an end is the winning of all of the arrows by one side.

Whether all or only part of the arrows have changed hands by the time that the rolling of the hoop is discontinued, these winnings are still only temporary. It is not easy to win at this game, for each arrow, if it is to be kept, must in reality be won three times—once when the opponent misses with it, again when the winner hits with the same arrow with which the loser missed, and once more at the close of the day.

The final event is as follows: On a straight course a sand mound about one foot high is built and the hoop is placed on top of the mound. A distance from which to shoot is agreed upon. Each boy, separately, then shoots at the hoop all of the arrows which he has won. Those that hit the target may be kept, those that miss are returned to their former owners—except that each boy has one last shot with one of his own arrows. If it strikes, the arrows which have failed to strike the target belong to him nevertheless. A great deal may depend on this last arrow.

Dart Throwing Game. This game is similar to the archery contest except that darts are used instead of bows and arrows. The same type of hoop comprises the target. The darts are made of corncobs which have feathers stuck in one end and a sharpened piece of greasewood in the other. In order to get feathers for their darts the boys sometimes enter chickenhouses at night and pull tail feathers from the chickens. Formerly bird feathers were used. Since corncobs are used in making the darts, the game is played in the fall when fresh corncobs are available. Sometimes a ring of watermelon is used as a target in place of the hoop. A further reason why this game is associated with the autumn is that the throwing of darts at a hoop occurs in a women's ceremony at that time. This tends to start the dart throwing game, although the game is played by boys and not by girls.

The participants are divided into two teams, as in the archery contest, and one side lines up and throws while the other rolls the hoop. When the hoop is struck, the opposing side throws at it, one boy at a time, each taking the exact position of the player who struck the hoop. The projectiles which miss the hoop, instead of going immediately to the opposite side, are gathered into four bunches and each bunch is tossed into the air. An opponent may temporarily keep any dart which he can catch in his right hand as it falls, but the boy who catches one must throw it into the air, and toss the target at it as it comes down. If the dart hits the target, he may keep the dart until the end of the day, when the final trials decide the future possession of the darts.

At the close of the game, when one side has won all of the darts or when the game is discontinued, the target is placed on a mound of sand, as in the archery game, and every dart which has been won must be thrown at it, the temporary winner losing all darts with which he misses the hoop, unless the final dart, which is his own, strikes the target.

Parchesi. The Hopi name for this game is *totolospi*. This is the name of the dice which are used as well as the name of the game. It is an indoor game which is played during the winter in the home or in the kiva. However, it is played only in daytime. Bets may be laid on the outcome of the game. The control of the dice is said to be in part a matter of skill.

The dice which are tossed to determine the moves of the player are sticks which have been split in half. Two or three sticks may be used. The moves to be made are dependent upon the number of split surfaces which lie upward after the sticks have hit the ground.

The course to be followed by the markers of the players is drawn on the ground, and units are marked off around the course. As stated above, the number of units which a player's marker may move is determined by the falling of the sticks.

The winner is he whose marker first completes the entire course. If the dice cause a man to move to a position already occupied by another player, the one who first reached the position must go back to the starting point.

The game is played by adults and by children, but girls and women do not play in the kiva.

Hidden Object Game. This game is common to many Indian groups, and is played at Hotavila, but we failed to get specific information concerning the rules of the game on Third Mesa. Four cups are used. Those who take part are chiefly boys and girls who are sixteen or more years of age. It is considered bad for married people to play it.

Non-Seasonal Games

A War Game. We shall describe the war game, although our informant says that because it is so dangerous it is no longer played.

The two leaders who start the game form teams by choosing alternately from among the boys who wish to play. In order to determine the first choice, each leader throws a rock. The boy whose rock goes the farther wins the right to the first choice of warriors.

The choices are largely in accord with prowess, rather than in terms of personal favorites. It is not a question of two gangs fighting each other, as a team disbands at the end of the game and there might never be another team with exactly the same membership.

The leader who is acknowledged as the stronger usually wants to represent the attacking side, and usually does so. He selects the tribe which he is to represent, Navaho, Apache, Ute or Havasupai.

The game is played at some distance from the village because of the danger of flying rocks. The team representing the Hopi takes up a position on the edge of a cliff and the enemy attack from below. During the attack, the weapons of both sides are rocks, thrown by hand or thrown by means of a sling. As a means of protection from the missiles, a boy may fold a heavy blanket over his left arm, forming a shield behind which he can duck his head. Nevertheless boys were often injured in the game.

Once the attacking side reaches the position of the Hopi, the game changes immediately from a rock throwing game to a wrestling contest. Each boy picks an opponent, and the two wrestle until one gives up. The boy who surrenders can no longer take part in the battle, but the winner may go to the aid of other members of his team. When all the members of one team have been vanquished, the game ends.

Álalatami. The name of the game is meaningless; it comes from the beginning syllables of the initial song of the game. It is played by girls and small children, and may be thought of as a method of entertaining the younger children. When children hear someone starting the first song, they come running. There is no limit to the number which may play. The game starts about sunset, and if the numbers are large, it may last until nightfall. The game consists in a series of disconnected parts which must be known by the leaders but which do not require memorization on the part of anyone else. The two leaders are girls of ten years or older who know the entire game.

To begin the game all the children join hands and circle while singing the traditional song.

The circle then stands still as the two leaders go around the circle, swinging each child on a seat formed by the clasped hands of the leaders, and singing a song which tells with whom each child will sleep—mother, grandmother, aunt, etc.

The leaders then choose sides, the leaders facing each other and the children forming a chain behind the leaders by grasping each other about the waist. The leaders grasp each other's hands and a tug of war follows.

In the next part, the children of each leader lie in a row. The leader passes down her row of children, lifting each child a small way, telling her what her mother does, and putting her back down. On the next trip, each child is pulled to sitting. When the leader again goes down the line she pulls each child to a kneeling position. On the following trip, the players are pulled to standing. On the final trip, the leader says to the first child, "This one will grow" and pulls her to tiptoe; to the second she says, "This one will be a dwarf" and pushes down on her shoulders, and so on alternately down the line.

The leaders now become jackrabbits, running about wildly and then hiding. The others try to find them and catch them. If one hiding place is discovered, the rabbit runs to another. Finally the leaders permit themselves to be caught. The smaller children pretend to skin the jackrabbits and put them in a cooking pit. The children then play at going to sleep. The jackrabbits jump up and run away. That is the end.

Breaking the Piki Stone. The game is played by girls from six to twelve years of age. The girls form a line in some sandy spot and each pretends to make a piki stone by smoothing the area of sand in front of her. She then makes a design on the smoothed area by letting sand drop between her fingers, as is done in making sand paintings. When the designs are made, the players exchange places at random, and each then rubs out the sand painting which is before her and makes a design of her own. Each then returns to her original place.

The first girl goes down the line of players, saying to each girl "Did you break my piki stone?", meaning, "Did you destroy my design?" The players are obligated to tell the truth. When the guilty girl is found, she is chased by her accuser until she is caught. The second girl then moves down the line and repeats the procedure, and so on until the last breaker of piki stones has been detected and captured.

Pursuit Game. In this girls' game, the leader makes in soft sand a complicated and twisting path which usually coils from the outside toward the center of the play area. When the path is made, the players line up in an outer section of the path, the leader taking a position behind them. The leader chases them as they run toward the center of the design. If a girl steps off of the crooked path, she must drop out of the game. The first girl to be caught by the leader becomes "it" and must chase the remainder of the players on the next trip.

Playing Witch. This pastime is for the older boys, and is played at night. One of the fastest runners is chosen as the witch. He takes with him a small drum, and hides at some distance. The other players try to find him. If the boys go too far in the wrong direction, the witch beats his drum, but he then slips to another hiding place. If he is seen, he is chased but he tries to elude the pursuers and to hide elsewhere. If he is caught, another boy is chosen to act as witch and the game continues.

Social Groupings in Play

In general a child may play with whom he chooses, although he should play with members of the same sex. Clan lines have nothing to do with play, nor do the society memberships of the child's parents in any way affect the social life of the child. The child may play wherever he pleases, although he should not go beyond the village without informing his parents of his destination. An older girl, as we have noted before, should not go about in the village unless a married woman is with her, but this restriction is breaking down even in Hotavila.

There are, however, some informal limitations upon the freedom of choice of playmates. If a group of siblings is known to steal or to fight, other children may be kept away from them. If a girl is known to be sexually immoral, parents may ask their daughters to avoid her. Particularly would they refuse to let a daughter spend the night with such a girl.

Families are quite often on the "outs" with each other. In such cases, their children may nevertheless play together. In this matter, as in many others, the attitude of the parents differs from family to family.

Some adults are said to be witches, although no one knows definitely who the witches are. Children are told who is thought to be a witch, and are warned to avoid the witch but to be very careful not to offend him or her. It may be that only one person in a family is a witch. In such a case, only the witch and not the entire family is subject to suspicion. Witchcraft is not hereditary, and children of witches are not shunned by other children as they are at Zuni.

The Joking Relationship

There is a joking relationship between a boy and the husbands of his father's sisters. In fun these uncles are called "grandfathers" by the boy. There is no such relationship among the girls and women. A grandfather may come and sprinkle cold water on the boy early in the morning, or may carry him out and dip him in the spring, or may continually tease him by word and manner or play practical jokes on him.

The boy retaliates in kind. The boy may offer to carry a load which his "grandfather" has just gotten to the top of the mesa, but upon being trusted with it, he may proceed to take it back down the trail and deposit it at the foot of the cliff. Another trick is to dig a shallow pit in a trail frequented by a "grandfather" and to camouflage it so that he will step into it. Other tricks are improvised as the occasion warrants. A "grandfather" is the only adult who may be teased by the boy; least of all would he tease his true grandfathers.

Story Telling

The telling of children's stories is engaged in only in winter time between the Wuwucim ceremony and Pamuyi, a period which is roughly the month of December. If one were to tell these stories at other times, he would be bitten by a snake, or other dire consequences would follow.

The stories told in December are thought of as children's stories, although they are enjoyed by all. They are told during the evening at home. Story telling occurs almost every evening during this period. Some member of the family may act as the story teller, or someone from outside the family who is skilled in this art may be called in. He is expected to tell the traditional stories, not to invent new ones or to elaborate on the old. Children are interested in the stories and stay awake to hear them, but, unlike the custom at Zuni, they are not forced to stay awake if they become sleepy.

The characters in the stories are largely animals—bears, rabbits, birds, coyotes—who are given human powers and tendencies. Many of the stories recorded by Voth at Oraibi about 1900 are children's stories.[7] In order to show the nature of these tales, two of them are reproduced here:

The Child Who Turned into an Owl

(Told by Sikahpiki of Shipaulovi)

Aliksai![8] They were living in Shipaulovi, and one time a child was crying bitterly. Its mother did not pity it and beat it. "You are crying,"

---

[7] H. R. Voth, "Traditions of the Hopi," *Anthrop. Series, Field Mus. Nat. Hist.*, 1905, 8, 1–319.

[8] A traditional beginning, perhaps translatable as "Listen."

she said: "I am going to throw you out to the Owl." Hereupon she dragged the child out of the house. A large Owl had been close by and had heard the moaning of the child. He came to the child and when he saw the latter still crying he put him on his back and carried him off. He lived in a little cave at the side of the bluff on which the village of Bayupki was situated. To this cave he took the child. The Owl had little children in the cave that were living there nicely.

When the mother of the child no longer heard the crying, she came out of the house and looked for her child, but it was gone. "Where has that child gone now?" she said. "It seems somebody came and got it," whereupon she went through the houses and inquired everywhere, but no one had it. In the morning she again went through the houses hunting her child, but could not find it. "Where may that child be?" she said. So she was without children.

Sometime afterward some men went after wood north of the village, some of them passing the cave where the Owl lived. They heard some one in a moaning voice sing the following song:

> Chavayo chavayo,
> Chavayo piva, chavayo piva,
> A hmhm, a hmhm.

Looking up they saw a child in the cave, which had already feathers, and the white spots of the Owl began to appear all over the body. The eyes of the child also began to become yellow. "Oh!" the men said, "whose child may that be?" One of the men then suggested that it might be the child that had disappeared, so when they returned to the village they said: "There in the cave of an owl, at Bayupki, is a child. It already has feathers and spots all over, and its eyes are already yellow. It is turning into an owl. Whose child may that be?" "It must be the child of that woman," the people said right away, so they told them about it. "Now, bestir yourself, bestir yourself, because that child is turning into an owl." So they hurried up and the mother and father and the men who had found the child then proceeded to the place.

When they arrived there the men who had found the child climbed up to the cave. In the back part of the latter was the Owl and his children. The little owl child was sitting alone. The men took it, brought it down and handed it to its father. The mother also took told of it. The Owl did not come out, but said: "You take the child with you, but when you get to your village you put the child into a room and keep it locked up there for four days. On the fourth day when the sun rises you open the door and let the child come out. It will then be a Hopi again. If you do not do that and open the door before that, the child will remain an Owl and come back again."

So they took the child to the village, put it into a room, placed some food in it and locked the door. The father watched in front of the door, keeping watch there during the four days. He heard his child move about in the room. After the first day the mother was anxious to open the door, but the father forbid her, saying that they were not to do that, because the Owl had forbidden it. So she waited and on the third day she was very anxious for her child and could hardly await the third day. During the night also, and it seemed to her as if the morning was very slow coming. Finally when it became light she went to the door, which, like the old Hopi doors, that were not made very well, had cracks. "It is light already," she said, "let us open the door." Hereupon she shaded her eyes and looked through one of the cracks. She saw her child walking up and down, but also noticed that it began to change into an owl again. "Let us open the door," she urged, "it is already light." Her husband protested, saying, that the sun had not yet risen, but she opened the door, and out rushed an Owl which immediately rose up and flew towards Bayupki to the place where it had come from. "Well, now," the man said, "there you looked in before the sun had risen, and yet the Owl had told us not to do so. You have done this, now you have done it and we have no children now. We were just getting our child back again, and now you looked in and it has turned into an Owl, and it will now remain an Owl."

The Chíro [9] and the Coyote

(Told by Qöyáwaima of Oraibi)

In Oraibi the people were living. At Ishmovala the Coyote lived. Away over there at Káhkangwovakaavi lived a great many Chíros, and they were always dancing there. One time the Coyote was walking about east of their village. The Chíros saw him as they were dancing. They were singing as follows:

> "Ishawu, ishawu, höhöongyanikay cölmoki
> Coyote, Coyote, to dance is longing,
> Ishawu, oomii höngina,
> Coyote upward dances,
> Aatkamii höngina,
> Downward dances,
> Machiwa, machiwa, chirorororo.
> Is called, is called chirorororo."

The Coyote was looking at them and wanted to dance along. "Very well," the Chíros said to him, whereupon each one of them gave him some feathers; one some wing feathers, another some tail feathers, and so on. They made for the Coyote wings and a tail, and put small feathers into his body, whereupon the Coyote was very happy. "Thanks," he said, "that you have made wings for me. I am going to dance with you now." Hereupon they danced, again singing the same song. The Coyote danced with them. Now they were flying upward somewhere, and arrived somewhere away high up. Now they crowded around the Coyote and said: "Why, this is my wing; why, this is my tail; why, these are

---

[9] A native bird.

my feathers"; some of them had given him these things, and now they took everything away from him, and alas! he began to descend. He arrived at the earth and died. The Chíros laughed at him. "Thanks," they said, "that you have died, because you very often do commit depredations on some one's property. That is why you were going about again."

Religious Training

The Kachinas. From the time that the child is a few months of age he is taken to see all public ceremonies, whether in the streets of the village or in the kivas. During his childhood he witnesses practically every ceremony which occurs. Ceremonials, therefore, are not something into which he is suddenly inducted, but events which have been a part of his life—the most interesting and colorful part of it—since he can remember. What is true of the ceremonies as a whole, is true of those supernatural personages who are impersonated,—the kachinas.

When the child is big enough to ask questions, he is told that the kachinas are powerful beings who control temperature and wind and rain. They live on Black Mountain, and on the San Francisco Peaks, which, although seventy miles away, can be seen clearly. Snow remains on the peaks during most of the year, but the kachinas are impervious to cold. In the mountains, the kachinas have farms where they raise the wonderful foods which they bring to Hotavila. They bring melons and fresh corn at the very beginning of the season, and beans in February when no plants could withstand the inclemency of Hotavila. The child is not told that the beans are raised in the kivas by the heat of wood fires. In the kivas are made the bows and arrows, the rattles, the shinny sticks, and the kachina dolls which the masked dancers bring to the children.

When the kachinas journey to Hotavila to dance for the people and to bring gifts to the children, it is said that they sometimes come on the clouds. The child is shown the place, just out of sight of the village, where the clouds land and from whence the masked dancers appear. Some dancers, however, come out of the kivas. In this case, they are believed to travel through the underworld, and emerge through a tiny opening in the floor of the kiva, which the child has seen and which he knows to furnish a connection with the dark world below.

The practicing of the kachina dances is carried out in a way which protects the child from learning the true nature of the kachinas. Dance practice is always held in the kivas after the usual bed time of young children. When practice is announced, the crier simply says "Men are invited to such-and-such kiva tonight." The children may be told that the kachinas are soon to appear and that the men are going to the kivas to smoke so that the kachinas will come. If a child should hear singing in the kiva, he is told not to ask questions about such things, as to do so is bad, or his inquiry may be turned aside with the remark that since the men have been smoking in the kiva perhaps the kachinas have come to the kiva.

When the kachinas do come, the childen are admittedly most interested in the presents which they are to receive, but they are also interested in the costumes and in the songs and steps of the dancers. The toys and food given to each child are provided by the boy's fathers, i.e., by his father and his father's brothers, and the child will later appreciate this fact although at present the kachinas are the ones who receive the child's thanks. If none of the child's fathers are dancing, the gifts are delivered by a dancer who is a friend of the father.

In some villages, all sorts of gifts are now being brought by the kachinas, including crackerjack and bottles of pop. At Hotavila, however, kachina gifts are restricted to the traditional toys and to farm products. The people of Hotavila do not want their children to think that the kachinas buy their presents from the stores.

The general attitude of the child toward the kachinas is a favorable and expectant one, although the child may be afraid of the gods because of their strange appearance. However, the child learns that there are unkind gods as well as beneficent ones. In some ceremonies, there appear whipping kachinas who, on certain occasions, whip everyone who remains on the dance plaza. While some adults receive the blows because they are good for rheumatism, mothers with children scurry out of the way, and the children learn to recognize these kachinas and to flee at their appearance.

We have already described the Soyoko kachina who formerly came specifically to punish children but who has not done so at Hotavila in recent years. This figure may be thought of not only as serving disciplinary ends but also as providing another strong element in the religious training of the child.

The Children's Initiation. The interpretation of the dancers as gods comes to an end at the time of the children's initiation, or as it is sometimes called, the first initiation. Initiation does not occur every year, so that the child at initiation may be from six years to ten years of age.

There are two forms of children's initiation, the Kachina initiation and the Powamu initiation. Either initiation reveals to the child the true nature of the kachinas and either entitles the boy to participate in the kachina dances. In describing the initiations, we must for a moment digress to the subject of the kachina dances in order to state that in these performances there are not only the kachinas, but also "kachina fathers," who do not dance but who help the kachinas or look after them, as by aiding them with their costumes, leading them to the dance plaza and by sprinkling corn meal on these impersonators of the supernaturals. The Powamu initiation entitles the boy to become a kachina father, although the boy who has been through this initiation may also act as a kachina. The girl who undergoes the Powamu initiation is expected to help cook for the dancers and to carry food and water to them. Since those who are initiated by means of the Powamu ceremony thereby obligate themselves to perform services for the kachinas, they are not flogged by the kachinas in the course of the initiation as are those who go through the other children's ceremc

It is the duty of the Kachina Clan and the Badger Clan to act as kachina fathers. Therefore the children who belong to these clans are subjected to the Powamu initiation. For the boy a godfather is chosen to conduct him through the initiation, and for the girl a godmother is selected. These godparents must not be close relatives of the child but must be of the Kachina or the Badger Clan. However, a child belonging to any clan may be put through the Powamu initiation if his parents choose his godparent from the two clans mentioned above. Since the Powamu initiation is the easier, parents often choose this ceremony for the child. If the child is to go through the Kachina initiation his godparent may not be from the Kachina or the Badger Clan nor may he be from the child's own clan.

Both initiations take place during the Bean Dance, which is a nine-day ceremony. The Powamu initiation occurs on the fifth day —and the Kachina ceremony on the sixth day. The Powamu initiates are present as spectators at the Kachina initiation.

Each initiation takes place in a kiva and each occupies a period of several hours. Since Voth has described the ceremonies in detail, we need not present a full description at this point. Each initiatory ceremony is composed of many of the same elements as make up other Hopi ceremonies: recital of prayers by the priests, singing of sacred songs, sprinkling the candidates with water and with corn meal, the tying of prayer feathers to the hair, the performance of rituals before an altar, the making of a sand-painting, the entrance of kachinas into the kiva and the dancing of the kachinas. Each ceremony is a serious affair, designed to impress the novices, and in this it would appear to serve its purpose.

In addition to the ceremonial elements mentioned above, the Kachina initiation involves the individual chastisement of each candidate by two Ho Kachinas, each using a formidable whip made of yucca. We quote Voth's account of this performance: [10]

. . . The dreaded moment which the candidates have so often been told about and of which they stand in such great fear has arrived. They are about to go through the ordeal of being flogged. Presently a loud grunting noise, a rattling of turtle shell rattles and a jingling of bells is heard outside. The two Ho Katcinas and the Hahai-i have arrived at the kiva. They first run around the kiva four times at a rapid rate, then dance on each side of the kiva a little while, beat the roof of the kiva with whips, jump on it, constantly howling the word u'huhuhu and finally enter the kiva. The two Ho Katcinas take a position on the east and west side of the large sand mosaic, the Hahai-i at its southeast corner, the latter holding a supply of whips. The children tremble and some begin to cry and to scream. The Ho Katcinas keep up their grunting, howling, rattling, trampling and brandishing of their yucca whips. All at once someone places a candidate on the sand mosaic, holds his (or her) hands upward and one of the Ho Katcinas whips the little victim quite severely. It is said that four strokes are supposed to be applied, but the Katcinas do not always strictly adhere to this rule. The girls have their usual dress on, but the boys are entirely nude. The persons holding them are also nude except for a scant loin cloth, and they wear their hair loose, as is customary in all Hopi sacred ceremonies. When one child has been flogged another one is at once brought forward and beaten and then another and so on until all have gone through the ordeal. One is flogged by one Katcina, the next one by the other, the two Katcinas constantly changing about. When a whip is worn out it is handed to the Hahai-i Katcina who exchanges it for a fresh one. Some of the children

---

[10] H. R. Voth, "The Oraibi Powamu Ceremony," *Anthrop. Series, Field Mus. Nat. Hist.*, 1901, 3, No. 2, 67–158.

go through the process with set teeth and without flinching, others squirm, try to jump away and scream. Occasionally a "sponsor," pitying his little ward, presents his own hip, snatching the child away, and receives a part of the flogging in the child's stead, in which case, however, the flogging is usually very severe.

With the crying and screaming of the candidates men and women mingle their voices, some encouraging them, others accusing the Katcinas of partiality, claiming that they whip some harder than others; in short, pandemonium reigns in the kiva during this exciting half hour. But the scene has not only its exciting, but also its disgusting features. As the whips are quite long they frequently extend around the leg or hip of the little nude boys in such a manner that the points strike the pudibilia, and the author noticed on several occasions that the boys, when being placed on the sand mosaic, were warned to protect those parts, which they tried to do by either quickly freeing one hand and pushing the pudenda between the legs or by partly crossing the legs. It was also noticed on several occasions that some of the boys, probably as a result of fear and pain, involuntarily micturated and in one or two cases even defecated.

When all the children have been flogged the Hahai-i Katcina steps on the sand mosaic, bends forward, raises the ceremonial blanket and is then severely flogged by both Katcinas, after which the two latter apply a thorough scourging to each other in the same manner, to the great satisfaction of the little novitiates who have just been so cruelly treated by these two personages. The Katcina chief then hands his baho and some corn-meal to one of the Ho Katcinas; his assistant hands the same to each of the other two, whereupon the three Katcinas leave the kiva.

In the course of each ceremony the children are admonished to tell no one what they have seen and heard, under threat of punishment by the kachinas. The children do not as yet know that the kachinas are men. This revelation is reserved for the last night of the Bean Dance, when the initiates see the kachina dancers perform without their masks. The initiation is then complete.

The initiation changes the status of the boy in several respects. His newly obtained knowledge about the kachinas, together with the fact that he has passed through the ordeal which children dread, act to make him feel much less like a child and more like a man. Prior to initiation, he cannot enter the kivas as men do. He can go with his mother to attend ceremonies in the kivas, but he can not come and go freely. After initiation he can even work and sleep in the kiva.

The girl's status seems to be changed less than is the boy's. At no time, not even as a woman, do the privileges of the kiva belong to her, except during the dance practices of the women's societies. The first initiation has nothing to do with her eligibility for membership in the women's societies, for these may be joined either before or after the children's initiation, although they are usually joined subsequent to this ceremony.

After the initiation, the boy may take part in the religious life of the community by participating in the public dances. The boys are anxious to do this and may begin to dance soon after their initiation. The winter kiva dances are easier than the all-day dances of the spring and summer, so that the child usually dances in the kiva first. If he becomes fatigued during a dance, he may drop out.

Before he participates as a kachina dancer, however, he is older, perhaps fourteen years of age or more. The practice for any of these dances starts in the spring and occupies one night each week until shortly before the date of the dance, when several sessions per week are necessary. If all of the songs are practiced, the entire night is required for the task, because the finished performance occupies about half of the daylight hours of a long summer day. Memorizing an entire day's program of songs and of dance steps is no easy task, and some persons have difficulty in accomplishing it. However, the men persevere in the attempt and most succeed in learning to perform the dance without error.

A boy may also begin to compose songs for the dances, after his first initiation but he is usually a mature man before he succeeds in producing songs which can be used. Part of the difficulty lies in learning to employ a special poetical vocabulary which he has had no practice in using.

The Second Initiation. At about fifteen or sixteen years of age the boy begins to think about his second initiation, which introduces him into adulthood. The nature of these initiations is secret, and only with extreme difficulty could one get much information about them. Since to seek such secret and prohibited knowledge would jeopardize one's friendly relations with the Hotavila community, we have not attempted it.

Each adult man is expected to belong either to the Warrior Society, the Horn Society, the Singer Society or the Wuwucim Society. They are exclusive societies; he cannot belong to more than one. At the present time, only a few adult men have not undergone the second initiation.

The society into which the boy is to be inducted is determined before his first initiation at the time that the godfather is chosen. The boy must join the society of his godfather. For the godfather, the guiding of the boy through the *first* initiation is a minor affair. The thing of greatest importance is that of seeing the boy through his second initiation.

In choosing a godfather for the boy, the father takes the most active part, the mother simply approving or disapproving of the father's suggestions. A maternal uncle would have a voice in the choice of a society only if the uncle expected the boy to succeed him in a society office.

The father usually wants his first son to belong to his own society, and consequently chooses as a godfather a friend who also belongs to his society. All of his sons may be placed in his own society, but usually this is not done.

Except for the father's preference for his own society, the consideration which is of greatest moment in determining a choice of societies for the son is the severity of the initiation. The initiations of the Warriors and the Horns are thought to be the hardest, and many parents hesitate to commit their sons to the hardships which membership in these societies entails. On that account, the Singers and Wuwucim, particularly the latter, which is considered to be the easiest, receive the largest number of boys. This is reflected at Hotavila in the fact that the Wuwucim has three kivas, whereas the other societies have only one kiva each.

The boys often resent the choices which have been made for them, most boys declaring they want to become Warriors or Horns. Whether they really do wish it is hard to say. The only circumstance which gives the boy any voice in the matter is the death of his godfather before the second initiation has been reached. In that event a second godfather has to be chosen and a boy who is fifteen or sixteen years of age may be permitted to make his own choice.

In the parents' selection of a society there is some attempt to choose a society for which the boy is fitted. Thus if he is unusually strong and brave, he may be put into the Warrior Society, whereas if he is weak he is likely to be placed with the Wuwucim.

Although the Warrior initiation is a severe ordeal, only a few candidates have failed to pass it. To fail at the tests of initiation of any society brings relatively permanent disgrace to the person.

Most boys become candidates for initiation at twenty years of age. Formerly this age was mandatory, but now some are permitted to become candidates when they are as young as sixteen years. Initiations at Hotavila occur only at intervals of six to eight years, although at Oraibi, when the population was greater, they were held more frequently. Initiations were held in Hotavila in the fall of 1938. There were about twenty candidates.

Candidates are announced a year before the initiation is to occur. The announcement is made for all societies at one time. The candidates have the ensuing year in which to prepare themselves for entrance into the societies.

The final initiations of all societies occur on the same day. The initiations are then announced at a public ceremony, and each man receives a new name which he uses throughout life.

The boy at that moment becomes a grown man. He is not expected to play with boys who have not been initiated; he is expected to refrain from fighting or quarreling as a boy might do. He has new religious duties, and he has access to religious lore and to sacred myths and songs which the uninitiated may not hear. In former times, he did not become eligible for marriage until after his second initiation, but this rule is no longer adhered to. However, girls are said to prefer as a husband a man who has been initiated. He is believed to be more mature, and stronger, and is said to have learned to lead a good life. A further consideration is the fact that a woman does not want to live with a man during his year of initiatory hardships.

The four men's societies exist on all mesas. When a man moves to another mesa, his society in the new village accepts him without question.

While every man must join one of the four societies mentioned above, such is not the case with the Snake and Antelope Societies. These are clan societies, and all boys of the Snake and Antelope clans must join. They usually join shortly after the children's initiation, and must in addition join either the Warrior, Horn, Singer or Wuwucim Society, as stated above.

While children and grandchildren of men of the Snake and

PLATE V

BOYS ON A DONKEY AND BOYS PLAYING HORSE.

Antelope clans are not members of these clans they may join the Snake and Antelope Societies, respectively, if they wish. Usually they join only if the society membership becomes very small, or if it is necessary for one of them to do so in order to keep an office within a family. No man may belong to both the Snake and the Antelope Societies because, since the societies perform simultaneously, a man could not do his duties in both organizations.

The women's societies are not analogous to the men's societies. Induction into the women's societies is not spoken of as a second initiation, and it is not compulsory. Nearly every woman, however, does join either Oaqöl or Lalkon and most women belong to both of these societies. For the women's organizations differ from the men's also in that they are not exclusive.

A girl may be inducted into the societies in any order but the first one which a girl may join is determined for her by her parents' selection of her godmother. She must first join her godmother's society. The usual age for joining the first society is from twelve to fourteen years. However she may even become a member as a baby, for if her mother carries her into a society meeting, she automatically becomes a member.

The motives for joining Oaqöl and Lalkon are largely social urges, rather than feelings of religious duty. The girl wants to be a member of the women's societies and wants to take part in the women's dances. All who wish to join are accepted. There is no relationship between clanship and society membership.

The Mamraut Society, however, is quite different from the Oaqöl and Lalkon and is much more like the Snake Society of the men. Mamraut is the women's society which is most important to the community, it is the most religious of the women's organization. It has only a few members and these are chiefly older women. Furthermore, to become a member of Mamraut one must belong to the Snake Clan or must have a godmother who is a Snake. The Mamraut ceremony alternates with that of the Snake Society, that is, they occur in alternate years and are thought of as related.

If a woman belongs to the Snake Clan, she may join Mamraut because of clan duty. If she is not a Snake clanswoman, she becomes a Mamraut member only because she was ill in childhood and was promised to Mamraut if she recovered. In this case, the child has no choice in the matter. No girl would join of her own accord, because membership in the society involves duties which offer no compensatory advantages.

A few men belong to each society and aid in directing the society ceremonials. In Oaqöl and Lalkon a man is chief of the society, but Mamraut has a woman chief. She is the only society chief in Hotavila who is a woman. The office is inherited by a younger sister, or if no sister is living, by a daughter. That is, it is inherited by a lineage but within the clan.

Courtship and Marriage

There is a natural sex education among the Hopi in the fact that the adults speak plainly of sexual matters. Nearly every boy and girl of eight or nine years knows of the sexual relationship between men and women and knows the cause and the origin of babies.

Young children are warned against erotic experimentation with members of the opposite sex by the pretense that even children may bear babies. A girl is told that if a girl of eight or nine years were to have a baby, all the people would die and the world would come to an end. In addition, the girl is appealed to not to disgrace her family. A boy is told that sexual experience will cause him to stop growing, so that he will be a dwarf. He is also warned that if he has sex relationships at an early age he will grow old prematurely. Both boys and girls are told that if they start acting as grown-ups in sexual matters, their parents will cease to support them; i.e., sexual maturity and economic responsibility go together.

At ten years of age, a strong attempt is made to keep boys and girls apart by insisting that a girl stay at home most of the time, and that she never go about except in the company of a married woman. In this respect the traditions of the Hopi come in conflict with American standards, for the Hopi girl learns in school that the American girl has greater freedom. In this regard, the Hopi girl is anxious to take over the customs of the whites.

No formal notice of physiological puberty is taken either in the boy or the girl. The boy's status does not change with puberty; neither his first nor his second initiation coincides with sex maturity. The situation is the same with the girl, for in her case also there is no formal recognition of physiological maturity.

The girl takes part in a grinding ceremony which signifies that she is old enough to marry, but the age at which she participates in this ceremony may vary by several years and while she would not go through the ceremony before puberty she may choose to do so at any time thereafter. Formerly, the grinding ceremony marked a change in the hair style of the girl, so that her marriageable status was visible to all. The hair whorls are not worn today but no doubt each girl's status is as well known as it was formerly, for a symbol is scarcely necessary in a small town. In former times it was mandatory that every girl go through the grinding ceremony before marriage, but today some girls dispense with this formality.

In Hotavila the ceremony is held every three or four years. A number of girls take part simultaneously, grinding together for four days in a house whose windows have been shaded so as to bar direct sunlight.

The girls grind continuously from morning until evening, not pausing for rest and not eating any lunch. Water may not be taken in the morning, and it should be drunk sparingly in the afternoon. A full meal is eaten at the close of each day's work.

The girl grinds for a different person each day. These persons are usually relatives, but one of them may be the godmother who has taken her through her first initiation and has inducted her into a women's society. The person for whom she is grinding brings the girl's supper to her at the close of the day.

After supper, the girls may engage in play or in conversation, but this does not last long, as they are tired, and must arise early the following morning. They may go out to relieve themselves only in the morning and in the evening, when they go out single file.

No one, except those concerned, may enter the house during the four days.

After the four days of grinding, there is a fifth day on which the girls take turns at making piki, as is done in the grinding party for younger girls which was described in the section on games. It will be seen that the grinding ceremony is very much like the grinding party but the latter is much less severe. In the grinding party the

girl's mother may substitute for her while she rests, and there is
no restriction upon eating and drinking or upon the eliminative
functions, nor is the house darkened during the party. The ceremony entails hardships such that a girl occasionally drops out of
the group because she cannot stand the rigors of the four days.
She is teased about this later.

It was formerly in the late afternoon of the fifth day that the
girl's hairdress was changed to that typical of the Hopi maiden.
About sundown on the fifth day the girls file silently out of the
village. Once beyond the village, the ordeal is over and their
silence is broken. They may have a good time among themselves.
Before dark they return, get their bedclothes from the house in
which the ceremony was held, and go home.

At the next dance, all of the girls who have been in the ceremony
stand together while watching the dance. They wear black shawls
instead of the usual colored ones, and on that account the boys
tease them by calling them crows.

Courtship may have started before this ceremony, because the
first meetings between boys and girls are not considered to be
serious steps toward marriage. The approved method of courtship
is for the boy to come to the outside of the girl's house after dark.
There is no daylight courting. The girl, if she is industrious,
should be grinding corn, but she is near a window, and the couple
talk through the window. In earlier days a very small opening
was left in the wall near the grinding bins, and this was called a
"courting window." These may be seen in Hotavila today, but are
not commonly used. It was customary for the parents to fasten
the door when they retired, leaving the boy and girl with the
small window as the only possible means of communication. If the
young man stayed too long, the girl's mother told her to go to bed.

Today it is common for the young man and woman to talk just
outside the door of the girl's home. They are not supposed to leave
this spot, but parents now complain that the young couple run away
from adult supervision. There is a considerable amount of sexual
irregularity among the unmarried, as is shown by the number of
unmarried mothers, and these nightly meetings outside of the
door probably furnish the chief opportunity for amorous en-
counters.

A considerable amount of promiscuity among the unmarried

occurs at the Snake Dance period. A certain degree of license has grown out of a custom which may, or may not, have been chaste in earlier years. At any rate, present-day parents insist that conditions following the Snake Dance are much more immoral than they used to be.

On the day of the Snake Dance,[11] and for three days afterward, a woman may snatch from a man any possession which he is carrying. This struggling over small possessions is the occasion of a great deal of fun and of practical joking. Any man carrying corn, a basket of fruit, or a melon, is likely to have it taken away from him by a woman or by a group of women. Only a married man who is accompanied by his wife is exempt from danger. Married women, as well as the unmarried, have the right to snatch things from the men, but married women participate in the sport only in the daytime.

For the unmarried, the game continues after dark, and a young man may exhibit some object—nowadays it is often a coin,—in front of a young woman in order to encourage her to pursue him to some secluded spot. In other words, the custom furnishes a ready means by which young men and women may escape from the village, and it is used as a convenient method of achieving clandestine meetings. At this season of the year parents worry most about their daughters. In the late evening they may be seen with lanterns seeking a girl who has disappeared from the village. While the sport of snatching from the men used to be limited to the three days following the dance, it now occurs, at least sporadically, for a period of a week or more.

Boys are the aggressors in sexual matters; the girl may consent to an intrigue but she does not propose it. Nevertheless, it is the girl who is supposed to exercise erotic control, and she, not the boy, is blamed for illegitimate children. The boy is not forced to marry the girl, nor to support the child.

If an unmarried girl becomes pregnant, it is common for her friends to cease their association with her. Her parents scold the girl, continually reminding her that she is bringing them extra work. She stays in the house when pregnant, and for some time after the birth of the child. It is pointed out as an instance of the

[11] H. R. Voth, "The Oraibi Summer Snake Ceremony," *Anthrop. Series, Field Mus. Nat. Hist.*, 1903, 3, No. 4, 271–358.

brazenness of the modern generation that unmarried mothers now often carry their babies about the streets, whereas formerly they would have been ashamed to do so. However, the disgrace of the girl is gradually forgotten, and she eventually marries, her husband accepting the responsibility of providing for the child.

Men and women marry at about the same age. The Hopi insist that formerly the age of marriage was quite late, often as late as twenty-five or thirty years. It was pointed out to a girl that if she were chaste, and did not marry until she was thirty, she might have only four children instead of bearing a large family. In earlier times, a man had to complete his second initiation before he could marry, which meant that he had to be more than twenty before taking a wife. This restriction no longer holds, and both boys and girls today occasionally marry as early as the sixteenth year. The average age of marriage is probably between eighteen and twenty years.

It is said that boys prefer pretty girls but that more mature men choose a woman who is industrious and who is of a good disposition. He does not want a wife who is cross, greedy, vain, gossipy or quarrelsome. The only limitation in marital choices is clan exogamy. A boy may not marry a girl of his clan and should not marry a girl of his father's clan, although this is sometimes done.

When a boy and a girl want to marry, they should obtain the approval of their families. The families perform the acts which acknowledge the marriage. This formality is breaking down today, and parents of a girl may suddenly find a son-in-law in their household without their having been consulted about the matter. But the wedding garments, woven by the boy's fathers, are still made in every case, and are considered very important.[12]

If a boy marries into a large household, he should build himself a house shortly after his marriage. If, however, he marries an only daughter or a youngest daughter, he may not need to erect a dwelling as his wife's mother may want the couple to live with her. Sometimes a man is accused of marrying an only daughter or a youngest daughter in order to avoid building a' house. To keep

---

[12] H. R. Voth, "Oraibi Marriage Customs," *Amer. Anthrop.*, 1900, 2, 238–246. Elsie Clews Parsons, "Getting Married on First Mesa, Arizona," *Sci. Mo.*, 1921, 259–265.

from being thought lazy, a man may construct a building which he does not really need.

With the birth of the first child, another individual enters the society which we have just attempted to describe. Today that society is changing more rapidly than it has changed in the past, but it has a culture which differs from ours, and which will continue to differ for at least several decades.

Hopi Expectations at Each Age

In dealing with different segments of the life of the Hopi child, it has been impractical to follow a strict chronological order. It has seemed best to deal, one topic at a time, with various aspects of child rearing, many of which operate simultaneously. Therefore at the close of this account of the conditions which surround the development of the child, it is advisable to summarize in chronological sequence some of the performances which Hopi parents expect of their children.

The Hopi infant stays on the cradleboard most of the time during the first six months, but he may occupy the cradleboard for a longer period. He gradually attains the freedom of the floor and of the ground, and is expected to begin to walk shortly after he is a year of age. Talking is also expected at this time.

By the time the child is two years of age he is usually weaned, and he is expected to have the proper toilet habits. He is much pampered, however, being permitted to eat nearly everything which he requests. He is carried about and constantly attended by an older sister.

In early childhood there is little or no difference in what is expected of the boy and the girl but from three or four years of age onward, we must distinguish between boys and girls, for the social rôles of the two are not the same.

By four years of age, both boy and girl become less dependent upon the older sister, and may go about alone in the village wherever they please. The boy is sufficiently grown up that he is expected no longer to cry at minor injuries and disappointments nor to shed tears. The girl, too, should cease to cry like a baby, but it is permissible for her to cry quietly throughout her life.

The work of the girl begins when she is very young. Even at

four years of age she may join her mother and her sisters in carrying water from the village spring, although her load would be a very light one. By the time she is five years old, the girl's responsibilities have increased so as to include tending and carrying a baby as well as bringing in fuel from the woodpile. The five-year-old boy has little work to do, although he may be sent on errands, but he has learned how to use the bow and arrow which the kachinas have brought him, and he can throw sticks, spin tops, roll hoops and run races.

At six years of age both the boy and the girl must start to school. This marks the beginning of the learning of English, for the native language is spoken exclusively in the home. The boy must begin to wear clothing. The girl has always been clothed, but now she may wear a pretty shawl over her head and shoulders as her older sisters do. At this age, the boy and girl know their clan and are fairly straight as to their relationship to the other people of the village. The boy begins to go with his father to the fields, and it becomes his duty to keep birds and other intruders away from the ripe fruits and to keep prairie dogs out of the corn fields.

Seven years is the most usual age for the first initiation for both boys and girls. The initiation is a landmark on the road to sophistication and maturity. After this event, the boy may begin to participate in the singing and dancing performances in the kiva, although he does not ordinarily do so until another year or two has passed. The initiated boy may enter the kiva at any time, just as the men do, and neither boy nor girl must tell the younger children that the masked dancers are not the real kachinas.

Children eight and nine years old are more advanced in regard to the type of work in which they can engage. The boy helps in the herding of sheep, and when near the village he may even herd them alone. He is permitted to join in the communal rabbit hunts, and perhaps kills his first game. The girl begins to learn to grind and to tend to the household fire. Play, of course, continues, and both boy and girl may occasionally be a leader in games in which previously they have been followers.

The period from ten to twelve years of age is marked for the girl by the fact that she loses the freedom of the village and loses much of her right to play. Her duties at home increase. She now grinds meal, and she begins to do part of the cooking. She must not go about except when chaperoned by an older woman. She becomes a member of one of the women's societies.

The boy at this age does not suffer any such loss of freedom. He does much more work in the fields than he did previously, but he may do as he likes when he returns from work. He becomes more skilled in games, as well as in work, and he learns to ride a horse, as the girl is not permitted to do.

By the fifteenth year, the girl progresses to the more difficult kinds of cooking. She can now make piki and somiviki, two of the most complex products of native culinary art. She is also beginning to make plaques of the kind which are made only on Third Mesa. The boy progresses in the learning of the practical arts in which the men engage in the kiva. He may learn to card and to spin the wool, although as yet he is scarcely able to weave. On the other hand, he has mastered fairly well the intricacies of knitting and is making socks and sweaters. At this time, he may be clearing some farming plots and may be cultivating them by himself. So long as he is single and lives with his father and mother, the produce of these fields is brought home and becomes the property of his mother, but his fields will later support his own wife and children.

Courting may begin in the sixteenth year, or even before that time. The young man's interest is definitely directed toward girls, and the girls reciprocate in this interest, although they do not take the lead in courtship. Sexual irregularities are condoned in boys but are penalized in girls, although such penalties may be relatively short lived.

Marriage may occur at an age as early as seventeen or eighteen years, both for the boy and for the girl, although it often takes place at a later age. Soon after marriage the young couple are expected to build a home of their own, and to become entirely self-supporting.

The second initiation of the boy may take place either before or after marriage, although formerly it had to be undergone before marriage was permitted. The second initiation occurs, in most cases, before the end of the twentieth year. This marks the young man's entrance into a man's society, and thereafter he is expected to act as a man. He receives a new name which is used throughout the remainder of his life. The initiation creates ceremonial affiliations which determine his ceremonial duties for the coming years.

The young woman, who undergoes no second initiation, is not expected to refrain from quarreling and fighting as a man does, and has few of the duties of religious participation which fall upon the man.

As the man grows older he learns more concerning the ceremonial forms and his knowledge of songs, ritual, and traditions may become greater and greater. His fields and flocks are more extensive, and he grows more respected in the community. He may fall heir to a ceremonial office, which will greatly increase his religious duties. But it is not our purpose to follow these changes in status which come during the adult years. The general pattern of life, for both the man and the woman, is established by the twentieth year.

CHAPTER IV

NEW ORAIBI AND MISHONGNOVI

NEW ORAIBI

W HILE Hotavila is the most conservative Hopi village, and New Oraibi is the most progressive, the road between is only six miles long. In a way the shortness of this distance in terms of our standards of travel symbolizes the fact that from our point of view the cultural separation of the towns is not great.

The progressiveness of New Oraibi consists in the abandonment of many Hopi customs, particularly in a neglect of the ceremonial life, and in accepting American innovations. Some of the American importations can be seen at first glance. There are several tin roofs in New Oraibi whereas Hotavila has none. It is doubtful that there will ever be any more tin roofs in New Oraibi than there are today, for the people have found that they are quite unsuited to their needs. The tin roofed house becomes extremely hot, whereas the earthen roof keeps a house cool on the hottest day. Furthermore the pitched roofs of tin are more likely to be damaged by the strong winds of spring, and are not as easily repaired as are the sun-dried adobe roofs.

New Oraibi houses are made of the same soft sandstone as are the most ancient structures in Old Oraibi which stand on the mesa above, for this sandstone is the only available building material. But many of the houses in New Oraibi are constructed of stone which has been carefully dressed by hand, and on that account they look quite different from the older homes. The homes of New Oraibi tend to be somewhat larger and to stand in greater isolation. Only a few houses have walls in common, and these belong to the same family. Whereas the older villages have rows of houses running in straight lines so as to form courts and streets, New Oraibi has no such arrangement. Many houses seem to have been built without regard to the placing of the other structures. The majority of the houses face eastward, however, as has been customary in Hopi villages for centuries.

Many of the homes of New Oraibi have electricity, whereas none have it in Hotavila. The New Oraibi homes are uniformly equipped with beds, tables, chairs, cupboards, and carpets, while such American furnishings are more rare at Hotavila. Some New Oraibi families have piped into their house water from the government tank which is filled from a deep well. Whether or not water is available in the house, it can be secured easily from one of several public outlets which are placed about the village. This fact saves New Oraibi women much of the labor which Hotavila wives expend in carrying water from a spring which is beyond and below the town.

A further advance toward Americanization consists in the introduction of outdoor toilets into New Oraibi. In all other villages, there are recognized places to which people retire for the purposes of elimination. But only in New Oraibi have outhouses been built. Not every home as yet possesses one, and they are thought of as being for the use of the women rather than the men. There are no indoor toilets in the native homes of New Oraibi, but a few families have installed bath tubs.

The people of New Oraibi have adopted American dress. Both men and women dress much as would white persons of comparable economic level. The dark blue woolen dress is no longer seen.

So far as infancy is concerned, the modifications have been slight. A white doctor is very seldom called in at childbirth, nor do many of the women go to the hospital for the delivery of a child. In cases of difficult birth, a native medicine man is more likely to be called than is the government physician. The room in which the mother remains is darkened during the period of confinement, although it is darkened by pulling down the blinds instead of by nailing blankets over the windows. The period of seclusion is often shortened to ten days instead of lasting for the traditional period of twenty days.

During this time the father's mother takes care of the mother and child as she does in the conservative villages, and ashes are applied to the baby until the vernix caseosa is removed. At the end of the period of seclusion the baby is carried at dawn toward the rising sun, as in olden times, and is given names by the female relatives of the father. An American name is given the child when he is about one year of age. The government nurse, who fills out the birth certificate and treats the baby's eyes, may be asked to supply an American name.

Only a few of the mothers of New Oraibi make use of the cradleboard. Instead a bassinet, or a basket, is used to replace the older device. At a slightly greater age, the child may be placed in a modern child's crib or bed.

Babies are carried about on the backs of their older sisters here as elsewhere, and the young children are largely under the care of girls from six to ten years of age. The taboos against tossing the baby in the air and against placing the young infant on his abdomen have been forgotten. Similarly changed are the practices regarding the time of the year at which the child's hair should be cut, but this much remains, that when the infant's hair is first cut it is closely clipped in accordance with the traditional manner.

The infant is nursed whenever he cries, and the practice of giving the child anything he wants to eat has not abated. At ten months or less he may have anything that is in the house—fruit, green or ripe, bread, meat, corn and coffee. At an early age, children go to the local stores with a coin for cookies or candy or pop. Our informant's nephew, who was only a little past two years of age, had learned to go to one store to get these things and to charge them to his mother. The things he ate gave him bad stomach-aches, but neither his parents nor the native clerks at the store put an end to the practice.

Obedience is due to the father and mother, and the mother of the child does most of the disciplining. The mother's brother may be called in to pour cold water over the child, or to roll him in the snow, if he is very bad. The smudge punishment is not used in New Oraibi, nor is the ceremonial treatment for enuresis employed.

The ceremonial situation in New Oraibi may be summed up briefly by saying that the sacred and serious parts of the ceremonies are gone, but that some of the public dances are performed for entertainment, and for social and esthetic reasons. The people of New Oraibi often attend ceremonies in other villages.

The child of New Oraibi receives gifts from the kachinas, and is told the usual stories about the nature of the kachinas, but there is no serious effort to keep him from learning the secrets. There is no initiation of the children, as there are no ceremonial officials and no societies to perform this. If the child has not learned about the masked dancers by five or six years of age, someone will tell him. He is threatened by Soyoko, and is afraid that she may come, for while he has never seen her in New Oraibi he knows that she does come to Second Mesa which is not far away.

The tasks of the boys and girls of New Oraibi are identical with those of other villages. The men of the village are all farmers. Although they may hold government jobs for short periods, this employment is temporary and is never looked upon as permanent means of livelihood. Nor is a position in a white city looked upon as a permanent way of life. All boys look forward to being farmers; they help with the corn, the fruits and the livestock as in the other villages.

The girl's work in New Oraibi may be slightly easier than in other villages, but it is of the same sort. Grinding is one of the chief labors of the woman even in New Oraibi, for, as we remarked earlier, there is no mill which will produce meal of the texture which the Hopi desires. In New Oraibi, the coarse grinding is done by means of small hand mills, but the meal must be finished on the grinding stone. Piki is still made, but perhaps not as often as in other towns.

While the work of New Oraibi is much like that of Hotavila, the pastimes have changed. The organized games which we described are not played in New Oraibi. Instead of these the young people play such games as baseball, basketball (out of doors), volley ball, hopscotch, flinch, and checkers.

Communal rabbit hunts are held by the men and boys, but the girls are not taken along.

In spite of the introduction of American games among the older children, the informal play of the younger children seems to be very similar to that which takes place in more conservative towns.

MISHONGNOVI

In the extent to which it adheres to old customs, Mishongnovi is much closer to Hotavila than it is to New Oraibi. The ceremonial system is intact, the native arts and industries provide the only means of livelihood, and there have been no sharp changes of any sort within the past quarter of a century. The differences between Mishongnovi and Hotavila are differences of native culture rather than differences in the degree of Americanization. The villages of various mesas, and indeed, the towns of one mesa, possess distinct characteristics, which often seem important to the Hopi. But to the outsider they appear as only minor variations within the same general pattern. In the present connection, the differences between Hotavila and Mishongnovi do not seem to us to warrant a detailed presentation.

The Beagleholes [1] have contributed much information about individual development at Mishongnovi. We have obtained data on some further points regarding child care. Below, we shall depict briefly some of the ways in which Mishongnovi resembles and some of the respects in which it differs slightly from the town of Hotavila which we have described with some fullness.

The economic life of the villages is identical, and the economic rôle of the children is the same. The social organizations are also in most respects identical. In Mishongnovi the family is matrilineal, there is female ownership of houses, and the maternal uncle has the relationship to the children with which we are already familiar from our knowledge of Hotavila.

Some slight differences in child care appear in the realm of punishments. While many of the same forms of punishments are used in the two villages, punishment by locking the child in a room is used at Mishongnovi and not at Hotavila. The maternal uncle, in both towns, is the person who makes use of the smudge punishment. There is no special cold water treatment for enuresis in Mishongnovi, although cold water may be used for any offense. If a child has misbehaved, any man may carry the child on his back and may ask any person in the village to throw water on the offender, but our informant felt that this was done as a joke rather than as a serious punishment. In general, only the family of the child has the authority to punish him.

We have indicated in earlier sections that Soyoko and her cohorts come to threaten naughty children at Mishongnovi, whereas they have not appeared in Hotavila or in New Oraibi in recent

---

[1] E. and P. Beaglehole, "Hopi of Second Mesa," *Mem. Amer. Anthrop. Assoc.,* 1935, 44.

years. Some fifteen or twenty years ago in Mishongnovi certain kachinas came and whipped severely, in view of the entire village, a girl who had told other children about the kachinas. Such punishment has not occurred on Third Mesa, so far as we could determine.

The games of the two villages follow the same general plan with occasional differences in minor characteristics. The snake game which at Hotavila is never played by the two sexes jointly, at Mishongnovi is sometimes played with boys and girls taking alternate places in the line. At the close of the snake game at Mishongnovi the leader is blindfolded and must catch another player, who is thus made responsible for starting the game on some later date. Our notes on the witch game are not complete, but it appears that at Mishongnovi the witch tries to catch other children, instead of attempting to escape detection as at Hotavila.

The details of cradleboard usage and of infant care are identical in almost every respect. We have no reason to believe that the differences in the child rearing practices of the two villages would have an appreciable effect upon the child.

PART II

THE BEHAVIOR
OF THE
HOPI CHILD

CHAPTER V

INFANT BEHAVIOR

REACTION TO THE CRADLEBOARD

THE unanimous testimony of Hopi mothers affirms that when the infant is tied to the cradleboard on the first day of life the process does not cause the baby to cry. It must be borne in mind that the restriction to which the child is subjected during the last three months of intra-uterine existence is even greater than the restriction of the cradleboard. This fact alone should make one unwilling to accept the theory that restraint, when applied at birth, will cause rage, yet Watson and Morgan [1] seem never to have considered the relation of prenatal conditions to the situation which they claimed would cause the newborn infant to exhibit anger.

However, there are differences between the position in which the child is held in utero and the position which he is forced to maintain on the cradleboard. In utero, the infant is squeezed into a flexed position; the extremities are bent, and the arms ordinarily are folded upon the chest of the fetus. The position which the cradleboard demands is one of extension. The trunk is extended, the legs are stretched out and the arms are bound so that the elbow may bend only slightly. Furthermore, the arms are held at the sides. That this difference between the prenatal and the postnatal positions of the Hopi infant does not cause crying may be due to the fatigued and relatively insensitive condition of the newborn child. It may be, of course, that at this age there is no tendency to react negatively to a marked change of position. In this connection it must be borne in mind that the freedom of the American neonate constitutes a contrast with prenatal conditions as great or greater

[1] J. B. Watson and J. J. B. Morgan, "Emotional Reactions and Psychological Experimentation," *Amer. J. Psychol.*, 1917, 28, 163–174.

than does the binding to which the Hopi infant is subjected at birth.[2]

When the Hopi infant who has become accustomed to the cradleboard is kept off of the board for a longer period than is usual he cries and does not go to sleep. We cannot say exactly how many weeks are required to cause the infant to reach this degree of dependence upon the cradle because the child is seldom taken from his home until he is four months of age and on that account there is little occasion for any irregularity in his usage of the cradle until after that age is reached. When, finally, he is taken from the house, he is ordinarily carried in arms or upon the back of the mother, and the cradleboard is left at home. Very generally, the mother finds that without the cradleboard the child will not go to sleep at the usual time, and that he frets and cries before finally closing his eyes.

Occasionally a child may be taken on a visit or to a dance before he is four months old. While such cases are few, they suggest that the infant at a very early age becomes so used to the board that he is restless when he is not on it. An Old Oraibi mother brought her baby to a dance at New Oraibi when he was five weeks of age, leaving the cradleboard at home. The child did not sleep well at the dance, but there were, of course, many conditions other than the absence of the cradleboard which may have operated to keep him awake. While we failed to observe other cases as young as this infant, our informants stated that even at one month of age the child will not sleep well without his usual bindings.

That this is true among older infants is more readily proved. One mother ceased using the cradleboard when her son was fourteen months of age. For a week he slept badly and cried at night. Another mother whom we knew also discontinued the use of the cradleboard when her son was fourteen months of age. This caused him to cry when he was sleepy during the day, and he woke up several times during the first two nights, but thereafter he was adjusted to his new mode of sleeping. Now and then a child is broken of the cradleboard habit with such difficulty that the mother permits him to use the cradleboard even after the child is able to walk. In

[2] W. Dennis and M. G. Dennis, "Cradles and Cradling Practices of the Pueblo Indians," *Amer. Anthrop.*, 1940, 42, 107–115.

such a case the child when sleepy may drag the cradling device to his mother and ask to be put to bed.

It must not be thought that all infants are as fond of the cradleboard as those to whom we have just referred. A child beyond the first six months of life may begin to fret and struggle when placed upon the cradleboard. If this happens, the use of the board is discontinued at an early age. Such restlessness under the restraint of the bindings need not be ascribed to a delayed appearance of some native or instinctive negative reaction to restraint. From three months of age onward the child enjoys freedom of movement for a larger and larger part of the day. During his free hours he has an opportunity to develop postures, activities and interests which may clash with the restrictions which are imposed by the cradleboard. The negative reaction to the cradleboard may be thought of as due to the development, through practice, of responses which are contradictory to the passivity which is demanded by the cradling device.

The question that may occur to the reader is this: What would happen if the child were not restrained at birth but were first hampered in his movements at a much later age? Fortunately, incidents occasionally transpire which give an answer to this problem. One of our informants from New Oraibi gave birth to each of her ten children at the government hospital at Keams Canyon, yet she placed them on improvised cradleboards when she came home. This unusual mixture of American and Hopi pediatric care presents an interesting situation. Additional cultural confusion is shown by the fact that in using a cradleboard, our informant placed a pillow upon it, which made it softer than the cradleboard as it is ordinarily employed. Her reason for using the board was that it kept the infant out of danger and made him more easy to handle. These advantages were especially important in her case because she often went to her husband's sheep camp, a trip which involved much handling of the infant. Although each infant came home from the hospital when about ten days of age, the mother stated that in every case he fretted when first placed on the cradleboard, but that he quickly adjusted himself to its use.

Other instances of delayed use of the cradleboard involve much later ages. One case concerns a girl who was born at Keams Canyon but whose mother did not attempt to tie her to a cradleboard

until the child was five months of age. The child cried and struggled and eventually got her arms free. The mother abandoned her
plan after the first attempt. This example is in accord with the general experience of mothers who have given birth to a child away
from the reservation, where cradleboards are not used, and who
have returned to their native village when the infant was several
months of age.

Even if the child has been habituated to restraint in early infancy, he does not readily adjust to it a second time after a period
of freedom has intervened. A Hotavila woman kept her son on a
cradleboard, but when he became ill at a few months of age she
permitted the nurse to take him to the hospital, where the native
cradle was of course discarded. When he returned after a few
weeks, he would not again accept the cradleboard. A Shungopovi
mother discontinued the use of the cradleboard for her daughter at
five months, and tried to put her upon it again at the end of the
first year. The girl cried and would not go to sleep. Both of these
attempts were given up after the first trial. It is possible that a more
prolonged effort might have met with a certain degree of success.

General Course of Infant Development [3]

The contrasts between the treatment of the Hopi infant and the
treatment of the white American infant raise the significant question as to whether these differences in the conditions which surround the two groups of children cause any differences in the behavior of the Hopi and the American individual during the period
of infancy.

Since our account of Hopi methods of infant care did not specifically call attention to the ways in which the Hopi practices diverge from our own, it will be desirable at this point to indicate the
manner in which Hopi infant rearing differs most markedly from
the situations which confront our infants.

Chief among these cultural variations is the binding of the Hopi
infant in comparison with the freedom of the American baby. The
cradling of the Hopi infant prevents a number of actions which our
babies commonly engage in, such as bringing the hands to the

[3] Much of the following material, together with facts on Navaho infant
development, will be found in an article by the present author, "Is Infant
Behavior Appreciably Affected by Culture?", *J. Soc. Psychol.*, in press.

mouth, playing with the hands, watching the hands, and putting the feet in the air. The Hopi infant retains the board for nursing and sleeping for a variable period which is only six months in some cases and which in other instances extends beyond the first year. Even when he is not in the native cradle he is not placed on his abdomen until he can turn himself from the supine to the prone position, which means that prior to that time he cannot practice the reaction of head up when prone or chest up when prone nor can he engage in any of the elements of creeping.

Another contrast betwen the Hopi and the white American child occurs in regard to feeding practices. Whereas the American infant is often bottle-fed almost from the beginning and is weaned at an early age, the Hopi infant is invariably breast fed, is seldom weaned under one year of age and frequently is not weaned before two years. Furthermore, the American infant is usually placed on a rigid schedule of feedings with an interval of several hours between feedings. Often he is expected to cry for some minutes before being fed. The Hopi infant, on the other hand, is nursed as soon as he cries, and consequently nurses frequently and cries very little. The breast is used as a pacifier even though the cause of crying is pain or fright and not hunger. Among the Hopi there is no feeling that crying is something to be expected from the infant; because of this there are but few frustrations during infancy and but little adherence to predetermined routines.

There is much less training of the Hopi than of the American infant. For example, the American mother and infant spend much time and energy on the early establishment of toilet habits whereas no training in this respect is imposed upon the Hopi child until he can walk and can understand simple commands, when he is told to go outside the door.

There is a great amount of avoidance training for the white infant. The American child, as soon as he can creep, is admonished not to touch radiators, windows, and electric fixtures; not to soil walls, furniture, curtains, books, pictures; and not to handle pieces of property such as spectacles, watches, jewelry, cigarettes, ash trays, and dishes, which are often left within his reach. The Hopi infant has few such prohibitions. In part this is because the majority of these pieces of property are not met with in the material culture of the Hopi. But even in regard to the property which the Hopi do have, there is less of the feeling that the child should let it alone. Nor is he exhorted to keep himself clean as is the white child. Only two objects of avoidance exist in his environment, the household fire which is often an exposed one, and the edge of the cliffs, from which he may fall. The Hopi expedient in the face of these dangers is to have someone with the infant always rather than to depend upon the effectiveness of infant training.

One aspect of behavior which the customs of child care undoubtedly influence is the frequency with which various infant behavior patterns are elicited. Crying provides a convenient response for a concrete example. The Hopi infant cries rather little. One can be in a village whose arrangement is more "intimate" than that of a modern apartment house and seldom be aware of the babies of the community. The reason lies in the facts just stated; namely that the infant is not denied food when he wants it, is not denied objects which he desires, is not put to bed when he is wide awake and is not fed when he has no appetite. The "goodness" of the primitive infant, which has often been noticed, issues from the fact that he is not provoked into crying. When such provocation is given, as occasionally it must be, the Hopi infant cries as readily as does ours and cries from the same causes.

Another effect of culture upon infant behavior is this: the infant in different cultures becomes conditioned to different objects and becomes accustomed to different procedures. This fact is as apparent in different homes among ourselves as it is between cultures. An infant who is hungry but who has never been fed from a bottle will not react to the sight of a bottle as does one who gets his nourishment from that source. No Hopi infant would react to the sight of a nursing bottle as many white infants do, because for the former it has never become a symbol for food. The culture determines what shall be symbolic for feeding.

The culture also determines the customary routine of the infant, and the infant, as we have seen in respect to the cradleboard, reacts to a breach of routine. The child who has come to anticipate a particular arrangement for sleeping will not readily go to sleep under different conditions. We would not expect a white child of six months to go to sleep promptly if at bedtime he were strapped to a cradleboard for the first time. Conversely we find that a Hopi infant who has slept nowhere except on the cradleboard becomes very restless and cannot readily fall to sleep when the board is not available.

However—and to our mind this is the most important point—the patterns of response of Hopi and the white infant are identical. The Indian infant may not cry as much as the white infant, but the cries are the same. Quite different things may keep the children of the two cultures from going to sleep, but the reactions are not distinguishable. The sleepy infant frets, fusses, tosses and cries, regardless of culture.

The behavioral similarity of American infants and Southwestern Indian infants needs to be examined in detail, especially at points at which we might expect a difference. One of these is motor development, for we have seen that Hopi cradling customs limit during most of the day the random activity of the infant, force the arms and legs into an extended position instead of the usual flexed position, prevent manipulation of the hands and make it impossible for the child to rest on the abdomen. Nevertheless, observation of a large number of Hopi infants of various ages shows that the behavior which is characteristic of the different ages is approximately the same for the two groups. In spite of the enforced extension of the limbs, the Hopi infant when freed from his bindings for the bath or for the changing of bedding, takes the usual flexed position. Although his hands are held downward perhaps twenty-three hours in twenty-four, when he is at liberty he puts them to the mouth and carries objects to his mouth as do white babies. He reaches for objects and handles them at approximately the same time as do white children. He reaches for his toes and puts his toes in his mouth. Sitting, creeping, and walking follow in the usual sequence.

Social behavior is identical in the two groups. The Hopi infant develops social smiling, social laughter, vocalization, crying at strange noises, staring at strangers, and crying at strangers just as does the American infant.

These conclusions are based on a considerable number of observations made during our two summers' residence at New Oraibi. The observations, however, refer chiefly to infants seen in other villages, as only a few families in New Oraibi make use of cradleboards and we wished to study children who had been subjected to the older native practices. It was not a part of our research plans to subject the infants to standardized tests such as the Yale or the

California series. An attempt to apply rigid conditions of examination would have met some difficulties among these people. At the time that the observations were made we did not think it wise to run the risk of losing the rapport which had been established by suggesting procedures which would be disliked by the Indian mothers. Fortunately it was possible to make many observations which did not require the introduction of test materials foreign to the native culture, and such observations were made on many occasions. These are summarized as brief individual protocols in the following pages. The descriptive terms are defined in a previous publication.[4]

It was impossible to record the same data in all cases. For one thing, some of the infants were seen at public ceremonials where the spontaneous behavior of the infant could be noted but where tests for other behavior could not be introduced. Likewise the length of the periods of observation varied. Some children were observed continuously for as long as an hour; others were seen for only a few minutes. The protocols in all cases refer to behavior which occurred when the child was not on the cradleboard, as when the child is on the cradleboard none but facial and vocal responses are observable.

PROTOCOLS OF THE BEHAVIOR OF HOPI INFANTS

No. 1. Boy, 2 months old—kicked, random arm movements, vocalized, turned head to fixate persons and moving objects.

No. 2. Girl, 4 months old—smiled at persons, vocalized to persons, reached for and grasped objects, stood supported under the arms, could not sit alone.

No. 3. Boy, 4 months old—smiled at persons, vocalized to persons, grasped own toes, reached for and grasped objects, sat with support, could not sit alone.

No. 4. Girl, 5 months old—held head erect, turned head to follow persons, smiled and vocalized at persons, hands clasped each other, grasped own toes, carried toes to mouth, hand to mouth, chewed own fingers, stood supported under arms, would not reach for objects held before her.

No. 5. Girl, 6 months old—stared at strangers, sat with slight support, reached for and grasped objects, objects carried to mouth,

<hr>

[4] W. Dennis and M. G. Dennis, "Behavioral Development in the First Year as Shown by Forty Biographies," *Psychol. Rec.*, 1937, 1, 349–361.

cried when object taken away, cried when put down, grasped own toes.

No. 6. Girl, 6 months old—smiled and vocalized at persons, reached for and grasped objects, sat with support.

No. 7. Girl, 6 months old—stared at stranger, then smiled, reached for and grasped objects, carried objects to mouth, patted objects, patted own feet, sat with support, could not sit alone, stood supported under arms.

No. 8. Girl, 7 months old—stared at strangers, sat alone, crept.

No. 9. Boy, 7 months old—reached for and grasped objects, sat alone, bounced while sitting.

No. 10. Girl, 7 months old—stared at strangers, reached for and grasped objects, carried objects to mouth, sat with support, stood supported under arms.

No. 11. Boy, 7 months old—smiled and vocalized at persons, reached for and grasped objects, carried objects to mouth, sat alone.

No. 12. Girl, 7 months old—sat alone, reached for and grasped objects, stood supported under arms.

No. 13. Girl, 8 months old—sat alone, pulled self to standing.

No. 14. Girl, 9 months old—cried at stranger, sat alone, stood supported under arms.

No. 15. Girl, 10 months old—stared at strangers, crept, walked when led.

No. 16. Boy, 10 months old—stared at stranger, crept, pulled self to standing, stood holding furniture.

No. 17. Boy, 10 months old—walked on all fours, pulled to standing, walked holding furniture.

No. 18. Girl, 11 months old—sat alone, pulled to standing, could not walk when led.

No. 19. Boy, 11 months old—sat alone, reached for and grasped objects, patted objects, carried objects to mouth, stood supported under arms, could not pull self to standing nor stand holding furniture, fretted when put down, crept, said Hopi baby word for "papa" and "mama."

No. 20. Girl, 11 months old—crept, pulled to standing, could not walk holding furniture.

No. 21. Girl, 11 months old—sat alone, crept, reached for and grasped objects, pulled to standing but could not walk holding furniture nor when led, smiled at strangers.

No. 22. Boy, 12 months old—crept, pulled self to standing, walked holding furniture.

No. 23. Boy, 12 months old—crept, stood holding furniture but could not walk.

The ages in all cases were determined by questioning the mothers. The ages are in terms of our calendar months and are quite accurate since young Hopi mothers know the birthday of their children. In each case which is included in the protocols the cradle-board was used for six months or longer.

It seems next to impossible to quantify data of the sort here obtained, but a careful examination of the records will convince the reader that the development of the Hopi infant is in essentials similar to that of the white infant.

Comparable data may be obtained from the recorded observations of the non-test responses of white infants. Recently the material of forty biographies of white babies has been compiled so as to show all of the responses which were reported for at least ten of forty infants.[5] *Every one of these responses was observed among the Hopi infants and no response was observed among the Hopi infants which had not been noted commonly among white subjects.*

It is worthwhile to check the report of an earlier author concerning one aspect of Hopi motor development. One of the first Americans to write about the Hopi was Bourke,[6] who witnessed the Snake Dance at Walpi in 1881 and subsequently wrote a book based on his brief visit to the Hopi country. At that time the Hopi made considerable use of the rooms on the second and third stories of their houses. Families living in these stories necessarily had to use ladders in going to and from their homes. Bourke reported in an incidental manner that children learned to go up and down these ladders before they could walk, an observation which probably meant little to Bourke but which is very important for theories of motor development. We have been able to determine that Bourke's casual observation was entirely erroneous. Mothers, both young and old, report that such a thing is unheard of and that children cannot go up and down the ladders before two and three years of age.

Effect of Cradleboard upon Age at Walking [7]

We have attempted to find the effect of the use of the cradleboard upon one response, namely, the onset of walking, by comparing

[5] W. Dennis and M. G. Dennis, "Behavioral Development in the First Year as Shown by Forty Biographies," *Psychol. Rec.,* 1937, 1, 349–361.

[6] J. G. Bourke, *The Snake Dance of the Moquis of Arizona,* Scribners, New York, 1884, 371 pp.

[7] This material has been presented by the present author under the title, "The Effect of the Cradleboard upon the Onset of Walking among Hopi Infants," *J. Genet. Psychol.,* in press.

the records of Hopi children who have been reared on the cradle-board with the records of those who have not been subjected to any restraint in early infancy.

Of the present-day Hopi villages, all make use of cradleboards, except the towns of New Oraibi and of Upper Moenkopi. Many of the parents of the latter two villages have become Americanized to the extent of giving up the use of the cradleboard. Nevertheless, their diet, their nursing customs, and their child rearing practices apart from the use of the cradleboard remain virtually unchanged. New Oraibi and Upper Moenkopi, therefore, furnish a nearly ideal comparison group for the purpose of contrasting Hopi infants who have not been placed on the cradleboard with those who have been subjected to this custom. However, some families in the progressive towns use cradleboards and a few families in conservative villages do not employ them. The use or disuse of the cradling device was determined for each child, and our classification was entirely on that basis and not on the basis of residence.

The first step in the gathering of the data for any pueblo was to contact a young woman who was a native and a resident of the pueblo. This was done through the assistance of a white person familiar with the village or through the aid of an older Indian woman whom we had previously met. Having been introduced to the native girl, we explained to her that we were interested in children and that we wanted to find out when Hopi children began to walk alone. We asked if she would be willing to take us to visit all the women of the village who had young children. In almost all cases, the first girl who was approached in this manner readily agreed to help us and cooperated fully. As a rule the interviews were conducted in English, but in some cases the Hopi language was used and our guide served as an interpreter.

Where it was possible, we saw all of the children of a village who were between two and six years of age. Children who were under two years of age are not included in the tabulations, as many children less than two years of age cannot walk and, hence, records of walking for this group would be necessarily incomplete. Only a few children over six years of age were included because we felt that the mother's memory would be less reliable if it covered a period of such length. In all, we secured data on sixty-three children who had used the cradleboard and on forty-two children who had not used it.

When asked at what age a given child began to walk, the Pueblo mother, after a few moments, gave a reply such as, "A year and one month and a few days," or "Two days before the first birthday," or something equally circumstantial. While we have no check on this point, we are of the opinion that the mothers who were interviewed gave information as accurate as that obtained from white mothers.

One indication of the relative accuracy of the data lies in the fact that there is no unusual grouping of cases in any one month, as shown in Table 1. The cases at one year and at eighteen months exceed those of the surrounding months, but scarcely more so than do the reports of white mothers.

In questioning the mothers, we asked how old the child was when he first began to walk by himself. If further definition was necessary, we asked when the first steps alone were taken. By examining a number of Pueblo infants who were just "beginning to walk" we were able to determine that the phrase "beginning to walk" and its Hopi equivalent meant taking one or more steps alone. This performance is a point of interest to Hopi parents and is noticed and remembered by them.

Our subjects were approximately evenly divided as to sex.

Smith *et al* [8] have held that children who begin to walk at an age greater than 21.0 months seem to make a separate group statistically and that all or nearly all such cases may be instances of retardation due to malnutrition or disease. We have computed averages for our data by two methods, one excluding and one including the most retarded cases among our subjects. The difference between these averages is approximately 0.5 of a month. Since we wished to compare our material with that of the authors referred to above,[9] our sigmas were computed with the retarded cases excluded, as was done by the authors just mentioned.

Table 1 presents the distribution of the ages of walking recorded by us, together with the averages and the standard deviations.

It will be seen that the infants who used the cradleboard and those who did not use it differ in average age of onset of walking

[8] M. E. Smith, G. Lecker, J. W. Dunlap and E. E. Cureton, "The Effects of Race, Sex, and Environment on the Age at Which Children Walk," *J. Genet. Psychol.*, 1930, 38, 489–498.
[9] *Ibid.*

by only seven hundredths of a month if we include all cases (the averages being respectively 14.98 months and 15.05 months) and by only four hundredths of a month if we exclude the cases beyond 21.0 months. This means a difference between the averages of from one to two days. The average age at walking of those who used the cradleboard, in both comparisons, is slightly *less* than those who did not. Since the differences are quite insignificant, there is no evidence of an effect of the cradleboard upon walking.

TABLE 1

AGE AT ONSET OF WALKING

Age in Months	Hopi Using Board	Hopi Not Using Board	Tewa
24–24.9	2	2	1
23–23.9	1	0	0
22–22.9	0	0	1
21–21.9	0	0	0
20–20.9	1	0	0
19–19.9	4	0	2
18–18.9	7	6	5
17–17.9	0	0	1
16–16.9	3	4	1
15–15.9	3	6	1
14–14.9	15	6	10
13–13.9	6	8	3
12–12.9	10	6	14
11–11.9	9	2	5
10–10.9	2	1	0
9– 9.9	0	1	2
Total cases	63	42	46
Average	14.98	15.05	14.45
Average excluding cases beyond 21.0 months	14.53	14.57	14.05
Standard deviation	2.62	2.24	2.60

Also included in Table 1 are the walking ages of forty-six children from the Tewa villages of Santa Clara, San Ildefonso, and San Juan. These data were gathered in the same manner as the data concerning the Hopi. It will be seen that the average age of walking among the Tewa children is half a month earlier than that of the Hopi groups, but the differences are not statistically significant.

We have shown in a previous communication that the Tewa use

a cradle only for daytime naps,[10] a practice which is intermediate to the customs of our two Hopi groups. The lack of a significant difference between the Tewa children and either of the Hopi groups tends to confirm the previous finding that cradling customs do not influence the age of walking. At the same time, the close agreement between the data of the Hopi and the Tewa groups—who differ considerably in language and culture—tends to show the reliability of our method.

We have shown elsewhere [11] that the walking of Hopi and Tewa children is retarded in comparison with American standards. The cause of this retardation may lie in poor nutrition or in the greater frequency of disease among Pueblo infants. It may, indeed, represent a true racial difference. At any rate, the lack of a significant difference between the conservative and the progressive Hopi villages shows that the use of the cradleboard is not the factor which produces the Hopi retardation. Hopi infants who have not used the cradleboard are just as retarded as those who have employed it.

[10] W. Dennis and M. G. Dennis, "Cradles and Cradling Practices of the Pueblo Indians," *Amer. Anthrop.*, 1940, 42, 107–115.
[11] *Ibid.*

CHAPTER VI

BEHAVIOR OF YOUNG CHILDREN

JEALOUSY

WE asked several of our informants if children become jealous when a baby sibling is born. The new arrival is usually a surprise to his immediate senior, although the older children are sufficiently acquainted with the signs of pregnancy to have guessed in advance that another baby is expected. Our informants' replies were to the effect that the next oldest child is often jealous of the new baby. He pushes the baby away from the mother, especially when the baby is being nursed. Toys may be taken from the baby by the older child. One informant believed that the child who is only two or three years of age when a sibling is born is especially likely to be jealous of the attention which the mother gives to the infant. Nevertheless, some children do not exhibit jealousy of the baby, and may even appear proud of the new member of the family.

A child may be jealous not only of a baby but of other siblings who receive attention from a parent, and he may be jealous when one parent approaches the other. A Mishongnovi informant spontaneously volunteered the information that a boy usually is jealous when the father, or when the other children, receive attention from the mother, and that he wants to keep others away from the mother, whereas a girl wants to monopolize the affection of her father.

An interesting case of jealousy is presented by the behavior of Elsa of Hotavila. When she was two years of age she slept on a bench beside her parents' bed. One day she said she was going to sleep with her father and that her mother could sleep on the bench. "But be careful not to fall off," she told her mother. At four years of age she frequently drove her older brothers from her father's lap.

109

FEARS

The young Hopi child displays the same fear of strange objects, persons, and places as does our own. Fear of strange people is common at about ten to fourteen months of age. Clowns and kachinas, since they are very strange in appearance, are often terrifying to a child who has not seen them before, or who has not seen them since early infancy (Clowns and kachinas do not appear between July and February). Our observations as well as the testimony of informants affirms that the child toward the end of the first year of life is often afraid of these characters.

Beyond the first year, the fears of the Hopi child are usually governed by what older children and adults tell him. He is told of Soyoko, although he may never have seen her. He is afraid of Owl and Coyote because it is said that they will harm him. (See the story on page 67.) These characters are used as bug-a-boos with which to threaten children who do not behave. He is also afraid of witches, about whose dangerous activities he has been warned.

TANTRUMS

The cause of tantrums, according to our informants, lies in keeping the child from doing something which he wishes to do; in other words, tantrums are caused by frustration. Other conditions may be contributory. The child is liable to have tantrums if he nurses when his mother is worried. Tantrums are more likely to occur in hot weather than on comfortable days, and are more frequent before meals than after the child has eaten, according to native observation. The frequency of tantrums will be considered in connection with the census of problem cases.

When a child has a tantrum he may engage in a variety of actions. Chief among these is crying and screaming, but he may also lie down or cast himself on the ground; he may throw things or strike wildly with whatever is in his hands; he may pull his hair and tear his clothes. When the child cries from fear, or from injury, or from disappointment or fatigue, he can be quieted by giving him the breast, but when he is having a tantrum he will seldom accept the breast, or if he does he may bite it.

Behavior Toward Animals

The lack of consideration with which the Hopi child treats pets and the small wild animals which he captures seems striking enough to warrant some comment as to its probable genesis. Mistreatment of animals is not specifically a childish characteristic among the Hopi; if the adult does not treat pets with as much hardheartedness as does the child it seems to be because of the fact that the adult seldom handles pets. On the other hand, the adult willingly turns over small animals to the mercy of the child.

In the harsh treatment of a pet there seems to be no element of intentional cruelty, and there is no indication that the Hopi receives any sadistic pleasure from the suffering of sub-human creatures. The facts are that the adult often gives an animal to the child in the same way that he would give the child an inanimate toy, and that the child subjects the living plaything to the same manipulative exercises which he has developed in his contact with a world of sticks and stones.

Several examples will make these generalizations more vivid. When we were once visiting in Old Oraibi in the company of a woman resident of the village and her daughter who was a year and a half old, we entered the house of a relative of our guide. Soon after our entrance, our guide's daughter became active about the house, and the hostess, in order to entertain the little girl, took from under a pan a young half-feathered bird which apparently had been placed there with such an exigency in mind. The child grasped the bird tightly, yanked first at its wing, then at its head, just as she might have handled an old rag. Fortunately the bird died during the first minute, but the child continued to play with the limp body during our entire visit which lasted for a quarter of an hour. No one said a word to the girl concerning her treatment of the animal, and the two native women paid no attention to her as they talked to us.

The incident was combined with another happening which gave us an indication of the relative unimportance of the bird. The second piece of behavior consisted in the young girl wiping her nose on her mother's dress. After we left the home, our guide, who had worked in American homes, spoke apologetically of this but said nothing about the bird.

Many similar instances of callous behavior toward animals were recorded. In a home in Moenkopi a girl of four years was playing with a half-grown kitten. She seized it by the front paws and dragged it up in front of the seven-month-old baby. The baby beat it over the head. The kitten escaped. At a dance at Mishongnovi a two-year-old boy carried a very young pup onto the plaza, holding it by the loose skin of its back. Held in this fashion, it squealed continuously for five minutes while a dance was in progress. The boy dropped it, then picked it up and threw it. Several of the adults smiled. No one offered any criticism. Finally a girl of about fifteen years seized the animal and carried it away.

The catching of young birds, prairie dogs, and rabbits is very common, and the rough treatment of them is no less frequent. While we were in New Oraibi, the children brought several such young animals for our daughter to see. We were given an immature prairie dog, one of whose legs had been broken, and were permitted to adopt a kitten which was similarly injured. The treatment of a captured rabbit by Sid is described in the diary record which forms a later section.

These observations would tend to show that generally speaking no sympathy for animals develops when there is an absence of training in that direction. We would suggest as an important factor in this failure to develop sympathy the fact that pets are given to children when they are so young that their manual habits are entirely inappropriate to the handling of small live animals. It may be that rough handling, established at an early age, tends to prevent the later development of sympathy for its victims.

THE DIRECTION OF AFFECTION

Despite the fact that many women are called "mother" and many men are called "father" the child when very young distinguishes his true parents, and his chief bonds of affection are to them. Aside from his father and his mother, the child seems most favorably inclined toward his father's brothers and sisters. They are interested in the child, they are affectionate with him, they spoil him and give him gifts, but they do not scold or punish him and have no responsibility for him. Those who are responsible for his conduct, in addition to his parents, are his mother's sisters and brothers. As we have seen, the mother's brothers play an especially important rôle in the matter of administering moral lectures and in meting out punishment. On this account, the uncles are usually feared and disliked. They are thought of as "mean" to the child.

In Hopi society the relations between the child and the father on the one hand and between the child and the maternal uncle on the other hand are very similar to the relationships with which Malinowski [1] has dealt among the Trobriand Islanders, and the psychological outcomes of the two situations seem quite similar. The Hopi child shows no fear or resentment of his father, but, to the contrary, is fond of him; the maternal uncle is often feared, resented, and disliked among the Hopi as among the Trobriand Islanders.

DRAMATIC PLAY

In our account of the traditional modes of play we named several respects in which the child imitates the activities of the Hopi adult. The question arises as to whether or not the child imitates any person who is not a Hopi and whether or not he imitates animals and objects. These facts may in the future have some significance for determining with what persons the child identifies himself, and may be useful in tracing the course of his socialization. At present, however, it would be unwise to do more than to present the relevant data.

We have had several occasions to mention the child's imitation of the activities of the kachinas. At two years of age or even when he is younger, the boy attempts to beat a drum as the kachinas do, he tries to duplicate the steps of the masked dancers, and practices snatches of the songs. The child is told that people become kachinas when they die. He has his favorite kachinas, and, according to our Hotavila informants, he sometimes says: "When I die, I am going to be such-and-such a kachina." The girl seldom if ever imitates the male dancers, but she duplicates the motions of the female gods, not knowing that they are really men dressed to impersonate the feminine supernaturals. The child does not know that these characters are really Hopi in disguise.

The child does not limit his play to the rôles which are occupied

---

[1] B. Malinowski, *Sex and Repression in Savage Society,* Harcourt, Brace, New York, 1927, 285 pp.

by the Hopi. He may play tourist, the type of American most frequently seen on the reservation. In the child's opinion all "bahanas" (Americans) are rich, and the child who plays bahana pretends to distribute money and gifts to the poor Hopi children. The missionary is another white person whose part is taken in play. The fact that airplanes are frequently seen whereas other aspects of American civilization are seldom visible on the mesas is the probable reason that aviators are imitated although very few other occupational classes provide any content for dramatic play.

The girl does not know of many non-Hopi rôles. Occasionally she plays at being a government nurse, but our informants state that the girl seldom plays at being a schoolteacher.

In dramatic play, the appropriate division of labor between the sexes is observed. A boy would practically never play at grinding, nor would a girl play at herding sheep. Other children would ridicule such activities, and this may be one reason for their absence, but, on the other hand, the child seems to accept without protest the rôle which is accorded to his or her sex.

CHAPTER VII

AN OBSERVATIONAL STUDY OF CHILD BEHAVIOR IN NEW ORAIBI

INTRODUCTION

THE house which we occupied in New Oraibi during the summer of 1938 was a one-room native structure, twelve feet wide and twenty-five feet long. Fortunately for our purposes it had one or more windows in each wall and the surroundings of the house were such that by moving from window to window we could obtain a complete view of the nearby section of the village. Beyond the western end of our residence was a level plot of relatively soft sand, suitable for child play. However, one of the chief environmental disadvantages here, as well as elsewhere in the village, was the absence of shade, for there were no porches in the town and practically no trees. Because of the need of protection from the midday sun, we caused to be constructed over this sandy space a native summer shelter of the type that is often constructed in the fields. Four forked posts were placed in the ground so as to protrude about seven feet above the surface. In the forks of the posts were placed beams, across these were put rafters and this was covered with a thick layer of bows of green cottonwood, bearing many leaves. (See Plate VI.)

The shelter, which provided a shady place to play throughout the day, was attractive to children, and it was seldom unoccupied. It was located immediately outside of a window. The window was kept open at all times. In consequence of this, when we were inside of our house we could see and hear what was going on in the shelter. In addition, we could see whatever play was in progress in the vicinity of the neighboring houses. We could observe also the play which took place in the road in front of our house, and that which occurred in an old school yard about twenty yards distant and in part of a small plaza whose open end was in our general direction.

Since we had other work to do, we could not spend too much of our time in the observation of children's activities. At times whole days passed without our making any record of play. But we attempted, when we were at home, to observe at least once per hour the play activities which were in progress. Occasionally we observed continuously for an hour or more. Our procedure in such cases was to watch the children about ten minutes, then to write down in summary form what we had seen, then to observe for another ten minutes, etc. The diary which follows reproduces our notes in full, edited only for grammar and for ease of reading.

In editing the notes we have chosen for each child a name which enables us to identify him but which will make him anonymous to all except those who know the village very well. Our own daughter, Mary, has been called by her true name. She was eight and one-half years of age at the time these records were made.

We give below a key to the sex, age and the siblings of all children who are referred to by name in the text. This is not a complete list of all of the children of the village, as some children did not come to play at our house, and a few of those who came only once or twice were not known to us by name. Likewise the lists of siblings are not complete but include only the siblings who came to the shelter.

It must be borne in mind that at the beginning of this record we were not complete strangers to the children. We had spent the preceding summer in New Oraibi, although in a house which gave us much less contact with the village. Mary had played with several of the girls during the preceding summer.

A DIARY ACCOUNT OF CHILD BEHAVIOR

June 27, 1938—8 P. M. We reached New Oraibi at 2 P. M., and found the person who had agreed to rent us a house and who took us to our home. Del, a girl who played with Mary last summer, and some other girls whose names we do not know, came to our house almost immediately and watched us through the windows as we unpacked. Mary went outside and played with them. From 4:00 until 7:00 P. M., eight girls and two boys, between eight and ten years of age, were outside the house almost continuously, either

PLATE VI

A SECTION OF NEW ORAIBI, SHOWING THE AUTHOR'S HOUSE (*extreme right*) WITH THE ATTACHED
PLAY SHELTER.

TABLE 2
LIST OF PLAY PARTICIPANTS

Name	Sex	Age	Siblings
Al	girl	6 years	
Ann	girl	2 years	
Ber	girl	10 years	Fen, Ru
By	boy	14 years	Edna, Del, Mat
Car	girl	6 years	Jan, Em
Del	girl	10 years	Edna, Mat, By
Ed	boy	4 years	Nin, El
Edna	girl	5 years	Del, Mat, By
El	girl	19 years	Ed, Nin
Em	boy	10 years	Car, Jan
Etta	girl	10 years	Win, Frank, Ral
Fen	girl	5 years	Ru, Ber
Fran	girl	8 years	Hal
Frank	boy	9 years	Win, Etta, Ral
Gie	girl	5 years	Shir, Lor, Gra
Gra	girl	10 years	Shir, Gie, Lor
Hal	boy	6 years	Fran
Har	boy	10 years	Sus
Jac	boy	11 years	Mar
Jan	girl	8 years	Car, Em
Joe	boy	2 years	Nephew of Etta, Win, Frank, Ral
Jun	boy	9 years	
Ken	boy	14 years	Min
Lor	girl	4 years	Shir, Gie, Gra
Mak	boy	8 years	
Mar	girl	10 years	Jac
Mat	girl	12 years	Edna, Del, By
Mer	boy	10 years	
Min	girl	10 years	Ken
Na	boy	2 years	Pete, Vie, Pam
Nin	girl	9 years	Ed, El
Pam	boy	12 years	Na, Pete, Vie
Pete	boy	6 years	Na, Vie, Pam
Ral	boy	12 years	Win, Frank, Etta
Reg	girl	10 years	
Ru	girl	7 years	Fen, Ber
Shir	girl	2 years	Lor, Gie, Gra
Sim	girl	10 years	
Sus	girl	8 years	Har
Vie	girl	10 years	Na, Pete, Pam
Vin	boy	11 years	
Win	boy	5 years	Frank, Etta, Ral

watching us or talking and playing. There was no strife or trouble of any kind.

When we sat down to supper they moved away from the windows and did not look at us, which is in accord with Hopi etiquette.

In the course of the afternoon and evening no child came into our house, nor did we ask any to come in, as our one-room dwelling is altogether too small to enable us to encourage indoor play.

When a light shower fell during the afternoon, the girls ran, each to her own home, but all of them returned soon afterward. Some older boys who were stripped to the waist, and some small boys who were naked, stayed out in the rain. One boy built a dam with his feet, impounding a small rivulet.

After the rain all the children seemed more lively, running and calling a great deal. Two boys, Em and Mer, played with auto tires. They raced the tires by hand, and also took them up a low hill and raced them coasting down the hill. At a later time they ran the tires toward the girls, making the latter dodge and run.

The girls engaged in building houses in the sand, each building her own house. They also played seesaw, using a log placed in the crotch of a forked post.

Three girls are still playing with Mary, although it is getting dark. Mary is inside the house sitting by a window. She covers her eyes and counts to five while Del, Vie, and Edna, hide nearby. Mary then tries to see them by moving about inside the house. If she cannot see them, they move into view. When she finds a player the girls laugh.

8:30 P. M. We have put Mary to bed on a cot by a window. Some of the girls came to the window to tell her goodbye and then departed.

June 28—9:00 A. M. We arose at 6 o'clock. Some chimneys showed that breakfasts were being prepared but no one was in view. Children did not appear until 8:00. At 8:30 Mary began playing in the sand beside the house, and some girls joined her. They built houses in parallel play in the sand which is still wet from a rain which fell last night. (The rain of yesterday and of last night is the first rain in two months.)

11:00 A. M. Mary and the other girls played in the sand until 10 o'clock, when all of them left except Vie and Reg. Mary and the two remaining Hopi girls played at sliding down a log, and then at Mary's suggestion played school, with Mary taking the part of teacher. Most of the suggestions came from Mary. Vie, especially, tended to stand and watch.

While the three girls were playing, a group of boys led by Em and Mer came by, stayed about ten minutes, and moved on. They appropriated the seesaw and more or less dispossessed the three girls, who moved aside. The boys threw stones at the houses which had been constructed and destroyed some of them. They chattered, laughed and were generally noisy.

The children this morning spoke in Hopi except when speaking to Mary.

At present Mary and Vie are on the seesaw, with Reg standing near. Mary bosses them about. We will ask her not to do this, as we want the Hopi children to initiate the play. Mary talks more and makes more noise than do the Indian children, although they laugh freely.

12 Noon. While Mary was inside Edna and Fen came and put three dead mice where Mary had been playing, then asked Vie to call Mary. As soon as Mary came, Edna and Fen ran away. Mary paid little attention to the mice.

When Mary was called to lunch, Vie and Reg went elsewhere.

1:00 P. M. Before lunch Mary gave Reg a book of comic cartoons. When Reg came back after lunch she brought Mary a small flat kachina doll.

Mary, Reg and another girl whose name we do not know are now playing outside at the usual spot, just west of our house. For half an hour they have been taking turns at walking up an inclined log. When a girl falls off or jumps off there is much shrieking and laughter. At times a girl is led up the log by the others, who walk on the ground on either side of her. Mary is again giving directions.

The gang of Em and Mer has hung together all day while the boys have been playing about the village. We cannot tell whether Em or Mer is the leader but the other three are smaller and obviously follow the two larger boys. Not long ago the group passed here, each riding a horse of untrimmed green cottonwood. Then each pulled the branches off the main stem of his horse and used the branches as whips.

3:30 P. M. We have been away from home visiting Miss Hartwick, a nurse, and Mrs. Wagner, a teacher. Del is now here with three new girls. Del was not here this morning. The group of five boys is broken up and Em and another boy are on the seesaw.

5:00 P. M. Del and her companions have been here since 3:30. The boys left soon after the girls arrived. For a while the girls played at seesaw with many variations, sometimes one girl on each side of the seesaw, sometimes two or more. At times they pushed the seesaw instead of riding it. Following this, they built sand houses. Now they are again at the seesaw.

The only toys which have been brought to the place of play are two auto tires and some pieces of tin, can lids, etc., which are used in furnishing the sand houses. We are not providing any toys or play materials.

6:00 P. M. We have not heard a child cry today.

The children seem to move about the village quite freely. At hard rain, the children go home, not only from our place but from everywhere, running in all directions. There were several showers today.

Not long ago we went to see Ho, whose sons fourteen and sixteen years of age are good at carpentry, to ask if they would make us some benches. Their father did not know where they were.

At the moment it is raining lightly and Mary is playing with Del and Jan the same peek-a-boo game which was played last night. All three players find it highly satisfactory. Del and Jan seem to wish to be found quickly.

7:00 P. M. When we were eating supper we heard a child crying. Going to the window we saw Jen, holding his three-year-old son, Na, on top of a post. A crowd of children gathered around. After a few minutes the crying subsided and Jen took Na inside the house. Shortly afterward Vie, his older sister, carried Na to the plaza. Mary went to find what had been the trouble. Vie said Na had fallen and hurt himself, but we believe he was held on top of the post because he had been having a tantrum.

A girl passed our house carrying a younger child in a shawl on her back and singing "bye-bye."

Just now a girl of about nine years smilingly struck a boy of six years with a cloth bag. He had a rock in his hand and drew back as if to throw it at her. She hit him again, playfully, and he picked up a second stone, but both children moved off in good humor.

7:15 P. M. Ed, a four-year-old boy, was playing with a string in front of his home when the string caught in the clothesline. He went into the house and came out pulling his mother by the hand to get her to release the string, which she did.

Later Ed and his older sister, El, were walking across the plaza. He repeatedly stopped and said in English "go." It was obvious that he wanted El to race with him, and this she finally did, after making several false starts.

Mary and four other girls played tag in the plaza. The girl who is "it" had to chase the others until she touched someone. Considerable shrieking occurred when a child was being actively pursued or when one was caught. There was no place of safety.

Vie did not play because she had Na to look after, but some of the other girls left their young charges on the sidelines in order to play. Vie, who is rather fat, moves slowly and takes little part in games. However, just now she grasped a young girl by the arms and swung her round and round.

7:30 P. M. The girls who were playing tag have moved to the play spot outside of our house and are using the seesaw. Del and Mat, sisters who are ten and twelve years of age respectively, are among the group. In coming from the plaza, Vie carried Na on her shoulders with his legs about her neck. This caused him to laugh.

In the old school-yard two boys and one girl, all of them about six years old, are doing stunts on the horizontal bar. The boys are hanging upside down by their knees, while the girl is hanging hammock-fashion by her hands and feet.

9:00 P. M. All the children left our place by 8:00.

As we were going to the school building, we passed Edna and By, sister and brother of five and fourteen years respectively, in front of their home. She was throwing stones at him and he was throwing sand into her face and hair.

Boys are calling and shouting in the village, but no girls can be seen. Four boys about ten years old just passed, rolling tires. A drum is sounding in the rear of James Brothers store; probably it indicates practice for the annual Indian Pow-Wow in Flagstaff.

June 29—11:30 A. M. We arose at 7:00. No children were in sight until 8:30 and none came to play before we left for Hotavila at 9:15. No observations from 9:15 until 11:30 because we were in Hotavila. As we returned, no one was visible. The village is very quiet.

2:00 P. M. Del came at 12:30 and played outside with Mary until both seemed affected by the hot sun. We asked them to come in, and they cut out cardboard dolls to make a marionette show. Nin, the nine-year-old sister of Ed, joined them at 1:30. They played quietly and cooperatively, Mary telling each what to cut from among the materials provided in a box of cut-outs.

It is raining lightly now.

2:30 P. M. Mary became shaky from continued application to the task of cutting, although the other two girls did not appear to be fatigued. She suggested that they go outside to play, a suggestion which the others accepted without a word. They are playing on the log and on the seesaw, and laughing.

3:00 P. M. It became cool after the rain. Nin, Del, Ed and Mary played tag, running, laughing and shouting. Two boys played at rabbit hunting, throwing sticks at a tin can. They threw while they ran.

It began to rain again. Mary came inside. Del, Nin and Ed sat on the step under the eve humming a Hopi song. The two girls then counted their fingers in English, spelling each numeral. After this they counted in unison in Hopi. The girls stood at the window singing a Hopi song to us, while Ed danced.

3:30 P. M. Del, Nin and Ed moved to the plaza. The two girls put capes over their shoulders and held corncobs in their hands and sang and danced a part of the Butterfly Dance. Ed moved about, beating two sticks together and singing. Two boys crept up behind some gasoline drums which were nearby, then stuck their heads above the drums and laughed at the girls. Del threw some sand at the boys, who ran, but the dance was discontinued.

3:40 P. M. The two girls are again dancing. A woman, standing nearby, is watching them.

5:00 P. M. When Nin and Del left our neighborhood, Reg came to play with Mary and the two girls have been making sand houses for half an hour.

Em came to the seesaw with a boy of his size and a smaller boy. The two large boys played on the seesaw, the small boy played in the sand, but did not go near the girls. The boys improvised stunts on the inclined log, using an auto tire on one side while the boys sat near the fulcrum on the other side of the log.

Mer, a boy of Mer's age, and a younger boy played near the store. We do not know whether or not this means a split between Em and Mer.

Joe, a two-year-old boy, ran down the lane toward the main road. His grandmother called for him to come back, and he obeyed.

A Navaho woman with four children has been in town all afternoon, staying chiefly in front of James Brothers store. During all of this time the baby which is about eight months old, has been on a cradleboard, but his hands have been free part of the time and his siblings have played with him. His mother has nursed him twice in the past hour. The other children, a girl of about three, and boys of four and six, also remain near the mother. At the moment, the four-year-old is chasing the girl back and forth from one side of the store entrance to the other. After each trip the girl laughs and encourages the boy to pursue her again.

5:45 P. M. The Navaho baby is off the cradleboard, sitting alone and eating a chocolate bar. The four-year-old is swinging on the screen door of the store.

Reg has been here. She brought with her a doll and a toy chair which came from a box of Cracker Jack. Reg and Mary have been seesawing. Reg left just now because we called Mary to supper. She arrived at about 4:30, and no other girls came, except two-year-old Ann, who lives only a few steps away, and who toddled down to play in the sand while her mother watched her from the door of her home.

6:15 P. M. The Navaho woman bought a box of crackers and a can of tomatoes at the store and gathered her family in a circle on the ground outside, where they ate by dipping the crackers into the can. The baby joined in the supper. Soon the father and a ten-year-old son rode up, each on a horse. The three-year-old girl ran to them, holding the box of crackers for them to see. The father and the son went into the store, but soon came out and joined the family circle. After supper, the two small boys tried to mount the horses but could not accomplish it. They then played about the gasoline drums and the hydrant, running, shouting and laughing. The little girl remained with the mother and the baby.

When the Navahoes left, the two oldest boys rode the horses, which had purchases from the store hung across their backs. The two youngest children ran ahead. The husband and the wife also went on foot, the man carrying the cradleboard. It was nearly dark as they left New Oraibi and it rained soon after they had gone.

Throughout the long afternoon not a Hopi child approached the Navaho children.

9:00 P. M. A group of girls played tag in the plaza, making a great deal of noise. Mary did not play with them because she was in her pajamas before they gathered. The girls have only now disbanded.

Six boys have been rolling auto tires. They too were noisy. Shouting and loud talking is still heard from their direction.

Earlier this evening three girls between eight and ten years of age were in front of Jen's house, two on one side of the fence and one on the other side. They were throwing sand across the fence, and their actions seemed not quite playful.

9:15 P. M. The boys with auto tires have been noisy again. We thought a man reprimanded them in Hopi, but we are not sure. At any rate, play has now ceased. The evening is cool, and this seems to have made the children very active. A very unusual amount of rain lately; it is again falling lightly.

June 30—1:00 P. M. We spent the morning at Hotavila. No children had come to play, and very few were in sight, when we left New Oraibi at 8:30. We returned at 12 and prepared lunch.

After lunch, Nin, Ed and Reg came to play. Nin and Reg seesawed while Ed interfered by giving pushes, laughing each time he did so. Nin and Ed left, leaving Reg and Mary who entertained themselves by seesawing, by walking the inclined log, by standing on the log on one foot and by jumping off of the log.

Ann, the two-year-old who has no siblings to look after her, walked down the lane and onto the main road. An automobile came when she was in the middle of the road. The driver stopped and sounded his horn, and Ann slowly got out of the way, retreating toward her home, but as soon as the car was gone she again started across the road. Reg then saw her, picked her up, carried her to a point near her home and put her down. Ann went home where she was picked up smilingly by her father, with no admonition.

1:30 P. M. Ed and Nin are walking with their arms about each other.

Reg and Mary are at the hydrant, washing their hands and drinking from the spigot.

2:00 P. M. Reg and Mary asked for crayons. After they received them, they went outside, found some vertebral bones of sheep, and colored them with the crayons so as to make bone tie holders similar to those seen at western curio stores. This, we learned, was done at Mary's suggestion. She and Reg are now in the house working on the materials for making cardboard marionettes.

3:30 P. M. Mary and Reg are outside, doing acrobatics on an iron pipe which is part of a fence.

Vie has made herself a shelter in her yard by putting an old blanket between some poles. She and Na are sitting in the shade.

Nin and Ed have been playing near their own home all afternoon. At present they are running a race.

One girl, whom we did not recognize, was seen rolling an auto tire. She is the only girl we have observed playing at this sport, and she was not proficient at it.

A child, not in view, cried for several minutes, the only cry that has been heard thus far today.

5:00 P. M. Reg left at 3:30 when we went to the school.

We visited Ro, who was taking care of Sid, a two-year-old son of Ro's brother. While we were there, Sid started to hit a pet rabbit with a hammer. Without reprimanding him, Ro distracted Sid while the rabbit got away. Ro's mother, Sid's grandmother, was making some sort of dough. When Sid put his hands in the dough, his grandmother gave him some of it to play with and to eat. He then tried to get green peaches from a tree nearby, but as nobody helped him he had to go without fruit. Sid is the boy who gets candy at Hubbell's store and charges it to his grandmother.

5:10 P. M. Ann's mother had a tub full of clothes in front of her home. Ann pulled some of the clothes out of the tub and put them on the ground. Her mother spoke to her in Hopi but otherwise she did nothing to the child. Finally the woman put the clothes back into the tub, smiling as she did so.

5:25 P. M. Ann started down the lane. Her mother came after her and carried her home.

Joe has been playing alone, naked, near his home.

5:30 P. M. Del and Ru are on the seesaw. They are reciting an English rhyme as they play on the teeterboard but we cannot hear it.

6:00 P. M. Del, Ru and Mary played at making houses by outlining the rooms on the earth. Sticks were used for people. Del made several suggestions.

Five boys, seven to twelve years of age, came by from the peach orchards where they had been guarding the fruit from the birds. The oldest boy carried an old gun.

Three boys rolled auto tires for a while. From time to time they carried the tires to the top of the slide in the old school yard and let them roll down.

6:10 P. M. When our supper was ready, Del and Ru went home. Vie and Na are sitting quietly outside the store.

6:30 P. M. Two boys about nine years old threw rocks at the backboard of the basketball goal which stands across the way. They made quite a noise hitting the board with the rocks.

Em rolled a tire. He has not been seen with other boys today.

Car and Jan, girls of six and eight years, are on the seesaw. Vie and Na are sitting by the store.

6:45 P. M. Vie and Na just now went home.

Car, Jan and Mary are playing on the seesaw. By the use of an additional log and another forked post, which was already in place, a second seesaw has been made at right angles to the first and so near to it that the two seesaws can be made to interfere. The girls are trying all sorts of variations on the seesaw game.

Aside from the seesaw and the sand, the play space outside of our house provides no materials, but nevertheless children play there almost continuously.

7:00 P. M. Nin and Ed have joined the other three children at seesaw play. Not always do the children sit on the log. On occasion they lean on it, pull at it, or hang to the end of it. Nearly continuous laughter.

7:10 P. M. Mary showed Nin some dancing stunts, clapping her hands behind her back in time with her dancing rhythm or clapping them under each leg as she stepped. Nin imitated, and all laughed.

El, Ed and Nin's older sister came by. Ed ran and jumped at her. As she leaned over, he put his arms around her neck and pulled himself up. She carried him home and Nin went with them.

Ann again ran toward the road. This is the third time that this has happened today, there having been one occasion which we failed to record. Her mother ran after her and led her back. As she returned we talked to the young mother, who said she was much worried that the child might be run over, but not once has the child been punished, or even strongly scolded, for her behavior.

After Nin and Ed left the group, Car, Jan and Mary played

circling games, pulling, struggling and laughing. They held hands and circled until they fell. At one time they sat on the rocks to rest, but after ten seconds they were circling again. Mary said rhymes as they played.

Three boys are rolling tires along the road.

7:30 P. M. Vie and another girl have joined the circling game, which has turned into London Bridge. The Hopi girls sing the song quite well. In the game there is much rough play and continuous laughter. The play, which has lasted for twenty minutes, is gradually becoming less fun than it was. Jan and another girl dropped out, watched the game for a while, and then walked off, arms about each other.

7:45 P. M. The game of London Bridge has stopped and the girls are resting.

Ann's mother is sitting in front of her house playing with Ann. She holds Ann above her head, lowers the child and puts her face in the child's neck, and hugs and pats her. Ann laughs. Her mother is sitting on the ground with her legs straight in front, the usual fashion for Hopi women.

8:00 P. M. Em and another boy played on the seesaw for five minutes and then left.

Mary, Vie, and Car threw rocks for a while, or rather they slung them in something of the way that a discus is thrown. Vie was the first to quit.

There are now seven girls and five boys outside the house. They are talking and arguing, using English most of the time. The boys and girls are joshing each other. Finally a boy says "Let's go" and they pick up the tires which are parked nearby and push off. Now each boy is swinging his tire around and around.

Mary must go to the school for her bath.

8:45 P. M. Vie and another girl were still here when we returned from the bathroom, but they left when we said that Mary must go to bed. No one is here now.

9:15 P. M. Three boys are in front of the store; they are sitting, their tires lying near at hand. The village is entirely quiet.

July 1—8:30 P. M. There are no play notes today because we were out of the village all day long, visiting Mishongnovi in the morning and working with our Hotavila informants in the afternoon. Tonight the village is very quiet, chiefly because many families have gone to Flagstaff for an annual affair which is called by its American sponsors the Pow-Wow.

Reg went to Flagstaff. Before she left, she gave to Mary the much-abused young rabbit which Sid nearly killed with a hammer.

Seba built the shelter today while we were away.

July 2—5:30 P. M. Again we worked with Hotavila informants, reaching home at 5:00 P. M.

The shelter is proving to be popular. Vie, Mar, and Sim have been playing there with Mary since we returned. They were rather rowdy, tickling and tumbling, shouting and laughing. Mary and Sim, who is half-white both in race and in culture, were the roughest of the lot. During this rowdy play, some woman came and spoke to the children in Hopi. She was not the mother of any of the girls. We do not know what was said, but soon after she had spoken, Mar and Sim left for a few minutes. When they returned, the play was much more quiet. Part of the time the girls sat and talked.

When Mrs. Dennis asked Mary to bring some sticks of firewood from the woodpile, the Hopi girls joined her and carried wood also.

6:00 P. M. After Mary was called to supper, the girls remained outside but they kept away from the windows. There was constant conversation while we were at supper, and while we could not hear it well enough to understand it, we could tell that it was in English. This was probably due to the fact that Sim, whose father is Hopi but who lived in Prescott until a few weeks ago, does not understand Hopi.

6:30 P. M. Mar went home. Sim, Vie and Mary went to the vicinity of the store. Vie was carrying Na, and Sim had her baby sister. Sim and Vie ran because a boy threw a torpedo, the first fireworks of the season. All laughed when it exploded.

7:00 P. M. Vie and Sim went home. In the shelter were gathered Del, Fen, Ru and Mary. They played on the seesaw and talked. Mary and Del hung to the rafters of the shelter and swung by their arms. Ru said, "Let's make a swing" and Fen, her younger sister, was sent home to get a rope. When Fen brought it she explained that the children could use it but it would have to be taken home when she quit playing. In order that they would have a permanent swing, we put up a rope which we had, tying it to the framework of the shelter.

Mary said: "Let's take turns, I'm first."

Del said: "I'm second."

Mary said to Ru: "You will be third and your sister will be fourth." There was no dissent. They took turns, each swinging ten times before giving place to her successor. All counted in English.

Fen folded her shawl and put it in the swing to make a seat.

Del was called home by her brother.

One girl swung until the count of twelve had been reached, instead of the customary number of ten. Now everyone swings twelve times.

7:30 P. M. When Del came back to the swing, she was given an extra turn because she had been away. Mrs. Dennis suggested they count in Hopi. One of the girls counted very slowly but they soon went back to English. Mary is chiefly responsible for the counting.

Mer and another boy sat near the swing for a while, neither asking or being asked to use the swing. Mer then made a swing of the rope which Fen had brought and the two boys used this swing.

Mary deserted the group and rolled Mer's tire. Del helped her manage it. The other girls called them back to take their turns in the swing.

The two swings move at right angles to each other. When Mary and a small boy were swinging simultaneously, their feet touched at the end of each excursion. This made them laugh and shout.

Mer sent the boy to find a board to make a seat for his swing. Mer and Del swung. Both tried to go so high that they could touch the ceiling of the shelter. The board which was in the boy's swing split and Mer fell out. While all of the children laughed, it seemed that the boy who had been sent to get the board laughed louder than the rest.

PLATE VII

CHILDREN IN AND ABOUT THE PLAY SHELTER.

7:45 P. M. As we took Mary for her bath, Etta arrived with a rope and began to put up a third swing. When we came back, both of the Hopi-owned ropes had been removed, and the rope of our swing had been thrown across the roof of the shelter. All the children had gone.

July 3—8:00 P. M. We have been away most of the day.

While we were at supper, Har and Sus, who are temporary residents, children of a white father and a First Mesa woman, stared at us through the window as no native child of New Oraibi has done. In their play outside, these children seemed to us more noisy and quarrelsome than were the Hopi children.

Two boys are standing on the roof of a house in the plaza and are trying to lasso girls as they go by.

July 4—6:00 P. M. The day was spent in visiting First Mesa and in attending the Hopi-Navaho races and horse show at Polacca. We reached home at 5:30.

Soon after our return, Etta and another girl, whom we did not know, came to the house and watched us through the windows. As we had American visitors, Etta immediately plied us with questions, wanting to know which of us were Mary's parents and asking who the others were.

Mary took a small doll and went outside to play with the two girls, but she soon returned, refusing to go out again. Etta had hit her on the chin, twisted the neck of her doll, and scratched her leg with a stone. It does not seem that Mary provoked these actions. Mary recalled that Etta caused trouble last summer.

6:30 P. M. Em was in the swing, but he left to go to the store where torpedoes are being exploded. When one explodes, everyone laughs; and when one fails to explode, everyone laughs.

7:00 P. M. Many children are in front of the store and on the plaza. Several are yelling shrilly and loudly. Nearly all of them were at the races today. Mer, who was there, is now at home rolling his tire again.

Mary and some of her playmates were sitting in front of the store, but Mary came home because Etta pulled her hair. Soon after this event Etta also went to her home which is just a few steps distant from us, and called to Mary to come up. Mary went. Vie also was there. The three girls had a tug of war with two boys. The girls won but the boys recovered their rope.

Mary saw a kitten in Etta's home and said she would like to have it. Etta's mother suggested that Mary take it home for a little while, and Etta watched through the window while we petted it. We learned that it belonged to Etta's younger brother Frank, who is in Flagstaff for the Pow-Wow, and told Mary we would see whether he would part with it when he came home. This satisfied Mary, and she returned the kitten to Etta, but Etta in receiving it pulled it away roughly and held it so tightly that it cried. Mary cried also. Etta said nothing and went home with the kitten.

8:00 P. M. After Mary had burned some sparklers in front of our house, Etta and Win came to watch. No other children were in sight. Mary offered to let each of the two visitors hold a burning sparkler. Win held one gingerly and silently but Etta, much older, was afraid to touch one, whereupon Mary brought out some flags and asked Etta to take one of them. This immediately precipitated a sham fencing match between the two girls, the flags being used as weapons. Mary took the initiative in starting this game, and we promptly stopped it before any casualties could result.

8:30 P. M. While Mary went to the school, Mrs. Dennis remained at home, and Etta and Vie helped her get a bucketful of water from the hydrant. Etta asked, with reference to our trips to the bathroom: "Why you have to take baths every day?"

July 5—11:00 A. M. Vie and Na have been in the shelter since 9:00, and Mary has been with them most of the time. The two girls made houses in the sand. Mary gave most of the directions, while Vie sat and helped with the construction. In this play, Na took no part, but sat watching them and a man who was working on a tire nearby. He occasionally played in the sand by himself. On one occasion he got sand in his eyes and began to cry. Vie went to him, held him, petted him, and talked to him, and he partially quieted. When Mrs. Dennis gave him an apricot, he stopped altogether.

Mer and a larger boy (we have had little opportunity to learn the names of the boys) came for a short visit to the shelter. After a little play on the seesaw and on the swing they departed. Although they played near the girls, they did not play with them.

Etta spent about half an hour in the shelter. She did not play at building houses, but tickled the others and wrestled with them.

Vie, Na and Mary started to swing. They took turns, as they usually do, but this time they did so without counting.

Later Vie and Mary, with the help of Nin, went about the nearby parts of the village and from street and trash pile gathered together a box full of odds and ends with which to play house. Bone dolls were included in the contents of the box.

At present Mary is indoors writing some post cards, while Vie and Nin outside are building separate houses, marking the walls with narrow upright strips of linoleum. Na is in the swing.

11:40 A. M. Na is still in the swing—this makes an hour he has spent there. He smiled when we played peek with him through the window.

Etta was here for a few minutes but did not build a house for herself.

11:45 A. M. When we told Mary it was time for lunch, all the children went away. The houses were left intact. Na cried at having to leave the swing but Vie persuaded him.

Mary reports that Vie moved her bone dolls about and spoke for them. Furthermore she had one doll who was Soyoko. "I am the old woman who steals children," Vie said, speaking for this doll. The Soyoko went to Nin's house where she stole some children, then to Vie's house where she stole more. Vie and Nin then caught her, fought with her, and put her in *jail*. When Vie's dolls misbehaved, she said, "Be good. The old woman who steals children is coming."

12:15 P. M. When we were leaving for Hotavila, Vie was experiencing some difficulties with Na, who was having a tantrum.

Vie tried to get him to ride on her back, and bent down in order for him to get on, but he refused to do so, striking Vie with his hands and continuing to cry.

7:00 P. M. While we were in Hotavila, Mary was kept by El, although in our own house. Mary staged a puppet show. The puppets were inside of a window, which served as a stage, and the audience was on the outside. Several of her acquaintances came to see the show.

During the afternoon, Nin and Etta were Mary's chief playmates. Etta caused no trouble at all. At El's suggestion they skipped rope, which is the first time since we have been here that this game has been engaged in.

Nin and El were turning a rope for Ed. El slapped Nin, who fought back, but it ended with Nin in tears. A little later Ed and Etta were throwing stones at each other in front of the store, Etta ran into the store.

7:30 P. M. Na, Pete and Pam have been using the swing and the seesaw. No girls have been in the shelter, except Mary, who has been talking to the boys. Just now we are starting for the school to get Mary ready for bed.

8:00 P. M. The boys are still here. They have been swinging Na very roughly. Na is laughing, but at times it sounds almost like crying. The boys have scratched on the rocks but we cannot see that they have drawn anything.

8:30 P. M. The boys have gone. Pam tried to get Na to roll his auto tire, but Na was too small to manage it. When they left, all of the boys had candy suckers.

9:00 P. M. Sixteen boys between ten and fifteen years of age have been in front of the store putting off firecrackers with no supervision of any kind and with not much self-restraint. Quite often a boy withdrew a few yards from the crowd, lighted a firecracker and threw it at the crowd. The boys ran away as quickly as possible, but the firecracker often exploded within a foot of one or more of the boys. There was much shouting and yelling and much talking in Hopi. We heard no English. Three small boys, between four and eight years, kept at a distance from the bigger boys, not joining in the fun.

Four girls came down the road. The largest was Vie. As soon as the boys saw the girls, they raised a cry and chased the girls a short distance, throwing lighted firecrackers at them.

The boys have now moved to the hill which is behind our house and are relatively quiet.

July 6—10:15 A. M. Nin and Ed came to the shelter at 9:00. Nin and Mary played house while Ed occupied the swing. Etta had to do some work this morning, but told Mary she would be here as soon as she was through with it.

Mat and another girl and a small boy came not long ago. When we took a peach to each of the children, each said, "Thank you."

Mary is giving a puppet show in the window. The spectators are quiet and attentive. A girl passing by, probably an older sister of Mat, said, "Mat, hurry up and come to work, you lazy thing."

10:30 A. M. The puppet show is still in process. The girls are watching, and Vie has joined them. Ed and Na are taking turns in the swing and have no interest in the stage, which is being watched only by girls.

10:45 A. M. The girls asked for more theatricals. Between acts, the girls hang by their hands from the rafters of the shelter.

11:45 A. M. Because of other work, we have not paid much attention to play in the past hour.

The puppet theater closed after a long continuous run. One of the girls said, "Mary, let's play doll." When Mary went outside, all of the girls were lying on the ground and as she approached they began to cry like babies. Then all laughed. This alternate crying and laughing continued for some time.

Ed and Na took no part. They are still busy with the swing.

12 Noon. The crying and the laughter ceased; the girls did not play doll in any other way than by crying.

Na and Ed exchanged places in the swing.

Although several children have been here during the entire morning, there has been no quarreling, struggling or crying, except the mock-crying which was described above.

1:00 P. M. As we started to the school at 12:30, Lor and Gie came to play. This is the first time they have been here. They have been in Flagstaff for the Pow-Wow and returned only yesterday.

6:00 P. M. When we reached home after spending the afternoon with informants, Etta was here with Win who had just returned from Flagstaff. They said nothing but it was obvious that they wanted to dispose of Win's kitten. We showed the boy a silver tie clasp with a turquoise set and asked if he would trade it for the cat. He was willing and Etta would have left the matter entirely to the judgment of the five-year-old boy, but we insisted that the children take the jewelry to their mother for her examination. They returned in a few minutes with the kitten, saying that their mother approved of the trade. Etta seemed genuinely pleased when Mary received the kitten which she had wanted so badly, and said, "Now it is all yours."

Mary reported that Etta had said earlier, concerning the pet, "She will have kittens and then you can sell them."

When the author was away for a few minutes, Gra brought our laundry, and as there was no money in the house, she had to wait for his return to receive the pay. Mrs. Dennis tried to engage her in conversation, but Gra would say very little and put her hand before her face when she spoke. At Mrs. Dennis' suggestion she went to see what was happening in the shelter, but she did not join the play even though Mary was friendly and tried to encourage her to take part. The other girls, however, paid no attention to Gra.

When Gra had gone, one girl said, "Where is the top?" referring to the top of a can which had been used in playing house. Mary replied that she did not know. The Hopi girls insisted that Gra had taken it.

7:00 P. M. Na has been in the swing for half an hour. Pam, his older brother, is with him, although Vie is there also.

10:00 P. M. The noise of firecrackers has just now ceased. Someone must have got a bargain in fireworks at the Pow-Wow (probably at its close) for at normal prices the display which has occurred this evening would be more than this village could afford.

The exhibition of fireworks has been almost continuous since 8:00 P. M. Most of the combustibles have been of the explosive type and very loud, there being scarcely any roman candles or rockets or fountains but many torpedoes and firecrackers. The fireworks have been put off entirely by the boys. No adults and no girls took part in this delayed celebration of the Fourth, nor did they gather to watch it, although without doubt the entire village heard it. As was the case last night, the boys often threw lighted explosives at each other. They also threw them so that they exploded high in the air. The technique of lighting the fuse and sticking the firecrackers under an empty can, so as to blow the can into the air, was also employed. Is this a borrowed trait or an independent invention? Explosions that were especially loud were followed by shouting.

Two small babies were kept awake beyond their usual hours and were set to crying by the noise.

July 7—8:30 A. M. Some children were seen out of doors as early as 7:30 but the first ones came to play only a few minutes ago. For once Vie is here without Na; perhaps he is still asleep. Lor is in the shelter for the first time, but she is merely watching. Win and Frank have been taking turns in the swing.

Yesterday we failed to note that the swing had been used so much that the rope wore out and had to be replaced.

8:45 A. M. Vie and Lor are sitting in the sand. Win sits on a rock eating a piece of melon. Mary is in the swing. Frank has gone away. No other children have come.

9:00 A. M. Lor is swinging. Win sits and watches. Vie and Mary are playing house very quietly.

9:45 A. M. Vie, who has been in the shelter all morning, says Na is still asleep. He was kept awake last night by the fireworks.

Mary is now in the swing. Vie, Etta, Lor, Win, and Ral are in the shelter, engaged chiefly in quiet talk. No one seems very energetic.

7:00 P. M. We worked with informants from 10:00 until 6:00. Mary was kept at home by El. Frank and Win were busy with the swing when we came home.

10:00 P. M. There were fireworks tonight from 7:00 until 10:00. We think they were not quite as loud as they were last night, but perhaps we are beginning to get used to it. Most of the celebration takes place in front of James Brothers store, which is only one hundred feet from our windows.

July 8—12 Noon. When we got up at 6:30, our usual time this summer, Frank and Ral were still asleep on the bed which stands in front of their house. Ordinarily they are out of bed before we arise.

Very few children have come to play in the shelter. The fruit is now getting ripe, and we saw several of Mary's playmates going to the orchards with buckets.

However, two girls, Fran and Al, eight and six years respectively, came to play. They used the swing for a while. At one time they twisted the ropes of the swing, making the child who was in the swing rotate rapidly as the ropes unwound. This is the first instance of this kind of play. Each girl told the other when she thought it was time for her to use the swing and there were no arguments. Following the play with the swing, the girls built doll houses in the sand. When playing by themselves they sometimes spoke English, sometimes Hopi. As Mary left for the school building, one asked us, "Where Mary Dennis went?" The children do not often ask questions of us.

After the girls departed, three boys of about eight or nine years came and swung and wrestled for a while. One of them was Frank.

7:00 P. M. The afternoon was again occupied by work with informants.

When we returned, Gra and Lor watched us through the windows for a while but did not play. Win, Frank, Mer and Em, all boys, have been taking irregular turns at the swing. Frank picked up Mer's tire, which was near, and threw it. Mer brought it back.

8:00 P. M. There has been very little play this evening and Mary, who stayed at home with Rom when we were away, says that scarcely any children came to play this afternoon. It has been a very hot day. Another reason for the quiet behavior of the boys this evening is the fact that a rabbit hunt was held today, a very fatiguing event. Tonight there are only a few firecrackers.

8:15 P. M. Lor and Shir played in the swing for a while.

July 9—8:30 A. M. We arose at 6:00. Lor came to play at 7:00, when Mary was still asleep. Lor waited outside and played by herself. We went to the school bathroom at 8:00, leaving Mary sleeping. As soon as we had gone, Lor called to Mary and awakened her, but Lor went away before we came back.

Now Win is here swinging, alone. Em is loafing about the store. Some small girls are carrying water from the hydrant.

12 Noon. While we have been working at home with an informant, we have kept on the watch for child play. Not a child has come to the shelter since 8:30. There are two probable reasons. In the first place it is a very hot day and heat seems to keep the children indoors (the houses remain quite comfortable). Secondly, there is a dance at Shungopovi and many families from New Oraibi have gone, or are getting ready to go this afternoon. A large truckload from Moenkopi went by not long ago. We ourselves are going to the dance soon.

8:00 P. M. Vie is just now beginning to carry her four-months-old sister, and brought the baby for us to see. Na was in the swing, being pushed by Pam. Na laughed when he was pushed with special vigor. He also laughed when we pretended to catch his toes as he swung near us.

Ann came toward the swing, and we asked her mother to let her try it. Ann did not know how to keep herself in the swing either by sitting properly or by holding on with her hands, but had to be held while she was swung.

Vie took the baby home at 8:30 and returned with Na. She seated herself beside us as we sat in front of the house. Na, however, wanted to swing, although he was obviously so sleepy that he could scarcely stay awake. Vie complied with his wishes. Soon Pam came and spoke to them in Hopi, apparently to tell them to come home, for they left us.

No fireworks tonight.

July 10—9:00 A. M. About 8:00, Vie brought the baby to the shelter and Na and Pete came with her. Vie sat on the ground with the baby against her shoulder, and rocked back and forth. Pete pushed Na in the swing. After ten minutes the baby began to fret, and all the children went home.

No one else has been here. There is another dance at Shungopovi today and a good part of the village is attending again.

9:30 A. M. No children have been here.

10:00 A. M. No one in the shelter. More truckloads are leaving for the dance.

11:00 A. M. Nobody in sight.

12 Noon. The village is dead. The thermometer stands at 100° in the shade.

3:00 P. M. Apparently there isn't a Hopi left in town. We too are leaving for the dance in a few minutes.

9:00 P. M. The dance did not end until nearly 8:00. There has been no play since we returned.

July 11—9:00 A. M. Win swung for a few minutes at about 8:00. No one else has been to the shelter.

Mar and Del and all of their brothers and sisters just passed the house, carrying buckets of apricots from the orchard.

11:00 A. M. Ed and Win are near Ed's home. Ed is sitting on his tricycle. Win is sitting on the ground not far from him. Neither is active, but they are talking.

No children have come to the shelter and very few have been seen. It is another hot day, nearly 100° now. Furthermore, there is a Niman Dance at Mishongnovi tomorrow, which people are preparing to attend.

Note that no boys have rolled tires for several days.

7:00 P. M. We were occupied by work with an informant during the afternoon.

When we returned to New Oraibi, Vie was attempting to take Na home, but he was yelling and refusing to go. Mrs. Dennis reported that after Na had been in the swing about fifteen minutes, Vie tried to get him to leave, but he had a tantrum, and engaged in ten minutes of continuous crying. Vie was not at all ruffled, but she spanked him a couple of times. He retaliated by hitting Vie. She picked him up and carried him to the store but he did not stop crying. She then walked him home, just as we entered the scene, and the trip home caused even louder crying. His father came to meet him and took him by the arm, but still the crying did not stop. His father then set him on top of a post in the yard, so that Na had to hold on to keep from falling. His father stood near. Within a few seconds the crying became less severe, whereupon his father took him inside, and the tantrum quickly subsided.

About five minutes later we saw him again coming toward the swing. Vie caught him before he reached his goal and took him home once more. He cried on the return journey but not as violently as before.

8:00 P. M. Vie, Fran, Min and Mary were in the shelter pulling each other in a circle and often causing each other to fall. Har, a small boy who was in the swing, was accidentally hit in the eye by one of the girls. He cried slightly but went home with dignity. The girls continued their former play. Note that it is much cooler tonight.

Min suggested that they play "I spy" but the suggestion did not take.

Pam, Pete and Frank came by rolling tires, and stopped to play on the seesaw. Pam with two tires balanced the two smaller boys. Pam made the log stand as nearly vertical as was possible, almost spilling the two smaller boys. The boys shrieked, yelled and laughed most hilariously. The seesaw play stopped after ten minutes and the boys watched the girls' game for a while. After this, the boys picked up the tires as if starting away and then ran them at the girls.

The girls began a game of tag, and the boys, to our surprise, joined the girls. The rules which evolved after a few minutes of play were as follows: One person is "it" until he tags someone else. A player is safe if he is touching a post or a rafter of the shelter, but only one person may touch each piece. When a second person touches a piece of timber, the first person is forced off. He may, of course, go to another timber and force someone else off.

This made a very active game and it was played vigorously and noisily for half an hour, when it became desultory and broke up. The rules were always adhered to.

In the course of the game, Ann came down the lane and stood in the shelter in the midst of the seven scrambling older children. She did not attempt to play, but merely stood and watched. The girls moved her outside of the shelter several times because she was in danger of being knocked over, but she returned each time. When the game ended, she started toward the main road. We brought her back to the shelter and her mother came for her.

July 12—5:30 A. M. We awakened at 4:30 in order to see the first part of the dance at Mishongnovi. It was still dark; there were no lights, no fires in the village and no one stirring. It became daylight at 5:00. Now, at 5:30, women are carrying water and building fires but no children are to be seen, not even the larger boys or girls. Frank and Ral are asleep on the bed in front of their home.

8:45 A. M. We returned from the dance at 8:30. It is a cool cloudy morning.

Win passed by rolling a tire. Etta has brought Joe to the swing. She, too, swings, holding Joe on her lap. Vie and Na have just come to the shelter.

9:00 A. M. Etta, without being asked, found a board which would serve as a seat in the swing and brought it to us. Etta has done nothing naughty since the first days of our residence here. Etta and Joe departed. Na sat in the swing and Mary pushed him. Vie built a house. Boys and girls came down the road carrying buckets of apricots from the orchards.

9:15 A. M. Etta and Joe returned, and Na let Etta swing Joe while he quietly stood by. After a few minutes, Etta gave the swing to Na and she and Joe went home. Na is in good humor this morning.

Vie and Mary are building houses by means of a new technique. They are digging into the sand which is firmly packed, making rooms by means of excavation. Steps lead down into the houses. Vie has furnished her building with a piece of mirror, and a bed which was improvised from a flat tin can. A bone doll rests on the bed.

9:20 A. M. Na watches while Mary swings.

9:25 A. M. Mary and Na watched while Vie used the swing. Then Vie put Na in the swing, wound the swing by twisting the ropes and let it unwind with him.

Etta and Joe are here again.

9:30 A. M. Win came, bringing his tire.

Etta sat in the swing for a few minutes, then swung Joe on her lap as Na and Vie watched.

Etta brought a small china doll, which Mary dressed.

9:40 A. M. Na took another turn at the swing, but the seat slipped, causing him to fall and to cry. Win got in next.

The girls are standing about talking, and looking at the doll.

10:30 A. M. There have been no detailed observations since the preceding note because we have had callers. The children have been playing tag.

11:00 A. M. The girls who are now in the shelter are Min, Fran, Gie, Lor and Vie. Na is with Vie. Two boys are outside the shelter but near it. The girls are taking turns at the swing, each claiming a turn, but they are not counting the number of swings.

Lor had a pop bottle filled with water which was the water supply of the group. Fran accused her of wasting it, and this accusation Lor denied. Fran said, "Then how did you get it on your shoe?" Lor said something in Hopi, and the girls struck each other on the legs, scowling at each other. In a few minutes Lor and Gie went away.

11:30 A. M. Har is in the swing. Mak and Jac are nearby. Mary is in the shelter digging a house of many rooms in the sand. The other girls have been sent to find furnishings for the house.

11:45 A. M. Now the boys have forsaken the shelter, and the girls have come back from their foraging expedition, bringing with them pieces of dishes, old combs and toothbrushes, scraps of cloth, fragments of glass and feathers, spools, sticks and bone dolls.

12 Noon. The girls are arranging the furnishings in two sand houses.

The boys are again here. Mak is swinging, Har is digging in the sand, Jac is standing and Na is sitting.

12:30 P. M. When Mary came in to lunch, the other children gradually departed.

1:00 P. M. On their way back from the store, Gra, Lor and Shir stopped to play with Mary. The girls who were here this morning have not come back as yet.

4:00 P. M. We have been working on other notes this afternoon and have not kept a complete account of play.

The large houses which had been dug and furnished so elaborately were deserted this afternoon. Most of the girls who worked at the houses did not return. Probably some of them went to the Mishongnovi dance.

Gie, Gra and Shir occupied the swing for a while. Gie cried once when Gra forced her out in order to get a turn for herself, and Shir cried when she also had to give way to Gra.

At Mary's suggestion, she and Vie dug a deep hole in the sand. Vie did most of the digging, using her bare hands part of the time and for the remainder using an empty can as a scoop. When the pit was completed, the girls sat in it.

Min, who was about the shelter much of the afternoon, went to the store and bought four suckers. She gave two to Mary, kept one for herself and then tossed the remaining one to the other children to let them scramble for it. This sort of thing is done at some of the Hopi dances.

9:00 P. M. This afternoon we again went to the dance at Second Mesa. There was no play after we returned.

July 13—8:00 A. M. We have been awake since 6:00 but no children have been seen. In fact, Frank and Ral are just now getting up.

8:10 A. M. Etta, Win and Joe are in the shelter.

8:30 A. M. To the three children mentioned above are now added Vie, Pete and Na, Gie and Lor, and Nin. All are idly sitting about, except Etta who is deepening the pit which was dug yesterday by Vie and Mary.

8:45 A. M. Etta is standing in the pit, filling cans with sand, and Win is taking them away and emptying them. Vie, Na and Joe are sitting and watching. Lor and Gie are alternating at the swing. Nin was swinging but has gone home.

8:50 A. M. Vie is now digging.
Joe seems sleepy and cross; he cries easily. He was sitting on Etta's lap and protested when she tried to get him to sit alone. When he cried, she hugged him and rocked him back and forth. Then she reached to the window sill and brought down a half-consumed sucker which apparently had been brought along with such a use in view. This quieted him, but he remained on her lap.

9:10 A. M. Etta, now free from Joe, is digging. She is being watched by Joe, Mary, Vie and Win. Na is swinging. Pete is operating the seesaw in solo play by hanging two tires on the end opposite himself.

While we were writing this note, Na talked loudly in Hopi (he does not yet speak any English). It appears that he had asked to get into the hole, for Pete took him from the swing and put him in the pit, which was so deep that only Na's head was above the level of the earth. He smiled and patted the ground. Pete and Win then pulled him out.

Joe cried briefly for some cause which we could not discover. He has the sucker, and also a runny nose.

Etta, Vie and Mary are taking turns at scooping sand from the bottom of the pit. The two who are resting count aloud as the other one works. Win is playing in the loose sand which they have piled up. Pete is watching. Na is swinging and Joe is watching Na.

Etta gives Na a few pushes in the swing, then takes a turn at digging. Win gets too near the edge of the pit and causes one side of it to cave in.

Mary: "Do you want to break it?"

Win: "No." Mary pushes and causes another landslide. All laugh.

Mary: "Now let's make another one (landslide). I'll hold my hand in there while you make another one." Win causes another landslide of sand. Play at the pit ceases.

Vie lies under the swing and pushes Na as he passes over her.

Etta comes to my window and asks us what we are doing. We reply that we are writing, as she can see.

9:15 A. M. The mother of Vie, Na and Pete came and spoke to them and they went home with her, Pete rolling a tire as he went.

Etta and Joe also went home.

Win got into the partially filled pit.

Lor arrived and used the swing.

9:25 A. M. Win scraped at the edges of the pit while Mary played in the loose sand outside of the pit.

9:30 A. M. Win went home, taking with him a piece of pipe which had been used to loosen the hard sand in the bottom of the pit. Mary played with loose sand and Lor stayed in the swing for

PLATE VIII
SOLITARY PLAY.

some minutes but when Reg came, Lor went home. (When a child walks away, as several have done in the past half hour, he says nothing and nothing is said to him.)

Reg and Mary are now the only ones who remain. Mary is explaining to Reg how the pit was made.

9:50 A. M. We asked Reg to stay while we took Mary to the washroom.

10:00 A. M. When we reappeared, Reg was standing in the pit which had been partially cleared and was making a house along the edge of the hole.

1:00 P. M. There is a gap in the play notes from 10:00 to 1:00 because of work on other notes.

Reg and Min played with Mary from 10:00 to 12:00, and waited at the store while Mary had lunch, returning to play afterward. We believe they had some lunch at the store; certainly they have not been home to eat since 10:00.

Min had twenty cents when she came. Part of this she spent for suckers which she shared with her two playmates.

Ann has come to the shelter.

8:30 P. M. No systematic play notes this afternoon because we worked at home with an informant.

Only a few children came to play. The heat of the day may have been a cause, the temperature in the noonday shade being 96°. Another factor is the peach crop, which is now being harvested and which requires work on the part of many of the children.

After supper Vie and Na came to use the swing. Vie slipped away for a few minutes while Na was in the swing. This is the first time that he has been alone in the shelter. When he discovered Vie's absence, he was slightly disturbed, but remained where he was. Some larger boys came, and he took turns with them in the absence of Vie.

When Vie had returned, we tried to get Na to play ball with us. We feel sure he understood from our actions what we wanted, but even after Vie had translated our request into Hopi, he was negativistic. A few minutes later he rolled the ball, on the ground, with Vie and Mary. He lets us push him when he is in the swing, and smiles at us in this situation.

We discovered that the swing rope was again worn to a single strand. Our notes on this point are incomplete, for although the notes do not show it, we are sure that this is the fifth rope that has been worn out.

In order to put up the new rope, we asked Na to get out. When Vie explained the situation to him in Hopi, he cooperated readily. He permitted us to lift him into the new swing.

9:00 P. M. Joe's father has been carrying Joe on his back and has been singing a Hopi song to him.

There is a slight recurrence of fireworks after several evenings of quiet.

July 14. No play notes today because of a visit to Mishongnovi, a session with an informant, and a speech by Mr. Collier at New Oraibi.

July 15—9:00 P. M. Today was occupied by a visit to Moenkopi.

Tonight as we sat in front of the house with a book Etta came to see what we were reading. She asks more questions and is more curious than any of the other children. In coming to see us, she slipped up quietly, not to spy, but to surprise us.

July 16—8:00 A. M. Frank and Ral got up at 7:00. Pete and Pam are still asleep on the roof of their home.

The village water pump is temporarily out of condition, so that water has to be carried from the spring. The women have been making trips to the spring since 6:00.

12 Noon. More work with a New Oraibi informant has prevented detailed notes on play this morning.

A small group of girls spent a great deal of the morning at making pottery. Those who participated were Fran, Fen and Mary. Fran was the leader. She suggested the occupation and showed

Mary how to do it. The girls went to the hill behind the village where clay is found and brought the clay to the shelter. After being moistened, the clay was shaped into pots by pressing it against the elbow. When the pottery was shaped the children wanted to fire it and asked Mrs. Dennis for matches. Mrs. Dennis refused, as she thought it dangerous to give them matches and was not certain that the parents of the Hopi girls would approve of it. But Fran got matches from somewhere and took the pottery to the hill. Since Mary wanted very badly to see the whole thing, and since we thought that playing with fire should be supervised, the author went along. This was useless as Fran would not fire the pottery so long as he was there. He finally returned, leaving Mary to the dangers of Hopi child ceramics, which, however, came off without mishap. Mary reported that Fran used for fuel cornstalks and dry sheep manure. When the pots were completed, they were brought to the shelter.

Lor has been in the swing lately. A small boy cried because Lor would not give him a chance at it.

10:30 P. M. The remainder of the day was spent in other work.

July 17—7:30 P. M. Today we worked with informants, part of the day here, part of the day away from home.

During the past two days a new fad in play has developed—rolling hoops. Hoops have been rolled to the total neglect of auto tires. While only boys play with tires, both boys and girls have been playing with hoops, although the boys predominate. The hoops are small, only about one foot in diameter and are obtained from the hubs of old wagon wheels. They are rolled by the use of sticks to which a piece of tin is nailed.

Boys often roll hoops in a group, three or more boys running single file or moving abreast, each with a hoop.

Tires are so neglected that Win, five years old, managed to gain possession of one. Usually they are claimed by the older boys.

When we returned from Old Oraibi today, we saw Nin with the seat of the swing under her arm. The swing rope had been tossed over the roof of the shelter. Apparently there had been some disagreement about its use.

Earlier today Vin struck Nin, who was in the swing, because she would not let him use the swing. Several blows were exchanged between the boy and the girl. At length our informant, who had witnessed the clash, spoke to them in Hopi and Vin went away.

Vin was not the only one to indulge in striking today for at another time Win hit Fen on the back as she sat on the ground. He had no apparent reason for the blow. Fen cried slightly, but did not retaliate.

When we started for Mishongnovi to bring an informant to our house, we asked Etta if she wanted to go along. She was anxious to ride, but we told her to get her mother's permission. Etta replied: "It all right. She not mad at me." However, when we insisted that her mother be consulted, Etta sent Win, her brother, to make the request. Win came back beaming, and without saying a word he also climbed into the car.

July 18–20. No play notes because of attendance at dances and because of a trip to Holbrook.

July 21—9:00 P. M. The day has been broken by visits to Mishongnovi, Shipaulovi, Bacobi and Hotavila.

During the part of the morning that we spent at home no children came to play nor were children to be seen anywhere in the village. It was a very hot morning, being 98° for several hours.

At 2:00 P. M. a heavy rain fell and for a while the temperature dropped to 66°. The children became active immediately. Soon after the rain there was much playing in the pools and in the mud. The children waded and splashed; one boy even sat down in a mudhole. Wheelbarrows were obtained from somewhere, and the big children wheeled the small boys and girls, occasionally wheeling them through a mudhole. When the ground became more firm, hoops were again the favorite toys, and they were pursued with vigor. Boys drove the hoops so as to make the hoops strike each other, sometimes colliding at right angles and sometimes head on.

At 5:00 P. M. a play rabbit hunt occurred in the space before our house. A hoop took the part of the rabbit. The hoop was thrown so that it rolled rapidly and the boys threw sticks at it while it was in motion. This sport caused excitement and noise. The boys were between seven and ten years of age.

At 7:00 o'clock a tag game was started in the shelter, the players being Min, Nin and four boys. They were extremely noisy and rough, so much so that we kept Mary out of the game. The rowdiest boy of the lot we did not know; he was about twelve years old.

July 22–23. No play observations were made.

July 24—9:00 P. M. Ethnographic work again kept us too busy to observe play.

Na had another tantrum about leaving the swing, and was carried home by his oldest brother.

July 25. Our day was occupied by the taking of notes in the morning and by attending the Niman Dance at Walpi in the afternoon.

July 26—9:00 P. M. We were busy with informants during the day.

In the evening several children played in the shelter. Gra, Mar, Nin and Mary romped and laughed. Em, with two boys of his size, came by and shouted at the girls. The Hopi girls threw rocks at the boys. The boys did not retaliate but only dodged and tried to hit the rocks with sticks. The girls moved forward, still throwing, and the boys retreated. The skirmish ended with everybody in good humor, as they had been throughout.

Some large boys played softball, the first we have seen here.

July 27. The day was spent at Mishongnovi, Old Oraibi and Bacobi.

July 28—5:00 P. M. Today we made a trip to Winslow.

After we returned, Gie wanted the swing entirely to herself. She refused to take turns, and forcibly pushed Gra out of the swing. She also threw rocks at Gra. When Mrs. Dennis reprimanded her, she pouted and went home.

Through all of this trouble about the swing, Na, who was nearby, was well-behaved and caused no trouble. He was in the care of Pete, Vie being occupied with the baby.

6:00 P. M. Our friend Clar from Old Oraibi came to call on us, bringing her six-year-old sister, Nita. Clar brought a kachina doll and a small basket as presents for Mary. Mary showed toys to Nita, who was charmed but speechless. Apparently she had not seen many dolls before. She especially liked a rag doll made to resemble a Hopi woman, which we had purchased on First Mesa. (It was not a kachina doll.) She held it and smiled at it. She held the American dolls also.

When Gra and some other girls came to the shelter, Nita and Mary went to join them. Nita soon returned. Mary said that the other girls, in Hopi, apparently made fun of the little girl from Old Oraibi, who was shy and not very well-dressed.

July 29–31. We were away from New Oraibi.

August 1—5:00 P. M. Ann has been in the shelter in care of a boy and girl whom we do not know. Ann saw an American doll in one of our windows and came around to the door to get it. We let her take it. She carried it to the shelter and played with it for half an hour, then left it and went home. The girl who was with her said to Mrs. Dennis, "Let me help you with the dishes wash."

Later, when some boys were in the shelter, Sim and another girl passed. The boys teased them by calling some boys' names at them. The girls answered saucily.

Ed's family is being visited by a woman with a two-year-old son. When the boy interfered with Ed by pulling at Ed's tricycle when Ed was riding it, Ed hit the boy lightly on the head. They exchanged a few blows. The younger boy cried, and went to his mother. Ed may have been scolded but he was not punished. Ed never takes his tricycle out of his own yard and never lets anyone else use it.

Ann went down the road just now. The boy who is at her home called, "Ann, pewi (come here)," and she returned.

7:00 P. M. Em and another boy have been alternating in their use of the swing. Vie and Na have been sitting in front of our house, swinging only occasionally.

Joe, Pete and Win are playing in front of their home.

August 2. There are no notes on play because of work with informants.

August 3—6:45 A. M. Nin and Ed came to the shelter at 5:45 A. M. and wakened us by talking and laughing loudly while they used the swing. We dressed and asked them not to make noise because we wanted Mary to sleep, and they soon went away. Ed rolled a hoop, and Nin did some chores for her mother, carrying some things to a neighbor.

At 6:00, however, Etta and Vie and Na came to the shelter. Vie swung, and Na held on to her knees, laughing loudly. As Mrs. Dennis and Mary dressed, the girls stood at the window, watching.

These are the earliest visitors we have had. The activity of the children at this unusual hour may be due to the coolness of the morning and to the fact that a rain last night caused everybody to sleep inside, where, we surmise, bedbugs caused the early rising.

7:00 A. M. Nin and Ed are in the shelter again.

Several children are at the store watching a truck get a tankful of gasoline. They are now running after a wagon which is passing by, and *Vie* is hanging to the rear of the wagon.

5:00 P. M. We worked with Hotavila informants. When we returned home, Na was trying to push Gie out of the swing and was hitting her with his fists. He stopped when we approached.

6:00 P. M. Both Vie and Ber have built a playhouse in the shelter. The houses are excavations in the hard-packed sand. Furniture has been made of strips of paper fastened together by fine wires. From scraps of cloth, Etta made two neat dolls and gave one to each of the two girls. Vie cut out a figure from a catalogue and put it behind a piece of glass and called it a picture.

Win, Joe and Na watched.

When Mary went to the store, Etta started to go with her, but Joe began to cry because of her departure and she returned. As we were unpacking some pieces of cloth, Etta asked where we got them and how much we paid for them.

August 4. Mary was ill with an upset stomach and stayed in bed all day. Vie, Mat, Nin, Gra and Ber came and each brought her a little present. They were most considerate.

August 5—10:00 P. M. No detailed notes because of other work.

During the afternoon two boys of twelve or thirteen years came to the swing for a while. There was much horseplay, including false counting of the number of oscillations in the swing. Later, when Mary was swinging, the two boys stood by and teased her.

In the evening, Del brought a plaque which her mother had made for Mary.

All children were up late because of bright moonlight, the cool air and an impending storm. Even Na was awake until 9:00. We put Mary to bed at 8:30 and thereafter sat in front of the house. Etta, Mat, Vie and Edna came and talked to us. At our request they talked to us in Hopi phrases and sang Hopi songs. Etta volunteered the information that she had twice danced in the Butterfly Dance, whereupon Mat said she had danced it once and Edna said she had not been in it at all. Vie said nothing. Na, who was in the swing, made Vie give him a push every few minutes.

August 6—5:30 P. M. We spent most of the day at First Mesa and at Awotobi.

Upon our return to New Oraibi, Em and Jan were in the swing but they left as we approached. A girl, about twelve years old, was crying on the other side of our house. She said Jan had hit her.

Vie and Na came to the swing. Vie swung Na on her lap and bounced him and played with him until he was half-crying, half-laughing. When Vie left for a few minutes, Na cried, but when she returned he quieted and played without expressing a desire for the swing.

Etta came to ask where we had been and what we had done. We are sure these interrogations are spontaneous on her part, and not instigated by her parents or by anyone else.

August 7. No play notes.

August 8—9:00 A. M. Nin was in the swing while Ed nearby was crying. We think it possible that he had destroyed some sand houses and that Nin had punished him. El, Nin's older sister, came over and slapped Nin and took Ed home. Nin, when she was slapped, held her hands over her face and tried to keep from crying, but she did cry a little.

COMMENTS ON CHILD PLAY AT NEW ORAIBI

Unfortunately there is no record of the play of American children which is comparable to that of the New Oraibi participants in regard to age distribution, the types of play materials which were available, and the relative absence of adult supervision. It is therefore difficult to determine in what ways the play which we have observed may be similar to, and in what details it may differ from, the activities of children of a different cultural background playing in the same immediate environment. Nevertheless some aspects of the record which we have just presented seem worthy of comment.

1. Proximity as a Determinant of Participation. Theoretically a Hopi child may play wherever he pleases within the village, but a consideration of the play diary shows that at least so far as our shelter was concerned it was patronized chiefly by children of the neighboring houses. As an index of participation we have counted the number of days on which each child came to play in the shelter or in the territory immediately outside of our house. This does not include all of the play which was recorded in our notes for some of the observations refer to play which took place near neighboring houses or in the road or in the nearby plaza. In order to receive a score in the tabulation a child had definitely to leave his own home and come to the immediate vicinity of our house. As stated earlier, we tabulated the number of days on which such behavior occurred in our notes. The tabulation does not show the actual number of days on which the child came, because play notes were not taken on all days and are seldom complete for a given day. Nevertheless we do not know of any respects in which our choice of observation times was selective, except that we seldom were in the village on dance days. This seems unimportant, as many of the inhabitants of New Oraibi were also out of town when dances were held elsewhere.

Table 3 shows the frequency of visits for each child who came on more than one day. Those who came to play most often were Vie, Na, Etta, Nin and Win. These children lived in the three houses which were nearest to us. Our house was located toward one end of the village. *All* of the children listed in the table came from the half of the village which adjoined our house. It would ap-

TABLE 3

NUMBER OF DAYS ON WHICH EACH CHILD CAME TO THE SHELTER

Ann 5		Lor 7
Ber 2		Mar 2
Del 6		Mat 4
Ed 5		Mer 3
Edna 3		Min 4
Em 6		Na 13
Etta 12		Nin 11
Fen 4		Pam 4
Fran 4		Pete 5
Frank 4		Reg 6
Gie 5		Ru 2
Gra 6		Shir 2
Har 2		Vie 18
Jan 3		Win 10
Joe 3		

pear, therefore, that while a child may play anywhere, he chooses to play at some spot in the vicinity of his home.

This apparent effect of proximity is not due to the fact that the nearby children had formed friendships which held them together. As a matter of fact some of the children who have relatively high scores did not play together and did not come to the shelter at the same time. Reg seldom came when any other children were about, yet she managed to come often. Gra, Gie, Lor and Shir, a family of four sisters who lived near us, were unpopular among the other children, but they too came to the shelter a considerable number of times.

2. Conflicts. It is our impression that in comparison with many groups of American children playing under roughly the same conditions the Hopi playmates got along with remarkably little trouble. During the period of our notes there was not an incident that could be called a serious fight, nor was any child injured more than slightly. There were several conflicts, to be sure, but generally speaking they were of a transient nature.

Since it is difficult to define conflicts objectively, we shall list all of the events which seem to us to deserve this title, citing the date of each and the persons who were involved. They are as follows:

> *June 28*—Edna and By
> *June 29*—three girls, names not recorded
> *July 4*—Mary and Etta
> *July 5*—Na and Vie
> El and Nin
> Ed and Etta
> *July 11*—Na and Vie
> *July 12*—Lor and Fran
> Gie and Gra
> Shir and Gra
> *July 17*—Vin and Nin
> *July 24*—Na and Pam
> *July 28*—Gie and Gra
> *Aug. 1*—Ed and visiting boy
> *Aug. 3*—Na and Gie
> *Aug. 6*—Jan and unnamed girl
> *Aug. 8*—Nin and Ed
> El and Nin

In several cases the cause of the conflict was not determined. Of the eleven cases whose cause was known, seven were attributable to the swing, the only piece of equipment in the shelter, except for the seesaws.

Twelve of the eighteen instances of conflict involved children of the same family, whereas only six cases of conflict between children of different families were observed.

The children who were involved in the greatest number of conflicts were Na and Nin. Na's difficulties arose as a result of his somewhat inordinate desire to use the swing. Nin's conflicts grew out of disagreements with her younger brother, Ed, and were increased in frequency by the fact that her older sister, El, often clashed with Nin on behalf of Ed.

3. Age Differences. When children of two to four years of age were in the shelter at the same time as somewhat older children, the notes reveal that there was a marked tendency for the younger children merely to watch the older ones. Na, Ann, Joe and Ed, who were the youngest of those who came to the shelter, usually sat on the sidelines and made no attempt to participate in group activities. The only exception to this rule occurred in the case of the swing, which the younger children were as anxious to use as were the older ones.

4. Sex Differences. It was quite common for the shelter to be occupied only by girls with their young charges, or by boys alone. If older boys and girls were in the shelter at the same time, they ordinarily engaged in quite different activities; that is, they did not play jointly. This is in accord with Hopi tradition. In fact, the only instance of cooperative play involving both boys and girls was the game of tag on July 11. Quite often there was a distinct, if playful, antagonism between a group of boys and a group of girls. On June 27 boys ran their auto tires at the girls. On June 28 Em and Mer and a group of boys drove the girls from the shelter and ruined some of the sand houses which the girls had built. Early in July boys on the roofs about the plaza lassoed the girls who were playing there. During the epoch of fireworks, boys on one occasion chased a group of girls by threatening them with lighted firecrackers. Late in July there was a mock fight between boys and girls in which the girls threw rocks, but it was in good humor, and the boys did not throw in return. On several occasions, there were arguments and mutual teasing between small groups of boys and girls. No similar behavior was seen between two groups of boys or between two groups of girls. There were no antagonistic gangs of the same sex.

5. Cultural Content of Play. Although New Oraibi has been affected by American influences, and although our daughter took part in most of the games, it is interesting to note that many of the activities of the children were probably specific to the Pueblo culture area, and some may be specific to the Hopi. The use of bone dolls we have not discovered in other Pueblo groups, nor do we know that the technique of roofing mud houses by first filling them with dry sand occurs elsewhere. The play rabbit hunts, and the threatening of the dolls with the Soyoko and the modeling of pottery probably take place in most of the Southwestern pueblos. Swinging is native, according to our informants, as is also the use of a log as a seesaw.

Some of the games which show acculturation are easily interpreted as the use of American materials in an old pattern. Racing is characteristic of the entire Pueblo area, and plays a large part in the ceremonial life as well as in the field of sports. In racing the runner follows a stick which he kicks along the course in front of him. It is therefore not at all surprising that the boys should develop an interest in racing by rolling an auto tire or a hoop before them. It is also understandable that tin cans should be put to good use in the imitative rabbit hunts.

We do not see that there could have been any aboriginal counterpart to the play with fireworks. This trait must have come in its entirety from the white man.

6. Fads. The various kinds of play ran through cycles of popularity and unpopularity even in the short period covered by our observations.

For several days after our arrival, both boys and girls played a great deal on the seesaws, and invented some ingenious methods of utilizing these logs placed in the forks of two posts. After July 1 play on the seesaws practically ceased. During the last days of

June the girls had spent a great deal of time walking up and down the logs. This also went through a period of high development and of later decline. These games may have been interrupted in part by the Fourth of July and the subsequent fireworks and also by the building of the shelter and the installation of the swing.

The swing provided the most consistently popular activity of the summer. There was not a day when it was not used, and on many days it was used almost continuously. It must be remembered that it was a Hopi girl who introduced the swing. We had not planned to provide any apparatus.

The boys rolled tires during most of the summer, but this sport was interrupted for the duration of the fireworks and it again came to a stop when hoops were introduced on July 17. Playing at rabbit hunting occurred twice, once late in June and again a month later. The two periods of popularity of tag games were also separated by approximately one month. The digging of the pit occupied a group of girls for several days, and this activity was not duplicated during our residence.

7. Temperature Effects. While we do not have enough cases to make for statistical certainty, our observations suggest that the Hopi children were relatively inactive when the temperature was between 90° and 100° and were most active on the occasions when the air became as cool as 70°. It also appears that in summer Hopi children are more active after sunset, when the air is invariably comfortable, than they are in the heat of the day. Both of these deductions from the play notes are corroborated by general native testimony.

It may be significant that of the eighteen conflicts reported in a previous section, twelve occurred between 12 noon and 6:00 P. M. Only three took place during the morning hours, and only three happened after 6:00, although evening was the time when the children played most and was the period when we were almost invariably at home to observe any conflicts which might have occurred.

CHAPTER VIII

CHILD BEHAVIOR AT KACHINA DANCES

W HENEVER we attended a kachina dance at any of the Hopi villages, we jotted down in brief form our observations concerning the behavior of the children who were at the ceremony. These records are presented below:

July 12, 1937—Kachina Dance at New Oraibi. This was a short dance, which took place at a late hour in the afternoon after the kachinas had returned from Moenkopi where they had performed on the preceding day.

The onlookers, children and adults alike, were quiet and attentive throughout. The only exceptions to this attentiveness were a few boys who rode a bicycle and a few who rolled auto tires in the village while the dance was in progress. They were not noisy.

Sid, one and one-half years of age, received an apple from one of the kachinas. He was the only child to receive a present.

A three-year-old boy kept his index finger in his mouth throughout the performance. No children were afraid of the dancers.

July 13, 1937—Niman Kachina Dance at Mishongnovi. The onlookers, who sat on the ground and on the roofs on all sides of the court, were quiet and serious. There was no gaiety or laughter. The dance lasted all day long, and we were there most of the day.

The children at the dance were quiet and did not run about or play with each other when the dance was in progress, but occasionally they walked in the court. Many presents were given to the children by the kachinas, bows and arrows to the boys, kachina dolls to the girls, and fruit, corn and candy to both sexes. When a child received a present, he smiled, but said nothing. No child was afraid of the kachinas. Presents of food were immediately eaten by the recipients.

One girl of about seven years exchanged blows with other chil-

161

dren, once with a boy and once with a girl. The blows seemed to be without provocation.

At least three boys asked us for money, without making any claim of need. (We do not accede to such requests.)

During a rest interval, a girl of about two years squatted in the court and defecated in the presence of several people. No one paid any especial attention to her.

July 17, 1937—A Kachina Dance at New Oraibi. This was a full-day dance, in which clowns participated during the afternoon. The crowd was serious except when the clowns were present, at which times the people often laughed hilariously. The children were quiet and well-behaved. We saw only one untoward incident. A girl of about ten years without apparent cause slapped another squarely in the face. The latter cried, went to the hydrant and washed her face, but did not retaliate. No one said or did anything to the offender.

Many children were given presents by the kachinas. The gifts consisted of oranges, watermelons, piki and cakes. One small boy ran away as soon as he grasped the gift which was held to him by a kachina. A baby seven and one-half months of age cried upon first seeing the kachinas but later watched them quietly. A child of two years cried loudly whenever the clowns came near him.

Toward the close of the dance an automobile driven by two Hopi boys from Winslow struck Gie, a four-year-old girl, who ran directly in front of the car. The child's mother became nearly hysterical and even left the child in order to berate the boys, who were quiet and apologetic but apparently not at fault. The crowd which gathered was relatively unexcited and the dance which was in progress was not interrupted. In a few minutes a government nurse came and took the child to the hospital at Keams Canyon. The girl was not seriously injured, but she remained at the hospital overnight.

We learned later that when she was struck by the car she was eating an ice cream cone, a comestible of which she had been very fond. She was very badly frightened by the accident. At the hospital on the day following the accident, her parents brought ice cream to her room on two occasions, but she asked them to take it away, as it nauseated her. She told them she never wanted to see ice cream again. A nice instance of emotional conditioning.

July 24, 1937—Niman Kachina Dance at Walpi. We spent at least three hours at the dance but saw nothing except casual and ordinary behavior on the part of the children.

During rest intervals the dancers retired to a cliff below the road which leads from Walpi to Sichumovi, where they unmasked and relaxed. Some Navahoes and some white people stood at the edge of the cliff and watched them, but the Hopi children who passed along the road never came to the edge of the cliff.

July 26, 1937—Shalako Dance at Shungopovi. A very large crowd of visitors attended this dance, as it is seldom given. A Niman Kachina Dance preceded it, the Shalako dancers not appearing until about 5:30 P. M. People were not much interested in the Niman Dance, and many persons loitered about the village without watching it.

There was a period of an hour and a half between the close of the Niman Dance and the beginning of the Shalako Dance, during which a considerable number of the visitors simply sat and waited, although others called on friends. Mothers of small children played with their infants, fed them and changed their position. The children under two years of age became quite restless during this period when nothing was happening. They fretted but did not cry loudly. There was no scolding, no irascibility on the part of the mothers. Several children who were old enough to be able to walk were observed nursing at their mother's breasts. One child pulled a zipper in the mother's dress to attain the goal by his own efforts.

The older children went about the village, but they did not make much noise. Some of the girls walked arm in arm. Some of the boys chased each other, while others teased dogs or teased the captive eagles. There was no fighting or shouting, and no excitement or hyperactivity. During the interim, we saw four children between two and six years of age asleep on a bed, arranged in a fashion which suggested that they had climbed onto the bed by themselves.

In two instances, a young boy in care of an older sister stumbled and fell. In each case, the sister picked up the boy and carried him.

There are two courts at Shungopovi, and the crowd was not certain in which of these the Shalako would appear. Eventually the entire assemblage was grouped about the walls and the roofs of the larger plaza. A rumor spread that the dancers would appear not in this place but in the smaller court. There was a hurried scramble for places in the second plaza. Every person left the first court and tried to find a favorable spot in the other. After ten or fifteen minutes, there was a similar scramble back to the main plaza, where, in fact, the dancers appeared.

When, at the close of the dance the Shalako dancers were unmasked, a leader shouted directions, and mothers covered the faces of all of the uninitiated children while the Shalako costume was removed from the dancers and was taken into a kiva.

July 30, 1937—Niman Kachina Dance at Hotavila. We saw the first dance of the day, which began at about 6 A. M., but we left soon after its close. Apparently every child and every adult arose in time to see the first dance. All were quiet and well behaved. Some children received presents at this initial performance. As is traditional at the Niman Kachina Dance, the boys were given bows and arrows, the girls were given kachina dolls, and both sexes were given native foods including melons, squash, and boiled corn. Some children ate their food immediately.

July 4, 1938—Hopi-Navaho Rodeo at Polacca. We spent from 10:30 A. M. to 3:30 P. M. at this affair, which was arranged and controlled by the Hopi Rodeo Association. The events were chiefly races. There were many horse races, several foot races, a burro race, a mule race, a relay foot race and a relay horse race. There was also a corn shelling contest for the women. A few stock-judging contests were held. Practically every event was competitive.

Both Hopi and Navaho contestants took part, although in some events, as in horse racing, there were separate contests for Hopi and Navaho entrants, followed by a joint contest for the winners of the earlier races.

The crowd was silent. There was no shouting or cheering and no urging of contestants, yet all of the spectators were interested and they watched the finish of each race very closely. The children, of which there must have been 200, were also quiet, and the older ones were attentive to the races. Only a few crying babies were heard. Refreshment stands, operated by Hopi concessionaires, were patronized by adults and children alike.

Em of New Oraibi was there, as well as several other children from our village. Em at one time was pestered by another boy. Both boys had lolly-pops in their mouths. When the other boy became too bothersome, Em dropped his lolly-pop on the ground and walked away.

July 9, 1938—Navaho Kachina Dance at Shungopovi: First Day. There were many visitors at this dance, partly because clowns were there. The clowns performed during most of the afternoon. The children were much more interested in the clowns than they were in the kachinas, often crowding close to the clowns in order to watch them. Many children left the plaza where the kachinas were dancing when they learned that a clown was riding a bicycle about the village. However, one small boy of about two years was very much afraid of the clowns, and cried so loudly that his father took him away.

Generally speaking, the children were well behaved. They were reserved, and did not annoy each other or bother the adults. They received presents of food from the kachinas. The gifts consisted chiefly of fruit, but a few boxes of crackers were dispensed.

July 10, 1938—Navaho Kachina Dance at Shungopovi: Second Day. We were at the dance from 3:30 P. M. until 7:30 P. M. There were many visitors from other villages, including a large part of the population of New Oraibi. We estimated that the persons watching the dance numbered about 700, of which 200 were children between two and ten years of age. During the four hours that we observed these 200 children there were no quarrels and no fights. One six-year-old boy threw a stone at two boys whose backs were turned, but this seemed to be for the purpose of attracting their attention. Two boys of about nine years wrestled in good humor for a short time. A girl, age ten years, gave a shove to a girl of five. We saw no other conflicts of any sort.

Some children moved about when the dancers were in the plaza but most of them were quiet, and in general the children did not display much energy. A few of the girls walked here and there with their arms about each other. No boys did this. Two boys of about six years played horse for a while, one boy holding a string in his mouth as he was driven by his companion. This was unusual, because so few of the children at dances engage in dramatic play of any sort.

A girl of five years cried when her grandmother walked away, leaving her alone. A few babies fretted occasionally during the afternoon, but were quieted by being offered the breast.

The kachinas again gave gifts of food to many of the children. The presents included fruit and piki, but also bakery cakes, Cracker Jack and even dyed eggs.

When the clowns passed out gifts of Cracker Jack and lolly-pops (probably in imitation of the acculturated kachinas) women and children struggled to get them, for clowns' presents, unlike those of the kachinas, are the property of any person who can seize them. Men, however, do not attempt to claim them.

When one old woman attempted to get a box of Cracker Jack for her four-year-old granddaughter, the child apparently thought that her grandmother was getting into a serious fight, for she cried frantically and pulled at the woman's skirts as if to get her out of the fracas.

Late in the afternoon, whipping kachinas appeared. The children and many of the women ran to places inside the houses or against the walls of the court where they would not be struck. The kachinas whipped only those who were in the front row. A considerable number of people welcomed the blows on the legs or on the back because of their beneficial effect. A girl of two years remained on the lap of her mother, who was toward the front of the crowd. The child as well as the mother was hit on the legs, and the child cried for some time.

Several girls from New Oraibi saw us at the dance. Etta gave Mary a stick of piki which had been given to her. Mat and Del at one time asked Mary to come stand with them. At another time Etta, Del and Nin came and stood by Mrs. Dennis.

On one occasion two Shungopovi girls, whom Mary had never before seen, came and sat by her. After a few minutes, they suggested that she go walking with them. We gave Mary a dime and told her to go with them to the store and buy candy for all. During the remainder of the afternoon Mary had a hard time escaping from them, as they stayed with her persistently.

Mary asked Reg to ride home with us, but Reg was in a stubborn mood and refused. Her father apologized for her.

Rom had arranged to go home with us, but when we decided to leave at 7:30 P. M., she decided to stay until the close of the dance.

July 12, 1938—Niman Kachina Dance at Mishongnovi. We attended the first performance, from 6:15 A. M. until about 8 A. M., and again went to Mishongnovi at about 4:00 P. M. to stay until the end.

At the first dance there were no visitors except ourselves, but it seemed that all of the inhabitants of Mishongnovi were present. There were several babies on cradleboards which were covered to keep the light from the infants' faces. Some two- and three-year-old boys were naked, notwithstanding the fact that the weather was quite chilly. The children were even more quiet than usual. Since this was a Niman Kachina Dance, the boys received bows and arrows and the girls were given kachina dolls. Other presents consisted of bundles of corn stalks bearing fresh ears, bundles of cattails, and watermelons and oranges. There were no cakes or confections.

While we were the only outsiders at the first dance, at the afternoon performances there were quite a number of Hopi from other villages in attendance.

In contrast to the behavior of the children in the early morning, their conduct during the afternoon was not exemplary. Some Hopi boys between fifteen and twenty years of age who were dressed in American clothing, and some of whom were in cowboy garb, strutted about noisily in their boots and talked and smiled in what we took to be a superior fashion when the ceremonies were in progress. During the very last dance of the day, the children seemed particularly ill-behaved; they were worse in conduct than any other group we have seen at a dance. Some boys between eight and twelve years of age pelted each other with orange peels. Another group of boys of this age teased some girls by shouting at them. The kachinas, it will be noted, were singing and dancing at the time. A boy sounded an auto horn about twenty-five feet from the dancers. A group of girls about ten years of age chased each other on the nearby roofs. Two girls of this age played at spitting at each other, and they displayed considerable proficiency.

A girl of between two and three years climbed on the kiva, which is forbidden ground for a child. An older sister was sent to bring her, but the younger child struck at her sister and refused to leave. Eventually her mother brought her away.

In contrast to the children, the adults were serious and quiet, but many left before the close of the dance. No one seemed to be concerned about the behavior of the children. No presents were distributed during the last dance.

July 19, 1938—Niman Kachina Dance at Hotavila. Our hours at the dance were from 9:00 A. M. until 11:00 A. M. and from 4:00 P. M. until 7:00 P. M. As is usual, the afternoon crowd was larger than the morning group. The morning performance was uneventful. In the afternoon, the children in general were quiet and well-behaved. It was a very hot day, and many children sprawled on the sand in the dance court. One group of girls, which included Vie from New Oraibi, drew figures in the sand. When a design was completed, the sand was smoothed to receive new figures.

Gra, Shir, Gie and Lor each received a kachina doll from the dancers. Mary also was given one by a dancer. We learned afterward that it came from the mother of the four sisters mentioned above. At Hotavila, the receipt of a kachina doll by a white girl caused quite a bit of native comment, and several Hotavila people asked our friends who we were.

After Mary received the doll, Etta came to see it. She looked it over, and then said quietly, "Something is walking on it." It proved to be a bedbug.

The afternoon was not entirely without expressions of aggression. One incident involved a woman and a six-year-old boy whom she was leading. When she came to a stop, the boy wanted to go on. At her refusal to go further, he ran at her and struck her in the abdomen, then lay down in the sand and cried.

Some of the misbehavior was on the part of Gra and Shir. On one occasion when Gra was holding Shir on her lap, Shir urinated, wetting Gra's new dress. Gra raised Shir and slapped her buttocks slightly, frowning all the while.

July 25, 1938—Niman Kachina Dance at Walpi. We witnessed the last two dances of the day, between 5:00 P. M. and 6:30 P. M. Since it had rained earlier, and was cloudy at this hour, the high village was cool. Despite the cool weather, there was no running about or shouting; the children were quiet and well-behaved. A boy of six hit a younger brother, but hugged him when he cried.

It appeared that all of the girls had kachina dolls, many of which were large and beautifully decorated, and every boy seemed to have a bow and arrow. At a distance from the dance, some of the boys were trying out their new weapons.

July 27, 1938—A Kachina Dance at Bacobi. Again we attended during the coolest part of the day, from 5:00 P. M. until the close at about 6:30 P. M. There were present about 100 children under fifteen years of age. Bacobi has very few children; most of those at the dance were from Hotavila and from New Oraibi.

The children had been given cattails by the kachinas. Many of the children tore off the long leaves and used them as whips with which to chase each other. Girls as well as boys joined in the sport, and some of the children actually whipped each other, but it was all done in good humor.

During a rest period, Shir was being led across the court by her mother when Shir suddenly refused to go any further, lying down in the road and crying. Her mother walked off, leaving her there. In a short time, Gra came and put Shir on her back and carried her away.

The kachinas who performed in the dance carried long staves which were painted in two colors and which had feathers attached to one end. At the close of the dance, certain small boys, from four to eight years of age, were expected to go to the kachinas and receive the staves as presents. Several of the boys were shy in approaching the dancers and ran away as soon as they grasped the long sticks, but all were highly pleased with their gifts.

COMMENTS ON BEHAVIOR AT KACHINA DANCES

Considering the fact that at each dance a great many children were present and that the period of attendance of those who live in the village is day-long and that for the visiting children it has a duration of many hours, we believe that the frequency of crying, of tantrums, of conflicts, of striking, of shouting and of yelling was extremely small.

It is likely that a very important factor in the good behavior of the children was the fact that throughout the day the dancers brought presents to the children, and that these gifts depended upon the children's conduct not only before the dance but during the dance. To misbehave would have endangered the child's chances of receiving gifts. Nearly all presents, however, were distributed before the last dance of the day.

In this latter fact may lie the explanation of the rather general misbehavior of the children of Mishongnovi during the last performance of the Niman Dancers on July 12, 1938. It will be recalled that earlier in the day their conduct was much better. However, our observations of the last performances of other dances show that such bad behavior during the last dance is not a general rule. Our Mishongnovi informant believed the present group of children in her village to be particularly troublesome.

CHAPTER IX

PERSONALITY SKETCHES OF HOPI CHILDREN

NO amount of general statement concerning the Hopi child can give a picture of an individual. We therefore wish to present brief descriptions of some of the children whom we knew best in order to give the reader an impression of the Hopi child in the concrete.

As we indicated above, the cases which are to be described were chosen because we knew them best. Most of them lived very near our house and were seen daily. The reader who has studied the diary account of play behavior will already be familiar with much of the material which is summarized in these sketches.

The sketches contain a disproportionate number of girls, most of whom are about ten years of age. This fact is due to the presence of our daughter. It was through her that we had our best opportunities of becoming acquainted with the children, and those who played with her were girls of about her own age.

Ann

(*Two years old*)

Ann presents a picture of imperturbability and fearlessness. She repeatedly went to the road where cars frequently passed. She also came to our house and to the shelter quite alone. This is in contrast to other children of her age for most of them scarcely could be separated from their older sisters. Ann's independence may have been due in part to the fact that as a first child she had no child caretaker, but this seems hardly to explain it as her mother was affectionate and attentive to her. Ann's wanderings away from home occurred when her mother was doing her usual work in the house.

When the little girl was carried back from her dangerous expeditions to the highway, she accepted her treatment without resistance and without any appearance of disappointment. Ann rarely cried. During the entire summer she did not have a tantrum. On the other hand, she seldom smiled or laughed. She was not very friendly, but she was not afraid of strangers. On one occasion she let us swing her, and at another time, as noted above, she came alone into our house where she had never been before. She entered the house to get a doll which she had seen in the window, and her treatment of the doll was typical of her general air of independence. She played with the doll for half an hour, then let it lie in the shelter and went home.

She was backward in the acquisition of speech or else she chose to talk very little, for in our hearing she scarcely said a word. If she had spoken loudly at her home, which was only ten yards away, we would have heard her. She seemed to understand what was said to her in Hopi, and gave no indications of deficient intelligence.

Ann's general emotional stability was more remarkable in view of the fact that in the course of the summer her mother separated from her husband and married another man. A very large part of the village was concerned over these domestic upheavals, but Ann's mother seemed to be less upset than many who were less directly involved. In this respect, the daughter greatly resembled her mother.

Na

(Two years old)

Those who have read the diary of play observations will scarcely need an introduction to Na, the boy who apparently would have been willing to stay in the swing from morning until night. In this he differed from Ann, who tried the swing only once. In a great many other respects Na provides an opposite to the girl which we have just described. Na lived on one side of our house in about the same position relative to the highway as did Ann, yet never during the entire summer did he go to the road alone. Despite his great love for swinging it was toward the end of the summer before he would come to the shelter by himself or would remain in the swing if his sister Vie left the vicinity. He cried easily when hurt and he had a bad temper. Several of his tantrums were recorded in our play observations. Informants told us that during the preceding winter he had been rolled in the snow because of his fits of crying.

But Na could be made to laugh as well as to cry. He laughed when he was pushed with special vigor in the swing, when he was played with roughly, and when one pretended to catch his toes. After prolonged play he apparently became half hysterical so that it was difficult to determine whether he was laughing or crying.

While he was dependent upon Vie, and Vie devoted much of her time to him, he seemed to take her services for granted. In a way he tyrannized over her, making her conform to his wishes and showing her no consideration. We never saw him exhibit any signs of affection. When he became angry, he even struck her.

Elsa

(*Three years old*)

Elsa is the girl who at two years of age decided to sleep with her father and told her mother to sleep on the bench beside the bed. Elsa had five older brothers and a baby brother. Since she was the only girl in the family, she was somewhat spoiled. She pushed the boys off of her father's lap, and occasionally had a tantrum when things did not go entirely as she wished. Her chief playmate was her brother, Lee, who was five years of age but not as gifted or as attractive as she. When Elsa and Lee got into difficulties, the parents usually intervened in favor of the younger.

Elsa was attractive, friendly and happy. We had several occasions to visit her home, and when we came we usually took a bag of candy or of fruit to the children. Ordinarily she came to meet us and to carry the bag to her mother who divided the contents among her children. After receiving her part, Elsa often brought the fruit for us to peel for her. Shortly after receiving her present she would go out to play. She was never at a loss for something to do. Often she made play houses in the sand. Once she came in fretting because a hen while scratching in the yard had destroyed a house. Lee went out with her to help in the repair work. At another time, she came in to report that Lee had made her fall, but when the parents paid no attention to her complaint she soon returned to her play.

During one of our visits, Elsa and Lee came in during the middle of the afternoon and were given piki to eat. Their mother attempted to get Elsa to drink some goat's milk also but she refused, and the matter ended with the mother giving the child some coffee. In the course of another afternoon Elsa made herself a Hopi equivalent of lemonade, namely, piki stirred into water. A further turn toward domestic occupations was shown on a later day when she entered the house and asked for a match in order to build a fire for the roasting of corn. The match was given to her, but two older brothers went to help with the fire.

Elsa impressed us as being above average in intelligence, well-adjusted, active and imaginative.

LEE

(*Five years old*)

Lee, Elsa's brother, was uncouth in appearance, his face and hands often being soiled, as was his shirt. His shirt was his only garment, and it came only to his hips. Lee had several convulsive seizures during his first year, and had them occasionally when we knew him, but we did not happen to see him while he was having an attack. The parents feared that the seizures may have done him some harm, and asked us if that were possible. They apparently were afraid that he would prove to be feeble-minded. He did not talk as much as did Elsa, his three-year-old sister, and it was our impression that his actions showed no greater mental age than did hers. Even in shooting a bow and arrow he did not do as well as most boys of his age.

He and Elsa played together a great deal, and in general they got along fairly well. Both took part in imitative games. On one occasion the family asked us to bring a sack of flour when we next came. Soon after seeing us carrying the flour, Lee filled a sack with sand, saying in Hopi that he was a rich "bahana." At another time, Lee and Elsa talked in gibberish, saying they were bahanas. One afternoon their play consisted of playing store; Lee was the storekeeper.

We have mentioned in our earlier sketch that Lee was not always kind to Elsa, but on the other hand, we never saw him really injure her or show any temper. He was not emotionally expressive. The rivalry between the two children over their father's attention when he came from the fields was exhibited mainly in shoving each other and in trying to monopolize his lap. Some of Lee's actions toward Elsa struck us as being mean although not vicious. When Elsa was making herself a drink of piki and water, Lee spit into it, apparently just to tease.

Lee was the only Hopi boy with whom we were well acquainted who openly handled his genitals, although we have heard of other cases of masturbation among the Hopi. In playing, or in running about, he often kept one hand on his genitals. We never saw him reprimanded for it. On some occasions he played with the genitals of his ten-months-old baby brother. Once his mother pushed him away and pulled the baby's dress down. At another time Lee tapped and patted the baby's genitalia for five minutes while an older brother was holding the child. Neither Lee nor the baby showed any sexual excitement.

VIE

(*Ten years old*)

Vie was a most dutiful and well-behaved daughter. She worked whenever her mother asked her, and was particularly helpful with the younger children. Having taken care of Na for a year, she was beginning to put Na somewhat on his own and to assume the responsibility of the baby. Toward both Na and the baby she was most considerate. She never neglected them and was never cross with them. Even during Na's tantrums Vie was unruffled.

Vie was not talkative. She seldom spoke to us unless we asked her a question, then she would often answer monosyllabically. Even when she was among girls of her own age, she did little talking, although she was capable of expressing herself.

There was but little vivacity and little leadership in Vie. Her actions were often controlled by the requests of others. We do not recall an instance of her starting a game. However, she liked to participate in whatever kind of play was in progress and was always cooperative. She played quietly even when the others were boisterous.

She seldom laughed, but she had a shy and quiet smile which showed that she was responsive to the events about her. She was liked by the girls, who were always willing to play with her.

It must be admitted that in movement Vie was slow though not awkward. She was, in fact, a bit fat. She seldom ran, and vigorous games such as tag did not appeal to her.

ETTA

(Ten years old)

On two occasions at the beginning of our second summer in New Oraibi, Etta for no apparent reason was rough and unkind to Mary and injured Mary's doll. This behavior appeared puzzling to us, for she was afterward consistently sweet and kind. Later we felt that we gained some understanding of this contradictory behavior. We learned that she had seizures which were described to us in such detail that they were recognized as undoubtedly epileptic attacks. They came approximately at monthly intervals, and one occurred shortly after our second arrival. It is likely that the condition which preceded this attack, or the knowledge that the attack was coming, made Etta somewhat disagreeable during the early days of our residence in the village.

Etta to some extent looked out for Win, her youngest brother, but most of the time she spent with Joe, the first child of her oldest brother. To Joe she was kind and gentle. She encouraged him to learn and to do things, and she liked to show him off.

Etta, after the first week of our visit, was cheerful and bright. She was something of a tease, although her teasing was never extreme. She paid more attention to adults than did most of the children.

She was by far the most inquisitive child that we knew, often asking us to explain our actions or our possessions.

REG

(Ten years old)

Reg demonstrates the fact that in Hopi society, as well as in our own, family discord often has its effect upon the child.

She was an attractive girl, of good disposition, with whom Mary liked to play. It was some time before we noticed that she seldom came to our house except when other children were away and that she usually left shortly after other children arrived. We did not guess that anything serious was wrong until we learned from Mor, Reg's sister, that Reg frequently stayed away from home all day long. For a time she ate no breakfast, no lunch and very little supper, and she grew quite thin. Mor pretended to be unable to understand Reg's behavior. From other sources we learned that her unsociability with other children was probably due to their ridicule of her parents' escapades and that her absence from home probably derived from parental discord.

The trouble had had its inception during the preceding winter, when Isa, Etta's older sister, bore an illegitimate son. Whether justly or not the child was attributed by some people to Reg's father. Reg's mother took this point of view and drove her husband from her home, so that he had to live with his sisters. Reg's mother went to the home of Isa, engaged her in an altercation, and threw a chair at her. The New Oraibi self-government council which has been set up by the Indian Bureau entered the controversy and decided that not Reg's father but another man was at fault and that this man must marry Isa. It also decreed that Reg's father and mother must again live together, although the relations between the two seem to have remained greatly strained.

The children of the village, as well as the adults, knew of the affair, and made fun of Reg at school. Her solution of the difficulty seems to have been to keep away from the other children as much as possible. On several occasions, Mary went to Reg's house for the afternoon. She reported that practically never did another child come to play.

We could never verify our surmise, but we believe that Reg's day-long absences from home were occasioned by fresh outbreaks of trouble between her parents. We learned that during the winter when her parents temporarily separated she wanted to accompany her father but was not permitted to do so.

GRA

(Ten years old)

We feel that Gra is probably another person who in her behavior showed the effects of family and community discord.

Gra was surly, suspicious, unfriendly and apparently unhappy. Her three sisters gave the same impression. They kept apart from other children most of the time, but often squabbled, quarreled and fought among themselves. There are several instances in our notes of the children of this family striking each other.

But unlike Reg, Gra and her sisters did not always avoid other children. They came to the shelter occasionally, but it was easy to see that no friendship existed between them and the other girls. They often had conflicts with the others, and frequently went home in something of a huff. Their playmates accused them of stealing and of other offenses. Gra delivered our laundry for us and saw us each week, and we knew her mother quite well and talked to her freely, yet Gra would scarcely say a word to us without the greatest embarrassment.

While such behavior may have had no relation to the social situation, the opposite view is more probably true. During the preceding winter, Gra's father had had an affair with a woman in the village. Gra learned of this at school while her mother was still ignorant of the matter and carried the news home. A teacher whom we knew believed that Gra felt the disgrace very keenly and that part of her shyness and surliness was due to the domestic situation. But Gra's troubles were somewhat more complicated. Gra's mother was a Christian, and had said sharp things about the native dances. Her husband, however, participated in these ceremonies. Gra's mother was told to stay away from the dances if she did not like them, and to keep her children away. On the day of a kachina dance in New Oraibi in 1937 Gra came to the ceremony late in the afternoon and stood inconspicuously by Mrs. Dennis. She stayed until the end of the last dance, because, she told Mrs. Dennis, the dancers would bring presents. But no presents came to Gra or to her brothers or sisters although gifts were given to nearly every child in the village. A deprivation of this sort, and a difference of this sort, must have been keenly felt by the children.

Toward the end of the summer of 1938 Gra's mother apparently changed her attitude, and at the Niman Dance at Hotavila she had the kachinas bring presents to each of her children. There was said to have been a reconciliation between her and her husband. We left the village before we could determine whether any change in Gra's behavior would result.

CHAPTER X

A CENSUS OF PROBLEM CASES

IN an attempt to find with what success Hopi methods of child rearing operate, we decided to determine roughly the frequency of each of several kinds of problem behavior in the villages which we knew best, namely, Hotavila, New Oraibi and Mishongnovi. The question of how to obtain a significant record of this sort was a difficult one. To do so by direct observation was out of the question, for no one could attempt to witness personally all tantrums, all instances of lying and stealing, etc. But fortunately for our purposes, in a Hopi town information concerning misdeeds in the community is common property. We do not claim that such popular information is always correct, but we feel that it is worth presenting. Whatever the objective truth may be, the testimony of an inhabitant may be said to give a local evaluation of the behavior of the village children.

We could find no way to obtain information of this sort from more than one informant in each village. To have attempted it with more than one would have caused us to run a greater danger of making the whole thing public. If it had been known that informants were giving data of this sort, the wrath of the village would have fallen upon informant and investigator alike. In many cases, however, we were able to check the facts given by our informants with the knowledge of the local white teachers and, in an off-hand manner, with the statements of Hopi acquaintances. It is our belief that other intelligent and wide-awake persons in the village would have given us substantially the same information as did the informants which we chose.

Neither Hotavila, New Oraibi or Mishongnovi had enough children to justify our presenting the data for the three villages separately. While the total number of children in each village was greater than 100, such figures become small when they are presented for separate age groups and for the two sexes. When groups of even 200 are broken down in this way, the subgroups become too small to warrant serious attention. We should like to be able to compare the three villages, but this is impossible on the basis of the children living in them at any one moment. When the three towns are combined, the number of inhabitants under twenty-two years of age, according to our census, is 525.

After we had obtained from an informant a complete list, by households, of the children of her village, we asked her to go through the list for each of the several kinds of behavior. We promised complete anonymity for the problem cases, and explained that we were interested not in individuals but in the frequency with which each sort of problem child occurred.

The types of behavior concerning which we inquired were: thumb sucking, temper tantrums, fighting and stealing. We made certain in advance that these terms had meanings for our informants which coincided with our connotation. The data referred to conditions as of the summer of 1938, and not to earlier behavior. That is, if a child had had temper tantrums formerly, but no longer displayed them, he was, of course, not listed as having them at the time of the census. The data had to do with conditions which were current.

The data which we obtained are shown in summary form in Table 4.

It is important, first of all, to note the per cent of children who were said to display none of these traits. These percentages are shown on the extreme right of the table. According to our informants, the majority of the children conformed to their parents' wishes in respect to avoiding the responses with which we are here concerned. Misbehavior of the kinds under consideration was the exception and not the rule.

On two grounds we might expect thumb sucking to be absent among the Hopi. The first of these is the frequent nursing which might be expected in itself to satiate the drive for oral satisfaction. The second consideration is the binding of the hands of the infant which might act to prevent the formation of the habit. But we have seen that the Hopi infant exhibits the "hand to mouth" reaction when the wrappings are removed. Beyond the age of six months the child has considerable opportunity to indulge in this reaction, and he frequently does so. We observed several instances of thumb

TABLE 4

INCIDENCE OF VARIOUS TYPES OF BEHAVIOR PROBLEMS

AGE GROUP (years)	NO. OF CASES	PERCENTAGE OF AGE GROUP SHOWING EACH KIND OF BEHAVIOR				
		Thumb Sucking	Temper Tantrums	Fighting	Stealing	None
BOYS						
0– 1.9	39	2				97
2– 3.9	33	7	20		3	75
4– 5.9	38	9	20	10	5	68
6– 7.9	23	4	12	10	16	70
8– 9.9	28	4	4	20	25	69
10–11.9	15		14	20	7	67
12–13.9	17		6	25	6	76
14–15.9	19			10	10	84
16–17.9	27			8	25	76
18–19.9	19					100
20–21.9	19				4	96
GIRLS						
0– 1.9	37					100
2– 3.9	27					100
4– 5.9	38	5	17	5	10	74
6– 7.9	28	4	4	8	14	82
8– 9.9	13	17		8	8	69
10–11.9	25	4				96
12–13.9	13				25	75
14–15.9	18				5	95
16–17.9	15				7	93
18–19.9	24					100
20–21.9	10				10	90

sucking. Native mothers, while they did not consider it to be a serious problem, stated that thumb sucking often occurred and they frequently had recourse to powdered chili in an attempt to cure it. In the census, the habit of thumb sucking was found in one child of nine years of age. Of the children between two and nine years of age, a total of 228, thirteen children or six per cent were definite cases of thumb sucking. This evidence should be sufficient to show that thumb sucking does occur in a primitive society where nursing through most of the second year is the general rule.[1]

Temper tantrums were found to be much more common

[1] M. Mead in "The Primitive Child," *Handbook of Child Psychology*, 2nd ed. rev., Clark Univ. Press, 1933, has made a generalization contrary to this finding.

among boys than among girls, as twenty-one boys and only seven girls were said to have tantrums. The age range for tantrums was from two to twelve years of age, with the greatest incidence falling in the two-to-six-year-old level. It would appear, therefore, that Hopi methods succeed in getting rid of tantrums, and that they usually succeed at a fairly early period.

Fighting shows an even greater predominance of boys over girls than do tantrums, the numbers being respectively twenty-two and five. The girls who were reported as fighting were between four and nine years of age. Some boys who fought were as old as sixteen, but none was older than that, a fact which shows that fighting ceases as the age of second initiation approaches. The greatest incidence of fighters was between eight and fourteen years of age. In this age interval, approximately one-fifth of the boys were said to engage in fights.

In regard to stealing, the boys outnumbered the girls twenty-seven to fifteen. Beyond four years of age, when the taking of other people's property begins to be considered intentional stealing, there was no consistent trend with age, until the age of eighteen was reached, when the rate dropped markedly. This again supports the view that the age of second initiation may be an important one. Girls do not have a second initiation, hence this cannot be evoked as an explanation in their case, but the girls contribute only a minor part of the problem behavior. Although fighting and stealing become less common as manhood is approached, it may well be that it is not due to the initiation itself but to a change in social position which begins to affect boys and girls alike irrespective of initiation. For as the time for marriage approaches, both the boy and the girl may be anxious for the approval of persons beyond the circle of relatives.

It should be pointed out again that at all ages the children who misbehave form only a small minority. A further fact which deserves notice is one which is not shown by the table, namely, that most of the problem cases come from a few families. It is the native belief, and the evidence supports it, that it is family attitude and discipline which determine the good behavior of the young child. Examination of the means of social control of the child will show that the parents and the maternal uncles provide practically all of the important social influences. The control by the kachinas provides no exception, for while the young child does not identify the kachinas with his relatives, they are in effect the same persons. It is the parents who must threaten that the kachinas will withhold gifts from a child who steals, just as it is the parents who must provide and interpret the gifts that are received. A dancer takes no responsibility for training or disciplining a child unless the child is his own son, daughter, nephew or niece, or unless the parents have given the dancer instructions. In effect, therefore, all child training, except those lessons which are administered by playmates, is received directly or indirectly from relatives. It is no one else's responsibility. There are no policemen, no truant officers, no youth organizations, no adult leaders of the young.

The census of Hotavila shows, in line with this analysis, that the instances of problem behavior, especially of the more serious forms, occurred chiefly in a few families.

In one instance the whole family was said to steal and to lie. The parents were very poor. The husband was described as peculiar in behavior and his own wife said that he was a witch. There was a daughter of five years who had tantrums, and who stole and lied, the only five-year-old girl in our records who possessed all of these faults. Next in age were three boys, six, eight and ten years old. They also lied and stole, and fought among themselves. Last winter they were rolled in the snow and whipped by their older sister. It is very unusual for an older sister to punish, and our informant did not know why she did so. It may have been because the parents had failed to do it themselves. The worst problem in the family was a boy of seventeen, who was possibly feeble-minded. He once robbed the store. The village chief and the members of the council, not being civil officers, did nothing about it, nor did anyone else do anything. Last spring he and three other boys stole corn by boring a hole into a storage bin. When they tried this technique a second time, the owner of the bin caught them red-handed. The parents of the boys should have punished them but they did not. It is even claimed that the parents of the boys encouraged them to steal. The father of the seventeen-year-old boy whom we are discussing said his son is a witch, an accusation by a person who is said to be a witch himself. These recriminations show that there was little love or unity within the family. The boy was very slow in school and it was claimed that he was guilty of stealing a teacher's watch. We have no record of misbehavior on the part of the oldest child, a girl of eighteen. Although she was married and had a son eleven months of age, she was still living in her mother's household.

There is a second family in Hotavila of which it was claimed that parents and children alike will steal. They went into neighbors' houses when no one was at home, a thing which no Hopi should do. They stole corn and sheepskins; the children stole toys as well. Even the two youngest boys, three and five years of age, stole; in addition they had tantrums. The youngest sucked his thumb. A boy of eight, who had the family weakness for other people's property, had the further fault of fighting and had ceased attending school. The next in the family, a boy of seventeen, stole, stuttered, and was stupid in school. A girl of eighteen was sexually immoral. Again the oldest, a girl of nineteen, was the best in the family, nothing being recorded against her present behavior.

These cases constitute the two worst families of Hotavila and are very decided exceptions. That delinquent families make up but a small part of the population is shown by the fact that of the sixty-six Hotavila families which appear in the census, only twelve families had any children who were said to steal. The situation is the same at New Oraibi and at Mishongnovi. A few families contain most of the problem cases, and a few problem cases contribute most of the misconduct.

These cases bring out clearly the fact that when the family of the child fails in his socialization, the Hopi community has no systematic means of attempting to do the work for itself. The majority of families, however, succeed fairly well in getting their children to conform to their ideals. When adulthood is reached, the situation changes, but it is not our purpose to discuss Hopi behavior at the adult level.

In discussing failures at socialization, we have said nothing at all about laziness. It is difficult to get any measure of parental success in inducing work habits. For one thing, failure in this direction affects only the parents, whereas stealing and fighting involve other persons and are common knowledge. It is our impression that nearly every boy and every girl is induced to help with the work of the household, but it is difficult to check this impression.

A few words may be said with regard to the fact that in the census of behavior problems the boys contributed more cases than did the girls. This situation is so much like the condition which prevails in our own very different and quite unrelated society that we are likely to see in it the result of fundamental differences between the sexes. In regard to the behavior of Hopi girls, we must call attention to a few facts which were presented in the account of child-rearing practices. During the early years, almost all girls have the responsibility of caring for younger siblings, a fact which may affect the chances of a girl's fighting with others of her own age and which certainly affects her opportunities for stealing, since she has an almost constant younger companion who cannot be trusted to keep secrets. Beyond the approximate age of ten years, the Hopi girl is expected to remain at home almost continuously, and to go about only when accompanied by a woman. This persistent supervision of the girl has no counterpart in the boy, and renders a biological interpretation of the sex differences in problem behavior very dubious.

CHAPTER XI

A SUMMARY OF FINDINGS

IDEALLY, the investigator who deals with the social psychology of the child should be able to compare the situations which confront the developing individuals of one culture with the conditions which are met in many other societies and should attempt to indicate the divergences in child behavior which result from the differences in adult treatment. In the case which is under discussion we should compare the Hopi child with the child of several other cultural groups. For the present, however, there exists in most respects only one standard of comparison, namely an account of the child as he has been studied by American and European psychologists. In the main the subject of these investigators has been the urban child. Usually the researchers have failed to describe the cultural backgrounds of their subjects and have used methods which cannot be applied outside of kindergarten, school and clinic. In view of these facts, a successful attempt to find the peculiar outcomes of Hopi child rearing by comparing Hopi child behavior with "American" child behavior is next to impossible in the present condition of child psychology. To a great extent, we are limited to an impressionistic approach. We are not too apologetic concerning our method, however, for the fault of child psychology in the past has lain not in impressionism but in the almost total lack of a comparative psychology of cultures. With this explanation before us, we may proceed as best we can to indicate what seem to us to be the most significant of our observations concerning the Hopi child.

INFANCY

We have pointed out previously that Hopi and American child-rearing customs diverge rather sharply in infancy. The binding of the infant on the cradleboard, the constant presence of an attendant, the frequent and long-continued breast feeding, the lack of early avoidance training and the unwillingness to let the infant cry, on the part of the Hopi, provide a set of practices which cannot be met with jointly among any group of American infants.

It is therefore not without significance to learn that Hopi and American infants throughout the first year engage in the same responses and exhibit roughly the same sequence of developmental items. Any small differences in the sequence and any minor variations in the rate of development of infant responses which may subsequently be found will not alter the fact of a great general similarity. We have found that, if mothers' reports can be accepted, Hopi infants begin to walk about six weeks later than do the groups of American infants which have been studied by the same method. We were able to determine that the cradleboard is not responsible for this difference, for Hopi infants who have been kept on the cradleboard walk as early as the infants of Hopi families who no longer bind their children. To what the difference in age of walking of Hopi and American infants may be due, we cannot say at the present time. It may reflect differences in nutrition and health.

Our observations tend to show that extensive cultural differences have little or no effect upon the infant during the first year.

CHILDHOOD

There is no denying that a very strong resemblance exists between the behavior of the Hopi and of the American child at all ages. This, we suppose, is a statement of the same meaning as the anthropologist's belief in "the psychic unity of mankind." It is difficult to be specific in regard to the points at which the similarities exist. Unless there were differences between Hopi and American *adults,* the two peoples would not be said to have distinct cultures. These differences extend into the period of childhood, for the behavior typical of the adult community is assumed gradually, not suddenly.

But we believe that all of the kinds of behavior which are treated in textbooks of child psychology are to be found among the Hopi children. Jealousy occurs, and its symptoms and causes appear similar to those of our own children. The tantrums of the Hopi child, also, are like those of the American child in their form and in the circumstances which precipitate them. The two chief kinds of fear in the Hopi child is fear of the unusual or strange, and the fear of injury. As among our children, so among the Hopi also, a great many of the fears refer to mythological and unreal entities.

Despite the fact that the Hopi are rightfully called a peaceful people, and that the men look upon open conflicts as unmanly and dishonorable, the Hopi boy, nevertheless, gets into fights. Possibly he fights as much as the boy of an American rural community. The play of the Hopi child reveals many similarities to the play of American children. We believe that almost every event which is described in our diary account of Hopi child play could be observed among rural American children. The only exceptions would be those activities which result from imitation of culture patterns with which our children are not familiar.

Hopi children are like American children in exhibiting very distinct personalities. Some observers have professed to see but slight individual differences in communities which are culturally homogeneous. Hopi culture patterns are homogeneous but they do not stamp out individuality, and marked personal traits appear among both children and adults.

The large number of similarities between the behavior of Hopi children and the behavior of the children of our own society is not necessarily contrary to the expectations of those who hold that child behavior is very responsive to social influences. To be sure, Hopi and American cultures spring from sources which have no known historical relationship, and the contacts of the Hopi with occidental culture since the advent of the Spaniards seem not to have influenced very much their patterns of social behavior. But even if Hopi and Americans had never met, there might still have been many points of resemblance in their patterns of child rearing. The principle of limited possibilities and the principle of convergence would lead to the existence of many common factors in any two societies. We must not be hasty, therefore, in supposing that identical child responses in historically unrelated cultures are a strong argument for the biological as opposed to the social origin of child behavior.

Let us turn next to the *differences* in the behavior of the two groups of children which we are considering. Some of these differences are inescapable outcomes of the two cultures, and are so obvious that they scarcely require mention. Hotavila children, of course, do not learn to swim, as there is no water in which they may swim. They do not go to movies, they do not ride in subways, they do not attend church. Differences of such kinds we identify as differences in the child rearing situation, rather than as differences in the resultant behavior. As psychologists, we are more interested in behavior which the situation does not absolutely demand but which nevertheless results, perhaps without anyone's intent to produce it.

The subtler differences between communities of children are probably matters of degree rather than of kind and hence require measurement. They are also, it is likely, primarily differences of attitude, which only occasionally show themselves in overt behavior. It is at this point that our measuring devices in psychology are least adequate, for few of our measures of attitudes are applicable to children, and those which might be used with young American subjects cannot reasonably be employed in another culture. Many of the statements and questions contained in these tests simply would not make sense to the Hopi child, and it would be pointless to attempt to apply them.

Through questioning, and through spontaneous remarks of our informants, we were able to determine one difference between Hopi and American attitudes, and thus to verify a finding of Malinowski. Because the maternal uncle functions as a disciplinarian, Hopi children dislike and fear him more than they do the father, who does not belong to their lineage and who is only slightly responsible for the child's conduct. As Malinowski has shown, these facts indicate that resentment of authority is a greater determinant of child attitudes toward a male adult than is the sexual jealousy which the Freudian theory hypothesizes.

Other characteristics of the attitudes of the Hopi child are more tenuous, and we note them as suggestions for later research rather than as findings.

It seemed to us that the absence of a culturally determined goal of power and prestige has its effect upon the younger members of the community as well as upon the adults. We thought we saw less rivalry than exists among American children, and less desire to be important, superior and distinguished. This does not mean, however, that the Hopi children make no invidious comparisons, for it will be remembered that they gave Reg a very bad time in this regard. But the ridicule which they deal out is as likely to be turned against the individual who tries to excell as against one who is aberrant in some other way.

Another guess which we hazard with respect to the Hopi child is that he has a strong feeling of social security. To be sure, individual homes are often in imminence of being broken, and we have cited several instances in which domestic discord has affected the child. But in case of separation of the parents, it is a foregone conclusion that the child will remain with the mother; there is no uncertainty about this. If the mother should die, there is a vast circle of relatives, all known to the child and living in close proximity to him who would accept responsibility for him. His is a world which he knows intimately, and which accepts him completely. A Hopi is never driven from his village; he is never an outcast; he never starves when others have food; he never lacks a place in which to sleep. While the child may early learn the unfriendliness of the climate and the danger of starvation which faces the entire village, he lives in a social world in which he has an indubitable place. He does not face an unknown vocation or an uncertain future, but looks forward to a life which even today is much the same as it was in the past. To know the effects of such surroundings upon the degree of tension and upon the amount of anxiety of the child would indeed be desirable.

THE FAMILY

We found that while the majority of Hopi children conform to an acceptable degree to the wishes of the community, a few do not. There are problem children in Hotavila, in New Oraibi, and in Mishongnovi as there are in any American town. A large part of the problem cases come from a few families whose standards are at some variance with those of the community at large. This situation is not unfamiliar, and suggests that the statement that the attitudes of the child are molded by those with whom he is in most immediate contact is a generalization which is applicable to more than one culture.

BIBLIOGRAPHY

Anza, B. "Diary of His Expedition to the Moqui in 1780." *Bull. N. Mex. Hist. Soc.*, No. 21. Pp. 47.

Arnim, S. S., Aberle, S. D. and Pitney, E. H. "A Study of Dental Changes in a Group of Pueblo Indian Children." *J. Amer. Dental Assoc.*, 1937, 24, 478–480.

Bancroft, H. H. *History of Arizona and New Mexico, 1530–1888.* The History Company, San Francisco, 1889. Pp. 829.

Bandelier, A. F. *Final Report of Investigations Among the Indians of Southwestern United States.* 2 vols. University Press, Cambridge, Mass., 1890–92. Pp. 323 and 591.

Bartlett, K. "Hopi History." *Mus. Notes of Mus. No. Ariz.*, 1934, 6, 55–60, 1936, 8, 33–37.

Bartlett, S. A. "An Observation on Hopi Child Burial." *Amer. Anthrop.*, 1937, 39, 562–564.

Beaglehole, E. "Hopi Hunting and Hunting Ritual." *Yale U. Publ. Anthrop.*, 1936, 4, 1–26.

———— "Notes on Hopi Economic Life." *Yale U. Publ. Anthrop.*, 1937, 15, 1–88.

Beaglehole, E. and P. *Hopi of Second Mesa.* Mem. Amer. Anthrop. Assoc., 1935, 44. Pp. 65.

Beaglehole, P. "Census Data from Two Hopi Villages." *Amer. Anthrop.*, 1935, 37, 41–54.

Beals, R. L. *Preliminary Report on the Ethnography of the Southwest.* U. S. Dept. of Interior, Nat. Park Service, Berkeley, Calif., 1935. Pp. 77. Bibliography of 36 pages.

Bloom, L. B. "A Campaign Against the Moqui Pueblos." *N. Mex. Hist. Rev.*, 1931, 6, 158–226.

Bourke, J. G. *The Snake Dance of the Moquis of Arizona.* Scribner, N. Y., 1884. Pp. 371.

———— "Vesper Hours of the Stone Age." *Amer. Anthrop.*, o. s., 1890, 3, 55–63.

———— "Bourke on the Southwest" [Journal, ed. by L. B. Bloom] *N. Mex. Hist. Rev.*, 1936, 11, 77–122, 188–207.

Colton, H. S. "A Brief Survey of Hopi Common Law." *Mus. Notes of Mus. No. Ariz.*, 1934, 7, 21–24.

Coolidge, M. E. *The Rain-Makers.* New York and Boston, Houghton Mifflin, 1929. Pp. 326.

Culin, S. "Games of the North American Indians." *24th Ann. Rep. Bur. Amer. Ethnol.*, 1907, 3–809.

Curtis, E. S. *North American Indians,* vol. 12. Harvard Univ. Press, Cambridge, Mass., 1922. Pp. 200.

Cushing, F. H. "Origin Myth from Oraibi." *J. Amer. Folk-L.,* 1923, 36, 163–170.

Donaldson, T. *Moqui Pueblo Indians of Arizona and the Pueblo Indians of New Mexico.* Extra Census Bull., 11th Census, U. S. Census Print. Off., Wash., D. C., 1893. Pp. 136.

Dorsey, G. A. *Indians of the Southwest.* Santa Fe Ry. Pass. Dept., Chicago, 1903. Pp. 223.

—— "The Voth Collection." *Amer. Anthrop.,* 1899, 1, 394–395.

—— "Hopi Indians of Arizona." *Pop. Sci. Mo.,* 1899, 55, 732–750.

Dorsey, G. A. and H. R. Voth. "The Oraibi Soyal Ceremony." *Anthrop. Series, Field Mus. Nat. Hist.,* 1901, 3, No. 1. Pp. 59.

—— "The Mishongnovi Ceremonies of the Snake and Antelope Fraternities." *Anthrop. Series, Field Mus. Nat. Hist.,* 1902, 3, 159–261.

Earle, E. *Hopi Kachinas* [Text by E. A. Kennard]. Augustin, N. Y., 1938. Pp. 40.

Eggan, F. R. "The Kinship System of the Hopi Indians." *Univ. Chic. Lib.,* 1936, 19–56.

Eickhoff, H. "Die Kultur der Pueblos in Arizona und New Mexico." *Studien u. Forsch. zur Menschen und Volkerkunde, Stuttgart,* 1908. Vol. 4. Pp. 78.

Fewkes, J. W. "Suggestion as to the Meaning of the Moki Snake Dance." *J. Amer. Folk-L.,* 1891, 4, 129–138.

—— "The Ceremonial Circuit Among the Village Indians of Northeastern Arizona." *J. Amer. Folk-L.,* 1892, 5, 33–42.

—— "A Few Summer Ceremonials at the Tusayan Pueblos." *J. Amer. Ethnol. and Archaeol.,* 1892, 2, 1–161.

—— "A Few Tusayan Pictographs." *Amer. Anthrop.,* o. s., 1892, 5, 9–26.

—— "Dolls of the Tusayan Villagers." *Internat. Archiv. f. Ethnog.,* 1894, 7, 45–74.

—— "Kinship of a Tanoan-Speaking Community in Tusayan." *Amer. Anthrop.,* o. s., 1894, 7, 162–167.

—— "Personages Who Appear in a Tusayan Ceremony." *Amer. Anthrop.,* o. s., 1894, 7, 32–53.

—— "Kinship of the Tusayan Villagers." *Amer. Anthrop.,* o. s., 1894, 7, 394–417.

—— "Walpi Flute Observance." *J. Amer. Folk-L.,* 1894, 7, 265–287.

—— "Destruction of the Tusayan Monster." *J. Amer. Folk-L.,* 1895, 8, 132–137.

—— "Comparison of Sia and Tusayan Snake Ceremonials." *Amer. Anthrop.,* o. s., 1895, 8, 118–142.

—— *Provisional List of Annual Ceremonies at Walpi.* Lieden, E. J. Brill, 1895. Pp. 24.

—— "The Oraibi Flute Altar." *J. Amer. Folk-L.,* 1895, 8, 265–282.

Fewkes, J. W. "Contribution to Ethnobotany." *Amer. Anthrop.*, o. s., 1896, 9, 14–21.

———— "The Miconinovi Flute Altars." *J. Amer. Folk-L.*, 1896, 9, 241–255.

———— "The Sacrificial Element in Hopi Worship." *J. Amer. Folk-L.*, 1897, 10, 187–202.

———— "Tusayan Totemic Signatures." *Amer. Anthrop.*, o. s., 1897, 10, 1–11.

———— "Morphology of Tusayan Altars." *Amer. Anthrop.*, o. s., 1897, 10, 129–145.

———— "Tusayan Katcinas." *15th Ann. Rep. Bur. Amer. Ethnol.*, 1897, 251–320.

———— "Tusayan Snake Ceremonies." *16th Ann. Rep. Bur. Amer. Ethnol.*, 1897, 267–312.

———— "The Growth of Hopi Ritual." *J. Amer. Folk-L.*, 1898, 11, 173–174.

———— "Feather Symbol in Ancient Hopi Designs." *Amer. Anthrop.*, o. s., 1898, 11, 1–14.

———— "Winter Solstice Ceremonies at Walpi." *Amer. Anthrop.*, o. s., 1898, 11, 65–87, 101–115.

———— "Hopi Snake Washing." *Amer. Anthrop.*, o. s., 1898, 11, 313–318.

———— "Winter Solstice Altars at Hano Pueblo." *Amer. Anthrop.*, 1899, 1, 251–276.

———— "Hopi Basket Dances." *J. Amer. Folk-L.*, 1899, 12, 81–96.

———— "Death of a Celebrated Hopi." *Amer. Anthrop.*, 1899, 1, 196–197.

———— "Alosaka Cult of the Hopi Indians." *Amer. Anthrop.*, 1899, 1, 522–544.

———— "New Fire Ceremony at Walpi." *Amer. Anthrop.*, 1900, 2, 80–138.

———— "A Theatrical Performance at Walpi." *Proc. Wash. Acad. Sci.*, 1900, 2, 605–629.

———— "Property Right in Eagles Among the Hopi." *Amer. Anthrop.*, 1900, 2, 690–707.

———— "Tusayan Migration Traditions." *19th Ann. Rep. Bur. Amer. Ethnol.*, 1900, 573–633.

———— "Tusayan Flute and Snake Ceremonies." *19th Ann. Rep. Bur. Amer. Ethnol.*, 1900, 957–1011.

———— "Lesser New Fire Ceremony at Walpi." *Amer. Anthrop.*, 1901, 3, 438–453.

———— "Owakulti Altar at Sichimovi Pueblo." *Amer. Anthrop.*, 1901, 3, 211–226.

———— "Interpretations of Katcina Worship." *J. Amer. Folk-L.*, 1901, 14, 81–94.

———— "Sky-god Impersonations in Hopi Worship." *J. Amer. Folk-L.*, 1902, 15, 14–32.

Fewkes, J. W. "Minor Hopi Festivals." *Amer. Anthrop.*, 1902, 4, 482–511.
———— "Hopi Katcinas, Drawn by Native Artists." *21st Ann. Rep. Bur. Amer. Ethnol.*, 1903, 21, 3–126.
———— "Note on Hopi Clans." *Amer. Anthrop.*, 1904, 6, 761–762.
———— "Sun's Influence on the Form of Hopi Pueblos." *Amer. Anthrop.*, 1906, 8, 88–100.
———— "Hopi Shrines Near East Mesa, Arizona." *Amer. Anthrop.*, 1906, 8, 346–375.
———— "Hopi Ceremonial Frames from Canyon de Chelly, Arizona." *Amer. Anthrop.*, 1906, 8, 664–670.
———— "Butterfly in Hopi Myth and Ritual." *Amer. Anthrop.*, 1910, 12, 576–594.
———— "Sun Worship of the Hopi Indians." *Ann. Rep. Smith. Inst.* for year ending June 30, 1918, 493–596.
———— "Fire Worship of the Hopi Indians." *Ann. Rep. Smith. Inst.* for year ending June 30, 1920, 589–610.
———— "Ancestor Worship of the Hopi Indians." *Ann. Rep. Smith. Inst.* for year ending June 30, 1921, 485–506.
———— "Use of Idols in Hopi Worship." *Ann. Rep. Smith. Inst.* for year ending June 30, 1922, 377–397.
———— "The Katcina Altars in Hopi Worship." *Ann. Rep. Smith. Inst.* for year ending June 30, 1926, 469–486.
Fewkes, J. W. and J. G. Owens. "Lalakonta: a Tusayan Dance." *Amer. Anthrop.*, o. s., 1892, 5, 105–130.
Fewkes, J. W. and A. M. Stephen. "The Na-ac-nai-ya: a Tusayan Initiation Ceremony." *J. Amer. Folk-L.*, 1892, 5, 189–221.
———— "Mamzrauti: a Tusayan Ceremony." *Amer. Anthrop.*, o. s., 1892, 5, 217–245.
———— "Pá-lü-lü-kon-ti: a Tusayan Ceremony." *J. Amer. Folk-L.*, 1893, 6, 269–294.
Fewkes, J. W., A. M. Stephen and J. G. Owens. "Snake Ceremonials at Walpi." *J. Amer. Ethnol. and Arch.*, 1894, 4, 1–126.
Fisher, A. K. "A Partial List of Moki Animal Names." *Amer. Anthrop.*, o. s., 1896, 9, 174.
Forde, C. D. "Hopi Agriculture and Land Ownership." *J. Roy. Anthrop. Inst.*, 1931, 61, 357–405.
Friere-Marreco, B. "Note on Kinship Terms Compounded with the Postfix 'e in the Hano Dialect of Tewa." *Amer. Anthrop.*, 1915, 17, 198–202.
Gilman, B. I. "Hopi Songs." *J. Amer. Ethnol. and Arch.*, 1908, 5, 1–235.
Goddard, P. E. "The Cultural and Somatic Correlations of Uto-Aztekan." *Amer. Anthrop.*, 1920, 22, 244–247.
———— *Indians of the Southwest.* Amer. Mus. Nat. Hist., N. Y., 1913. Pp. 191.
Gray, L. H. "Hopi," article in *Ency. of Relig. & Ethics.* N. Y., Scribners, 1908–12.

Haeberlin, H. N. "The Idea of Fertilization in the Culture of the Pueblo Indians." *Mem. Amer. Anthrop. Assoc.,* 1916, 3, 1–55.

Hawley, F. "Pueblo Social Organization as a Lead to Pueblo History." *Amer. Anthrop.,* 1937, 39, 504–522.

Hewett, E. L. *Ancient Life in the American Southwest.* Bobbs, Merrill, Indianapolis, 1932. Pp. 392.

Hodge, F. W. [ed.] *Handbook of American Indians.* Bur. Amer. Ethnol., Bull., No. 3. 2 vols. 1907.

——— "Pueblo Snake Ceremonials." *Amer. Anthrop.,* o. s., 1896, 9, 133–136.

——— "Hopi Pottery Fired with Coal." *Amer. Anthrop.,* 1904, 6, 581–582.

Hough, W. "Hopi in Relation to Their Plant Environment." *Amer. Anthrop.,* o. s., 1897, 10, 33–44.

——— "Music of the Hopi Flute Ceremony." *Amer. Anthrop.,* o. s., 1897, 10, 162–163.

——— "Environmental Interrelations in Arizona." *Amer. Anthrop.,* o. s., 1898, 11, 133–155.

——— *The Moki Snake Dance.* Santa Fe Ry. Pass. Dept., Chicago, 1898. Pp. 58.

——— *The Hopi Indians.* Little Histories of the N. Amer. Indians, Torch Press, Cedar Rapids, Iowa. 1915. Pp. 265.

——— "The Sio Shalako at the First Mesa, July 9, 1916." *Amer. Anthrop.,* 1917, 19, 410–415.

——— "Revival of the Ancient Hopi Pottery Art." *Amer. Anthrop.,* 1917, 19, 322–323.

——— "Hopi Indian Collection in the U. S. National Museum." *Proc. U. S. Nat. Mus.,* 1919, 54, 235–296.

Hrdlička, A. *Physiological and Medical Observations Among Indians of Southwestern United States and Northern Mexico.* Gov. Print. Off., Wash., D. C. 1908. Pp. 460.

——— "The Pueblos." *Amer. J. Phys. Anthrop.,* 1935, 20, 235–460.

Ives, J. C. *Report upon the Colorado River of the West.* Exec. Doc. 90, 36th Cong., 1st session. Wash., 1861.

James, G. W. *Indians of the Painted Desert Region.* Boston, Little Brown, 1903. Pp. 268.

Kennard, E. A. "Hopi Reactions to Death." *Amer. Anthrop.,* 1937, 39, 491–497.

Kroeber, A. L. "Native Cultures in the Southwest." *Univ. Calif. Publ. Amer. Arch. and Ethnol.,* 1928, 23, 375–398.

Lewton, L. "The Cotton of the Hopi Indians: a New Species of Gossypium." *Misc. Coll. Smith. Inst.* 1912, 60. Pp. 10.

Lockett, H. G. "The Unwritten Literature of the Hopi." *Univ. of Ariz. Soc. Sci. Bull.,* No. 2, 1933. Pp. 101.

Lowie, R. H. "A Women's Ceremony Among the Hopi." *Nat. Hist.,* 1925, 25, 178–183.

Lowie, R. H. "Notes on Hopi Clans." *Anthrop. Papers Amer. Mus. Nat. Hist.*, 1929, 30, 309–360.

———— "Hopi Kinship." *Anthrop. Papers Amer. Mus. Nat. Hist.*, 1929, 30, 361–388.

Mearns, E. A. "Ornithological Vocabulary of the Moki Indians." *Amer. Anthrop.*, o. s., 1896, 9, 391–403.

Mindeleff, C. "An Indian Dance." *Science*, 1886, 7, 507–514.

———— "Localization of Tusayan Clans." *19th Ann. Rep. Bur. Amer. Ethnol.*, 1900, 635–643.

Mindeleff, V. "A Study of Pueblo Architecture." *8th Ann. Rep. Bur. Amer. Ethnol.*, 1891, 8, 3–228.

Nequatewa, E. "Truth of a Hopi and Other Clan Stories of Shungopavi" [ed. by M. R. F. Colton] *Bull. Mus. No. Ariz.*, No. 8, 1936. Pp. 114.

Owens, J. G. "Natal Ceremonies of the Hopi Indians." *J. Amer. Ethnol. and Arch.*, 1892, 2, 163–175.

Parsons, E. C. "Hopi Mothers and Children." *Man*, 1921, 21, 98–104.

———— "Hidden Ball on First Mesa, Arizona." *Man*, 1922, 22, 89–91.

———— "Oraibi in 1920." *Amer. Anthrop.*, 1922, 24, 283–294.

———— "Getting Married on First Mesa, Arizona." *Sci. Mo.*, 1921, 259–265.

———— "The Hopi Buffalo Dance." *Man*, 1923, 23, 21–26.

———— "Hopi Wöwöchim Ceremony in 1920." *Amer. Anthrop.*, 1923, 25, 156–187.

———— "A Pueblo Indian Journal, 1920–1921." *Mem. Amer. Anthrop. Assoc.*, 1925, No. 32. Pp. 123.

———— "Ceremonial Calendar of the Tewa of Arizona." *Amer. Anthrop.*, 1926, 28, 211–229.

———— "The Kinship Nomenclature of the Pueblo Indians." *Amer. Anthrop.*, 1932, 34, 377–389.

———— "Hopi and Zuni Ceremonialism." *Mem. Amer. Anthrop. Assoc.*, 1933, No. 39. Pp. 108.

———— "Early Relations Between Hopi and Keres." *Amer. Anthrop.*, 1936, 38, 554–560.

———— *Pueblo Indian Religion.* Univ. of Chic. Press, Chic., Ill., 1939, 2 vols. Pp. 1275.

Parsons, E. C. and R. L. Beals. "The Sacred Clowns of the Pueblo and Mayo-Yaqui Indians." *Amer. Anthrop.*, 1934, 36, 491–512.

Roberts, F. H. H., Jr. "Archeology in the Southwest." *Amer. Antiquity*, 1937, 3, 3–33.

Solberg, O. "Über die Bahos der Hopi." *Archiv. f. Anthrop.*, N. F., 1906, 32, 48–74.

Stephen, A. M. "Legend of the Snake Order of the Moquis, as Told to Outsiders," *J. Amer. Folk-L.*, 1888, 1, 109–115.

———— "Tribal Boundary Marks." *Amer. Anthrop.*, o. s., 1889, 2, 214.

———— "The Po-boc-tu Among the Hopi." *Amer. Antiq. and Oriental J.*, 1894, 16, 212–214.

Stephen, A. M. "Hopi Tales." *J. Amer. Folk-L.*, 1929, 42, 1–72.

———— *Hopi Journal of Alexander M. Stephen;* edited by Elsie Clews Parsons. Col. Univ. Contrib. to Anthrop., 1936, vol. 23, 2 vols. Pp. 1330.

Steward, J. H. "Notes on Hopi Ceremonies in Their Initiatory Form in 1927–28." *Amer. Anthrop.*, 1931, 33, 56–79.

———— "Ecological Aspects of Southwestern Society." *Anthropos*, 1937, 32, 87–104.

Titiev, M. "A Hopi Salt Expedition." *Amer. Anthrop.*, 1937, 39, 244–259.

———— "The Problem of Cross-Cousin Marriage Among the Hopi." *Amer. Anthrop.*, 1938, 40, 105–111.

Tucker, M. *Books of the Southwest: A General Bibliography*. Augustin, N. Y.: n.d. Pp. 105.

Voth, H. R. "Oraibi Marriage Customs." *Amer. Anthrop.*, 1900, 2, 238–246.

———— "The Oraibi Powamu Ceremony." *Anthrop. Series, Field Mus. Nat. Hist.*, 1901, 3, No. 2, 67–158.

———— "The Oraibi Summer Snake Ceremony." *Anthrop. Series, Field Mus. Nat. Hist.*, 1903, 3, No. 4, 271–358.

———— "The Oraibi Oáqöl Ceremony." *Anthrop. Series, Field Mus. Nat. Hist.*, 1903, 6, No. 1, 1–46.

———— "The Traditions of the Hopi." *Anthrop. Series, Field Mus. Nat. Hist.*, 1905, 8, 1–319.

———— "Oraibi Natal Customs and Ceremonies." *Anthrop. Series, Field Mus. Nat. Hist.*, 1905, 6, No. 2, 47–61.

———— "Hopi Proper Names." *Anthrop. Series, Field Mus. Nat. Hist.*, 1905, 6, No. 3, 66–113.

———— "The Oraibi Marau Ceremony." *Anthrop. Series, Field Mus. Nat. Hist.*, 1912, 11, No. 1, 1–88.

———— "Brief Miscellaneous Hopi Papers." *Anthrop. Series, Field Mus. Nat. Hist.*, 1912, 11, No. 2, 99–149.

Wallis, W. D. "Folk Tales from Shumopavi, Second Mesa." *J. Amer. Folk-L.*, 1936, 49, 1–68.

APPENDIX

THE SOCIALIZATION OF THE HOPI CHILD
Wayne Dennis

REPRINTED FROM : *Language, Culture, and Personality*
Menasha, Wisconsin, pages 259-271

ANIMISM AND RELATED TENDENCIES IN HOPI CHILDREN
Wayne Dennis

REPRINTED FROM : *The Journal of Abnormal and Social Psychology,*
Vol. 38, No. 1, January 1943.

THE PERFORMANCE OF HOPI CHILDREN ON
THE GOODENOUGH DRAW-A-MAN-TEST
Wayne Dennis

REPRINTED FROM : *The Journal of Comparative Psychology,*
Vol. 34, No. 3, December 1942.

ARE HOPI CHILDREN NONCOMPETITIVE?
Wayne Dennis

REPRINTED FROM : *The Journal of Abnormal and Social Psychology,*
Vol. 50, No. 1, January 1955.

THE SOCIALIZATION OF THE HOPI CHILD

By WAYNE DENNIS

INTRODUCTION

IT IS A TRUISM that the individual at birth has no behavioral characteristics which mark him as the member of any social group, and that a few years of residence in one society serve to cause him to resemble other members of his social world. But the processes by which the developing individual is caused to conform, to some extent, to the customs of his fellows are far from being thoroughly understood. Notwithstanding the fact that the recognition of the existence of a process called socialization is old, the social sciences in the past have often ignored it, or given it scanty attention. Anthropology and sociology have been concerned with the description of societies. They have seldom directed their attention to the socialization of the individual. Psychology, which might have been expected to investigate the process, was driven into a social blindness by the glare of the laboratory. If today these sciences are directing their attention to a greater degree than has been the case in the past to the individual within society and to the psychological aspects of social life, we must name as one of the instigators of this movement Sapir, who saw the inevitable woodenness of findings derived from disciplines which treated man as if he were a marionette and who urged that social sciences not ignore the emotional and intellectual life of the individual.

In those instances in which the socialization of the child has been dealt with, authors not infrequently have written as if there were no real psychological processes to be observed. Human nature has sometimes been characterized as plastic to such a degree as to possess no other attributes. The fitting of man to a social pattern has been likened to the pouring of wax into a mold, as if human material were not at all refractory. The simile infers that the metaphorical wax, neurological, glandular, and otherwise, which comprises the human individual has no tendencies toward shapes of its own. At times a pseudo-psychological impulse to imitate or to conform has been hypothesized. This advances the wax-mold analogy one step farther in the direction of absurdity, for when an impulse is added to the wax, the wax does not have to be poured into the mold—it jumps in of its own propulsion. Sapir criticized theories which hold that the plasticity of human nature is unlimited. His interest in psychoanalysis, we believe, grew partly from his recognition of the need of a psychology which gave cognizance to human tendencies and desires. Through the influence of such ideas there is emerging a social psychology which will do better justice both to cultural patterns and to individual tendencies than have the discussions of the past.

The aim of the present paper is to contribute in a small way toward the development of such a social psychology by suggesting how the child becomes adjusted in one small society—a Hopi village in northern Arizona.[1] While our information is specifically concerned with Hotavila,[2] the account is descriptive of nearly all of the Hopi villages, and a great deal of it may also be characteristic not only of the Hopi but of the majority of the Southwestern Pueblos. Just how widely distributed are the practises to be described we do not know because the details of child rearing and of child development have received but little attention in anthropology. Within the limits of this chapter we must avoid a comparative or an historical interest and deal solely with Hopi child-rearing without discussion of its relationship to the practises of other groups. It is to be understood that we specifically disclaim any notion that the Hopi originated the child-rearing customs which they observe.

NECESSITY FOR SOCIALIZATION

If it were doubted that the Hopi child requires an active socialization, observation shows that such doubts are in error. Hopi parents are very lenient and Hopi customs impose almost a minimum of frustration and repression upon the child, yet the child may fail in many respects to meet Hopi standards. Only after a series of social influences are brought to bear upon him does he gradually approach the Hopi norms. A comparison of Hopi child behavior with the behavior of children of other groups would show that conformity to Hopi standards is not spontaneous and universal.

Foremost among the expectations of the Hopi parent is the requirement that the child shall work. The industry of the Pueblo peoples is well known, and is a precondition of existence in the arid region in which they live. The child is expected to join in the work of the household, although his contribution is proportionate to his size. Despite the model of his parents, the child does not do his tasks with the same willingness with which he plays; work, in the beginning, has no "functional autonomy" and we shall need to examine the means whereby the child is caused to perform his assignments.

Next to work in importance is the ceremonial life, which in native ideology is allied with work, for without proper attention to the ceremonies, industry would not be productive. The child's place in ceremonial life is small; nevertheless, it is necessary that he acquire some knowledge of ceremony and of the supernaturals who are associated with it, and that he have the proper attitude and demeanor in regard to the performances which take place in the plaza and in the kiva. Few difficulties seem to be encountered in the

---

[1] The material of this study was derived from informants and from direct observation in the course of two summers' residence among the Hopi. In the present connection our findings have been much abbreviated and our presentation has been limited to those topics which bear upon the question of socialization. A full account of the child-rearing practises of Hotavila and of New Oraibi, together with observations on Hopi child behavior, will be found in a book by the author, entitled *The Hopi Child* (New York, 1940). We are indebted to the Social Science Research Council and to the Institute for Research in the Social Sciences at the University of Virginia for financial assistance in the field study from which the following account is derived.

[2] Many data similar to those presented here, but for the village of Mishongnovi, are contained in the monograph by Ernest and Pearl Beaglehole, *Hopi of the Second Mesa* (Memoirs, American Anthropological Association, No. 44, 1935), p. 65.

child's adjustment to the religious observances, but socialization is no less important when it operates smoothly than it is when it proceeds with difficulty. The religious training of the Hopi child is interesting not only in itself, but also because the impersonators of the supernaturals are employed to encourage industry and good conduct as well as to inculcate respect for the gods.

A further general field in which the Hopi child requires socialization is the avoidance of open conflicts and the respect for the rights and the property of others. Hopi men seldom display strong emotion and almost never fight or quarrel, but the Hopi child has temper tantrums in which he screams and kicks and throws himself on the ground as no adult Hopi ever does. The child comes into conflict with other children over property, and these conflicts lead to hitting with the hands and with sticks, to pushing and shoving, and to the throwing of dirt and of stones. The pugnacity and aggressiveness of the child must be overcome so that in adulthood the behavior of the Hopi will approximate the Hopi ideal of a person who causes no trouble.

This list of the ways in which the Hopi find it necessary to modify child behavior is of course fragmentary. In addition to the socialization mentioned above, weaning must be accomplished, toilet habits must be established, taboos against indecent exposure must be inculcated, and many other standards of conduct must be interiorized. In discussing Hopi socialization within a limited space, we must of necessity restrict our treatment to those items which seem to us to be of greatest importance. A discussion of other topics is to be found in another publication by the author.[3] The present discussion will be limited to the topics named above: work, ceremonial life, and avoidance of conflict.

HOPI MEANS OF SOCIALIZATION

Parental Approval and Disapproval. Until he or she marries and establishes a separate home, the Hopi is a dependent member of his parents' household. The house belongs to his mother. The mother also possesses and dispenses the stored food supply of the entire family, while the father brings this supply into the possession of the mother and is directly responsible for clothing the family. Formerly the clothing was provided by his own work with skins and with textiles, but at the present time part of the clothing is obtained by purchase. The housing, feeding, and clothing of the child by the parents, and other less tangible services of the parents to the child, create bonds of love and of gratitude and of dependence which are used to influence the child toward observance of the parents' wishes. In some cases the desire to please the parents which grows out of the parent-child relationship may be almost sufficient in itself to cause the child to do what the parents wish in regard to helping with the work of the family and in conforming to the family pattern of religion and of deportment. If this is not sufficient, the parents have means of reward and punishment which can be brought into play. The child may be praised for his actions, although praise does not seem to be utilized to a great degree. One sees no indication of ex-

[3] *The Hopi Child.* Appropriate references to the literature on the Hopi are also cited in this work.

cessive pride on the part of parents or of much emphasis upon the superior qualities of one's own offspring; such feelings are restrained, and praise, too, is restrained in its forms.

Gifts are sometimes given to reward a task well done or to encourage an interest in work. The boy may be given a ewe, whose offspring will be his if the sheep receives proper care. The girl may have a small vessel for water-carrying which is all her own. Other rewards are received from the hands of the impersonators of supernaturals, the kachinas, as we shall see later.

On the negative side, scolding and nagging must be set down as of common occurrence. The child is quickly told when he displeases, although his parents are moderate in their expression, not raising their voices greatly in pitch or loudness and not losing their tempers easily. But scolding is very persistent; the child who has committed a misdeed is reminded of it at appropriate times for years afterward. The following illustrative incident occurred at Zuñi, but we feel that it expresses the spirit of Hopi discipline as well. Two boys who were playing with matches accidentally set fire to a barn and a team of horses was killed by the flames. We asked our informant in what way the boys would suffer for their offense. She said that for years they would be reminded of the great loss which they had caused the family, and that this would be brought to mind particularly when the boys needed new shoes or new shirts, or when they wished anything which must be purchased, for the horses could have been sold for money.

The Hopi are not averse to corporal punishment, although corporal punishments are not cruel or excessive. They are administered to young children, never to boys and girls of twelve or more years of age. The most usual form of corporal punishment is whipping the legs with a withe or a strap. The chastisement ordinarily is administered by that parent who has been disobeyed or offended, but, since the small children remain in the village and do not go to the fields, this is usually the mother. The mother would not be able to get the father to punish for her. She can, however, ask one of her brothers to punish the children, as we shall see later. No one except the parents and the maternal uncles has the right to punish the child, although anyone in the village may inform these persons of the child's misbehavior. The parents are financially responsible for any damage which is done by the child, and they, not the person whose property has been damaged, would discipline the child in such a case.

The most frequent cause of punishment, however, is not damage to property but failure to do the tasks which it is the child's duty to perform. The boy may be whipped for neglecting to keep the prairie dogs from the cornfield, or the girl for failing to come home to take care of the baby. Talking back to the parent or speaking impolitely to a parent are other causes of punishment, as are stealing and lying.

The parents may punish the child by withholding, or by threatening to withhold, some favor. Food, however, would never be denied in any case. To withhold food which is already in the house is never done, although the parent might refuse to buy candy or some other delicacy from the trading post. The most usual threat of deprivation is to threaten to leave the child behind when the family goes to a dance in a kiva. Occasionally this threat is carried out. To execute it is considered very severe, for all children want to go, and practically everybody in the village is in attendance. If the dance is one which is held out of doors in the child's own village such a threat is not made, for children are never kept at home under these circumstances.

The Role of the Maternal Uncle. As in many other societies, descent is matrilineal. Since the child belongs to the mother's clan, he shares the traditions and the history of that clan. Although the child is related to his father's people also, he is distinctly a member of his mother's household. While the child's parents jointly occupy the home, the home belongs to the mother. In case of separation, the father departs and takes up residence with his mother or with one of his sisters. Because the child belongs to a lineage which is not that of his father, it is felt that some male member of the child's lineage should be responsible for his conduct. The men who are most closely related to the child are the brothers of the child's mother, and they are responsible in a measure for the child's behavior. Any maternal uncle has the right to correct or to punish a child, but this duty is likely to be assumed by the oldest uncle, or by a particular uncle who is willing to accept the responsibility. The uncle, who is married into another family, comes to the homes of his sisters on winter evenings to lecture the children on their duties. He also punishes them if they fail in their duties, coming either at the mother's call or on his own initiative.

He does not correct minor and occasional offenses, but only misdemeanors which are serious or persistent. He may take disciplinary action if a boy injures other children, or if a son will not do as his mother tells him, or if the boy steals. If he thinks the offense requires it, he may whip the child severely, or he may punish the child by holding him in a smudge. The latter is considered the most severe form of Hopi child punishment. The uncle builds a small fire of green juniper twigs and holds the child, face downward, in the stifling fumes. This punishment is seldom used, perhaps only once in two or three years in an entire village, and it is never employed by a parent, but only by a maternal uncle. It is used for both boys and girls.

The uncle often punishes an entire group of brothers, though he may know that only one boy was guilty of the offense and may even be able to identify the culprit. Whether he similarly punishes a group of sisters we did not learn. When group punishment is used, it may take the form of whipping or of use of the cedar smudge. The boys are treated in proportion to their size, the young ones being punished only slightly.

Our informants gave no native rationalization of group punishment but we wish to suggest one way in which it fits into Hopi patterns of thought.[4] The Hopi often state that misbehavior, especially on the part of a participant in a ceremony, will cause the supernaturals to bring retribution not only upon the offender but upon the entire village. Group punishment for the offense of one boy would seem to be an effective way of illustrating the principle that the bad behavior of one person brings ill results to others. This sort of

---

[4] Group punishment is found elsewhere, and may, of course, be made to conform to quite different ideologies.

interpretation, on the part of the child, would be furthered by the fact that group punishment is not practised by his parents but by a representative of that large group of relatives, the clan.

Kachina Reward and Punishment. From the age of four months, when he is old enough to be taken out of doors, the Hopi child may witness the performances of the kachinas. These events take place in the months between February and July. The kachinas are men who impersonate the supernaturals, but the young child is told that they are the real gods. The kachinas have bodies like men, but their heads are different from those of men, being cylindrical, and having extraordinary eyes, ears, noses, and mouths. (These masks are carefully and skilfully made.) There are many kinds of kachinas, each kind having a distinctive head and often other distinctive characteristics as well. The kachinas are richly dressed in embroidered kilts and foxskins, and they wear a great deal of turquoise and silver jewelry.

The child is told that the kachinas come in the clouds and also travel in the regions under the earth. They govern the rain and wind and snow; they control good and bad fortune generally. The Hopi must please them, for unless this is done, the rains will fail, the springs will disappear, and the Hopi will perish. To please the kachinas, one must lead a good life and faithfully perform the ceremonies.

The kachinas are described as living in the San Francisco Peaks, which, although many miles away, are visible from Hotavila. There the kachinas have villages and fields much like their Hopi counterparts, but the kachinas have the power to grow beans even in the wintertime and to produce corn and melons when the Hopi plants are still immature. During the autumn and the winter, the kachinas remain in the mountains, impervious to cold. But in spring and summer they visit the Hopi from time to time, performing the dances in which the Hopi find so much pleasure.

The kachinas do not forget the children. When they first visit the Hopi each year in February, in the so-called Bean Dance, they bring the children bunches of fresh bean plants and also gifts of kachina dolls to the girls and of shinny sticks and tops to the boys.

Each child is given presents by one of the kachina impersonators, who may be the father or some other relative of the child but who the child thinks to be a supernatural. The child is told by his mother, or by others, that the present is brought because he has been a good child. The child looks forward expectantly to these occasions on which he receives fine gifts. He is warned by his parents that if he misbehaves the kachinas will bring him nothing. Such a threat is seldom executed, but a child who has been so warned may not receive his present until the kachinas make their last appearance of the day, which is near the hour of sunset. This entails an entire day of doubt and suspense, as the first public dance occurs shortly after sunrise. During this interval the child will have been reminded of his offenses by his parents, and he will have repented and promised to reform, whereupon the omniscient kachinas will take cognizance of his better heart and bring him a present. The possibility of not receiving gifts when all other children publicly receive them is said by informants to insure good behavior during a large part of the season of kachina dances. The kachinas bring presents to the children not only at the Bean Dance but at other dances as well.

At the public dances the kachinas are in the village in large numbers. At other times they appear singly and in small groups to perform other ceremonial functions. The child is thus frequently reminded of their presence in the vicinity, and he is impressed by the respect and the obedience which is given to them even by the adults. The child is thus surrounded by immediate supernaturals who take a direct interest in the affairs of the village and, he is told, in the child's personal behavior as well. The impressiveness to the child of these appearances of the gods in person can scarcely be overlooked.

To make this impression still more personal to the child, there occasionally appears a horrible female kachina, Soyoko, who with equally terrifying cohorts, goes about in the village demanding the children. At the first glimpse of these ogres parents and children alike wildly scramble inside and bolt the doors. But Soyoko and her companions, who are armed with saws and other vicious instruments, and who carry ropes and baskets with which to take away the children, come to each door, call the inhabitants by name, and loudly demand the sons and daughters. In order to render the parents willing to part with a child, the sins of the child are recited. "She does not grind enough meal." "He is lazy in the fields." "He is always fighting." The parents, who have informed Soyoko in advance in regard to what should be said about the child, hold the door against the invaders and defend their offspring and promise that he will do better in the future. After the passage of minutes which seem like hours to the child, the parents persuade the kachinas to leave by the device of giving them food, which lessens their appetite for children. The act is repeated at each door in the village.

The tradition of Soyoko is in every town and all children are afraid of Soyoko because they know that this personage does exist. In Hotavila Soyoko has not appeared for several years, but the mention of her name is still effective.

Initiation. When the child is between six and ten years of age he undergoes an impressive initiation which contains all of the elements of the elaborate Hopi ceremonialism. At the close of this he learns that while the real kachinas formerly came to visit the Hopi, they do not do so today. He learns that instead of the kachinas dancing for the pleasure of the Hopi, as he had thought, in reality the Hopi dress in the manner of the supernaturals and dance to please the gods. This secret must not be revealed to the uninitiated under pain of a very severe flogging by the kachinas. He learns that kachina presents have been the work of his own relatives, and that Soyoko, like all other kachinas, is impersonated. He is told that he himself may now please the gods by taking part in the masked dances, an art which he never before knew that a mere man could perform.

Our informants state that while knowledge of the nature of the masked dancers is often the cause of great disappointment to the child, it does not cause disillusionment or bitterness. The gods become not less real but more distant. The figures who dance in the village are mere men, not the powerful personages that the child once thought them to be, but the real gods are now free to become more powerful than the child could have conceived them as being in the form in which they danced in the plaza. It is more important to please the gods, now that the child is older, than it was when his powers of understanding and his possibilities of misbehavior were at the infantile level.

The impersonations, while they are recognized as such, still recall much of the emotional reaction which they did when they were thought to be real. A twenty-five year old informant from Mishongnovi, who had been terrified as a child when Soyoko on one occasion suddenly appeared near her without warning, confessed that she is still frightened when certain kinds of kachinas appear. The threat of calling Soyoko is effectively applied even to children who have been initiated.

Initiation is a milepost in the child's socialization. Not only does it mark a change in his conception of the gods, but it introduces a change also in his ideas concerning himself. Since early childhood he has heard of and dreaded the whipping with yucca blades which is a part of the children's initiation. He is now successfully past the ordeal. He possesses information which is not dreamed of by the uninitiated, and which he must keep from them. He may even dance in the kachina dances. He has risen one step toward adulthood; he is no longer a small child, and he should not act as one. This new feeling of maturity and of superiority encourages a control of tantrums, of shirking, and of dislike for hard tasks, because he is told that such things are characteristic of the uninitiated.

At a much later date, from sixteen to twenty years of age, the boy (but not the girl) undergoes a second initiation whose details are kept from the uninitiated (including anthropologists) with great secrecy, and which is said to be very much more important than is the first initiation. The second initiation marks the boy's entrance into manhood, and he is obligated, in order to be worthy of his new status, to put aside all childish things. He may no longer play with young boys, may not quarrel and fight as boys sometimes do; he should assume the character of a Hopi man. Refraining from quarreling and from malicious talking is not expected of the Hopi woman, because she does not undergo this second initiatory ceremony.

Other Children as Socializing Agents. The child's playmates and companions have little or no formal part in his socialization. Even his older sister who takes care of him when he is very young does not have the right to punish him, but is supposed to appeal to the parents to make him behave. Nevertheless, there is no doubt that in an informal manner the children exert an influence upon each other. We have seen young girls sufficiently exasperated to spank their younger siblings, regardless of their theoretical inability to do so. No doubt a child who does things which are displeasing to other children will have occasion to discover this fact. Hopi children ridicule each other, and they dislike very much to be ridiculed. However, not all of this ridicule works in the direction which the parents would wish. In New Oraibi recently one boy would not wear a clean shirt to school because the boys called him a woman when he did so. His father had to whip the boy in order to make him wear the laundered article of apparel.

Training in Games. Among the Hopi eternal vigilance is the price of security, a security which at its best is precarious. Corn may grow nearly to maturity to be washed away by a thundershower or to be stunted by a final failure of moisture. Crops are threatened at all times, not only by unfavorable weather but by worms and by prairie dogs, and by any burro or sheep or goat which escapes the watchfulness of its owner. Harvests are never safe until they are in the storage bin; not until then can the Hopi be certain of a season's yield.

One is tempted to draw a parallel between the training toward unceasing effort which characterizes adult life, and the rules of certain boy's games which may be said to embody a principle of difficult victory. These games exemplify the demand for continuous application and constant alertness which typify Hopi agriculture. In these games, success in the early phases is meaningless unless it is followed by success later in the game. Failure at any point causes the player to lose credit for his earlier successes.

This is illustrated in a stick-throwing game. The contestants are divided into two sides. The leader of one side throws the goal stick in a fashion such that it goes out of sight behind some obstacle. The other players must then throw without being able to see the goal. The team which owns the stick which falls nearest to the goal receives a score of one point. If a stick touches the goal two points are scored. When either side reaches a score of four, it is in a position to try for a victory. If in the course of the next trial the leading team wins the fifth point, it is declared winner. If, on the other hand, the team fails to earn the final point, both teams lose all of their points, and a new game must be started.

A similar principle is seen in an archery contest in which the participants direct their arrows at the rim of a small hoop of cornhusks. When one boy hits the target, the members of the opposite team must take the position of the successful archer and let go at the hoop from that position. The arrows which miss go to the boy who originally hit the target, but he retains them only if he can hit the target with the same arrows with which the opponent missed. At the close of the game he must shoot at a new target all of the arrows which he has temporarily won, and may keep only those that hit this second target. However, a great deal depends on the final shot, which is made with one of his own arrows. If the final arrow hits the target, he may keep not only those arrows which have hit this target but the ones which have missed it as well. A game of the same sort is played with darts. Among the girls there are no similar games.

Reciprocity. The Hopi child performs many services because he wishes to receive the services or gifts which will accrue to him in return, or because he feels obligated to recipro-cate for favors which have been done for him in the past. Hopi life is full of reciprocal obliga-tions; we can present here only some instances. The boy catches small game for the captive eagles because he will receive feathers in return when the eagles are killed. He helps his fa-ther's brothers, since when he marries he will wish them to make wedding garments for his bride. The girls make a special corn pudding when they are asked to accompany the boys on a rabbit hunt, for the game secured on such a hunt becomes the property of the girls. At a grinding party, the girl will grind meal for her godmother who saw her through the children's initiation and who inducted her into a woman's society. There are many such exchanges of services in childhood as well as in later life, and these are important forces toward conformity.

SUCCESS AND FAILURE IN SOCIALIZATION

The success of socialization may be measured by determining the relative number of successes and failures. We obtained from our Hotavila informants and from informants at Mishongnovi and New Oraibi a complete census of children, listing them by households. We then had our informants go through this list in regard to several kinds of problem behavior while we marked each individual who was said to possess each of the undesirable characteristics. The census includes all unmarried persons up to 22 years of age, a total of 525 cases, about equally divided as to sex. At the lower age levels there are approximately 30 children at each year; at the older levels, about 20 at each year.

Temper tantrums are found to be much more common among boys than among girls, as 21 boys and only 7 girls are said to have tantrums. The age range for tantrums is from two to twelve years of age, with the greatest incidence falling in the two to five year old level. It would appear, therefore, that Hopi methods succeed in getting rid of tantrums, and that they usually succeed at a fairly early period.

Fighting shows an even greater predominance of boys over girls than do tantrums, the numbers being respectively 22 and 5. The five girls who are reported as fighting are between four and nine years of age. The boys who fight are sometimes as old as sixteen, but none are older than that, a fact which tends to show that fighting ceases as the age of second initiation approaches. The greatest incidence of fighters is between eight and thirteen years of age (ages are inclusive). In this interval, approximately one-fifth of the boys are said to engage in fights.

In regard to stealing, the boys outnumber the girls 27 to 15. Beyond four years of age, when the taking of other people's property begins to be considered intentional stealing, there is no consistent trend with age, until the age of eighteen is reached, when the rate drops markedly. This again supports the view that the age of second initiation may be an important one. Girls do not have a second initiation, hence this cannot be evoked as an explanation of their conduct. However, the girls contribute only a minor part of the problem behavior. If fighting and stealing do become less common as adulthood is approached, it may well be that it is not due to the initiation itself but to a change in social position which begins to affect boys and girls alike. As the time for marriage approaches, both the boy and the girl may be anxious to gain the approval of persons beyond the circle of relatives. It should be pointed out, however, that at all ages the children who misbehave form only a small minority, since only a small proportion of the 525 cases engage in each form of misconduct.

A few words may be said with regard to the fact that in the census of behavior problems the boys contribute more cases than do the girls. This situation is so much like the condition which prevails in our own very different and quite unrelated society that we are likely to see this similarity as the result of fundamental differences between the sexes. In regard to the behavior of Hopi girls, we must call attention to a few facts, some of which we have had no occasion to mention at an earlier point in this discussion. During the early years, girls have the responsibility of caring for younger siblings. This fact may affect the likelihood of a girl's fighting since her contacts are predominantly with a younger child. Her position as nurse-maid certainly affects her opportunities for stealing, since she has an almost constant com-panion who cannot be trusted to keep secrets and whose presence would make deception difficult. Beyond the approximate age of ten years, the Hopi girl is expected to remain at home almost continuously, and to go about only when accompanied by a woman. This per-sistent supervision of the girl has no counterpart in the boy, and renders an interpretation of sex differences in biological terms very dubious.

It is the native belief that family attitude and family discipline determine the behavior of the child. Examination of the means of social control which were described earlier will show that the parents and the maternal uncles provide practically all of the disciplinary in-fluences. The control by the kachinas is no exception, for while the young child does not identify the kachinas with his relatives, they are in effect the same persons. It is the parents who threaten that the kachinas will withhold gifts from a child who steals, just as it is the parents who provide the gifts and interpret them as a reward for good conduct. A dancer takes no responsibility for training or disciplining a child unless the child is his son, daughter, nephew, or niece, or unless the parents have given the dancer instructions. In effect, there-fore, all forms of child training, except those lessons which are administered by playmates, are received directly or indirectly from relatives. It is no one else's responsibility. There are no policemen, no truant officers, no youth organizations, no adult leaders of the young.

Examination of our census of behavior problems in Hotavila shows, in line with this analysis, that the instances of misconduct, especially of the more serious forms, occur chiefly in a few families. This is especially true of stealing.

The most outstanding example is a household all members of which are said to steal and lie. The parents are very poor. The husband is described as peculiar in behavior and his own wife says that he is a witch. There is a daughter of five years who has tantrums, and who steals and lies. She is the only five year old girl in our records who possesses all of these faults. Next in age are three boys, six, eight, and ten years old. They also lie and steal, and fight among themselves. Last winter they were rolled in the snow and whipped by their older sister. It is very unusual for an older sister to punish, and our informant did not know why she did so. It may have been because the parents had failed to do it themselves. The worst problem in the family is a boy of seventeen, who is possibly feeble-minded. He once robbed the trading-post: the chief and the members of the council did nothing about it, nor did anyone else. Last spring he and three other boys stole corn by boring a hole into a stor-age bin. When they tried this technique a second time, the owner of the bin caught them red-handed. The parents of the boys should have punished them, but they did not. It is even claimed that the parents of the boys encourage them to steal. The father of the seventeen year old boy whom we are discussing says his son is a witch. These recriminations show that there is little love or unity within the family. The boy is very slow in school and it is claimed that he is guilty of stealing a teacher's watch. We have no record of misbehavior on the part of the oldest child, a girl of eighteen. She is married and has a son eleven months of age, but she is still living in her mother's household.

There is a second family of which likewise it is claimed that parents and children alike engage in thievery. They go into neighbors' houses when no one is at home, a thing which no Hopi should do. They steal corn and sheepskins; the children steal toys as well. Even the two youngest boys, three and five years of age, steal; in addition they have tantrums. The youngest sucks his thumb. A boy of eight, who has the family weakness for other people's property, has the further fault of fighting and has ceased attending school. The next in the family, a boy of seventeen, steals, stutters, and is stupid in school. A girl of eighteen is sexually immoral. Again the oldest, a girl of nineteen, is the best in the family, nothing being recorded against her present behavior.

These cases constitute the two worst families of Hotavila and are very decided exceptions. That delinquent families make up but a small part of the population is shown by the fact that of the sixty-six Hotavila families which appear in the census of children, only twelve families have any children who are said to steal. There is only one other family, in addition to the two treated above, in which almost all members of the household steal.

These cases bring out clearly the fact that when the family of the child fails in his socialization, the Hopi community has no systematic means of attempting to do the work for itself. The majority of families, however, succeed fairly well in getting their children to conform to their ideals.

In discussing failures at socialization, we have said nothing at all about laziness. It is difficult to get any measure of parental success in inducing work habits. For one thing, failure in this direction affects only the parents, whereas since stealing and fighting involve other persons they are to a greater extent common knowledge. It is our impression that nearly every boy and every girl is induced to help to some extent with the work of the household, but we are unable to measure the degree of industriousness.

In the field of religion, there is little possibility of failure. In Hotavila, there are no conflicting doctrines, although missionaries have entered other villages. Furthermore, the child has practically no religious duties. The child does not doubt what he is told. His attitude toward the supernaturals is one of awe and respect. He may dance if he wishes but there is no feeling that he should do so. Childhood is the period in which the elementary religious ideas are implanted, but religious observances come later.

SUMMARY

The Hopi Indians expect the child to perform part of the work of the household, to avoid conflicts, and to respect property rights. Other demands upon the child, while real, are of less importance. That he will absorb the chief religious ideas of the Hopi is so certain that it is taken for granted and does not become a cause of parental anxiety.

To insure conformity to Hopi patterns, parents make use of approval and disapproval whose effectiveness is based upon the strong personal ties within the family. The father is no more potent a disciplinarian than is the mother. The duty of lecturing and chastising the child falls upon the maternal uncles of the child. In the matrilineal Hopi society, they are expected to correct the behavior of their sisters' children, who are of their lineage and clan. Some of the forms of corporal punishment which are at the disposal of the maternal uncles are relatively severe.

While the correction of the child is in reality the function of the parents and of the maternal uncles, the child is made to think that the supernaturals, whom he identifies with the kachinas or masked dancers, also take a direct interest in his conduct. The kachinas bring gifts as rewards for good behavior and threaten the child with abduction and cannibalism when he is bad.

The children's intiation gives the child a higher status in the community, disabuses him of his belief that the gods appear in person, and grants him the privilege of impersonating the supernaturals and of participating in the ceremonies. By drawing a line between the initiated and the uninitiated, it encourages the former to give up "childish" ways.

The performance of many of the duties of the Hopi child is encouraged by the strong custom of reciprocity; nearly every action brings a well-defined reward, or creates an obligation on the part of the recipient of the favor.

A census of cases of problem behavior shows that failure to conform occurs in a small number of instances. Since the responsibility for socialization is familial and is not a function of the community or of community agents, it is not surprising that the majority of problem cases come from families whose adult members themselves fail to conform to expectations of the village as a whole, and whose child training is defective. Some misbehavior, however, arises in "good families," presumably because among the Hopi, as elsewhere, not all individuals are equally susceptible to socialization.

UNIVERSITY OF VIRGINIA
CHARLOTTESVILLE, VIRGINIA

ANIMISM AND RELATED TENDENCIES IN HOPI CHILDREN *

BY WAYNE DENNIS
Louisiana State University

INTRODUCTION

ALMOST all of the investigations of children's ideas which have been based on the work of Piaget have been conducted in Western civilizations and have made use of Indo-European languages. The question arises, therefore, as to what extent the thought tendencies of the child are the result of particular cultural and linguistic influences and to what extent they are universal outcomes of child experience and of incomplete mental development.

In order to answer these questions it will be necessary to have extensive data, gathered by Piaget's methods, on children in other cultures. It is for that reason that the following data on Hopi children are presented. In undertaking this research there was no assumption that the Hopi are a particularly valuable group for such research. The Hopi happened to be a group with whom we had an opportunity to work. While it has turned out that they do provide some valuable information with regard to thought tendencies, it is likely that many other groups would yield results just as interesting.

Before research of this type in a society other than our own can be interpreted, it is necessary to know the intellectual world of the adults of that society, the methods of child rearing of the group, and the nature of the language. Fortunately, for the Hopi, the first and second types of information are available. Pueblo ideas concerning cosmology, magic, and religion have been extensively studied, and the results for all the Pueblo groups, including the Hopi, have been summarized by Parsons (13). The Beagleholes (2) and the present writer (3) have described child care, and Sim-

* The research here reported was made possible by a grant-in-aid from the Social Science Research Council, for which we wish to express our gratitude. We wish also to express our appreciation of the complete cooperation which we received from those associated with the Hopi Schools, particularly Mr. Paul L. Fickinger, Associate Director of Education, Office of Indian Affairs, Mr. Carson Ryan, Principal of the Hopi Schools, Mr. R. D. Brinkerhoff, Principal of the Hopi High School, and Mr. Sam Rosenberg, Principal of the Polacca School.

mons (24) has edited an autobiography of a Hopi which contains much material on children. Unfortunately, practically no material on the Hopi language is available in print. The late Benjamin J. Whorf, a brilliant student of language, gathered extensive materials on the Hopi language, which it is hoped may be published soon. We had the good fortune to attend Mr. Whorf's seminar on the Hopi language and to be with him for a short time in the field. However, our own work with regard to the language has been limited almost entirely to an attempt to explore the vocabulary and meanings associated with animistic concepts. A wider knowledge of Hopi would be most helpful to the interpretation of the data to be presented and would be almost a prerequisite to more intensive work on the development of concepts in Hopi children.

When intelligent adult Hopi, well acquainted with English, are questioned with regard to objects in nature which the Hopi consider to be living, it is found that they do not by any means limit life to plants and animals.[1]

The Hopi include among living objects the sun, the moon, the stars, the wind, the clouds, permanent springs of water, permanent rivers, and fire. They do not include as living a rainstorm, a flash of lightning, or an arroyo which carries water only after a rain, or a temporary or intermittent spring. These events are brief and transient. Mechanical devices are not living, and sand, stone, and bare earth are not living because they do nothing by themselves. Perhaps one can best describe the quality which causes the Hopi to classify objects as living as some sort of enduring power.

In the Hopi language, there are two verbs which express the idea of being alive or having life.[2] They are "tayta" and "kata." The third person singular nominative pronoun "pum" is used for both sexes and also for neuter objects. Thus "it (or she or he) is living" may be expressed as "pum kata" or "pum tayta." The verb is made negative by the prefix "ka." Consequently, "it is not living" is stated in Hopi as "pum kakata" or "pum katayta."[3] The pronoun is very commonly omitted.

---

[1] In addition to objects in nature, the Hopi attribute life to a number of supernatural beings. Most English-speaking people likewise believe in supernatural characters which they consider to be alive. However, our present discussion will be limited to the animate and inanimate dichotomy as applied to natural objects.

[2] The information which follows was obtained independently from three informants.

[3] Since accurate phonetics are not essential to this discussion, we have not attempted to indicate in precise terms the value of the symbols used above.

RUSH!
NEW SUBSCRIBER ORDER!

BUSINESS REPLY MAIL

FIRST-CLASS MAIL   PERMIT NO. 1222   BOULDER, CO

POSTAGE WILL BE PAID BY ADDRESSEE

BETTER HOMES AND GARDENS® Magazine
PO BOX 55220
BOULDER   CO   80323-5220

սլ.ւ.ււ....ււ..ււ.ւ.ւ.ւ.ւ.ււ.ււ..ււ.ււ.ւ.ւ.ւ

Better Homes and Gardens®

one free year

Two Years (24 Issues) Just $15
(plus $3 postage)

Two Years For The Regular Price Of One!

PLEASE PRINT

Name _____

Address _____ Apt. # _____

City _____

State _____ Zip _____

Send no money now — We'll bill you later!
MAIL TODAY! Subscription prices subject to change. Add $24
for Canadian and other foreign subscriptions. Please allow 4–6
weeks for delivery.   **4JSB8**

The linguistic situation with reference to animism is complicated by the fact that both of these verbs have more than one meaning. "Tayta" means to look or to peer intently, as well as to live; but "tayta" also means "moving by itself," "in working condition," or "capable of normal activity," in much the same way that our words "live" and "dead" are used when we speak of a live battery and a dead motor. Thus our informants stated that a watch and an automobile are "tayta" when they are working, but they are not "really living." The third meaning of the word indicates "alive in the same way that people are," and this, as we indicated earlier, is said of heavenly bodies, rivers and springs (if permanent), fire and wind, in addition to plants, animals, and supernaturals.

"Kata" has the meaning "to sit" or "to be resting on the ground." In this sense it can be used to describe any object or person. It also has a meaning identical with the third meaning of "tayta" (*i.e.,* really alive), but "kata" in this sense is used properly only with reference to plants and animals, including man. There is no implication that life is restricted to animals and man—the word is synonymous with "tayta"—but it is improper to use "kata" to refer to objects, whereas "tayta" can be used for objects as well as for plants, animals, and man.

In reviewing these Hopi concepts it will be seen that the Hopi adult stage is quite different from the adult stage in our own culture. However, one meaning of "tayta" is very close to Piaget's Stage III, if not identical with it.[4] In Stage III, everything is living which is thought to move by itself. This is true with one usage of "tayta." All examples which we secured of "tayta" in this sense referred to manufactured objects, such as automobiles, batteries, and windmills. It seems likely that this usage is a recent metaphorical extension of "tayta" to cover new mechanical objects brought in by white people.

It will be noted that neither "tayta" or "kata" are used by Hopi adults to express meanings similar to the Stage I and Stage II degrees of animism.

[4] The stages distinguished by Piaget are as follows: Stage I: everything which is useful, unbroken, and in good condition is alive; Stage II: only things which move are alive; Stage III: only things which can move themselves are alive; Stage IV: only plants and animals are alive.

THE ANIMISM INTERVIEW

In questioning Hopi children with regard to their conceptions of animation, it was decided to question them in English. A major factor in this decision was the inadequacy of the investigator, who, while he could probably have understood simple answers in Hopi, could not have coped with unusual answers. It is hoped that examinations in the Hopi language may be conducted at a later time. Even apart from the limitations of the experimenter, it seemed best, since the subjects were bilingual, to explore first their responses in English.

All Hopi children learn first the Hopi language and seldom hear English until they enter school at six years of age. The Hopi, even the most highly educated ones, converse with each other in their native language. Aside from the school situation, they use English only when talking to a white person or to a Navaho or to some other non-Hopi Indian. On the reservation, the need for speaking English arises only seldom. Consequently, English has the status of an auxiliary language. It is likely that most Hopi, when employing English, definitely translate from their native language. That is, we believe that they do not have two independent sets of language habits. It is our conviction that if the examinations had been conducted in Hopi the results would have been the same.

The standardized procedure devised by Russell and Dennis (21) had to be modified for use among the Hopi, since the original procedure was not designed to reveal the concept of the Hopi adults. In order to make it possible to detect this concept certain items of the earlier list of twenty objects were replaced by other objects, the total number of items in the new list as well as the old list being twenty.

The items previously employed by Russell and Dennis (21) and also used with the Hopi subjects, numbered according to their position in the Hopi list, were (1) knife, (2) mirror, (3) stone, (4) broken button, (5) comb, (6) broken dish, (7) watch, (10) lightning, (12) pencil, (13) clouds, (14) moon, (17) wind, (19) dog, (20) tree. The following original items were removed from the list to make room for new objects: Chair, river, bird, bug, flower, grass. These were replaced by (8) automobile, (9) smoke, (11) windmill, (15) a spring of water, (16) fire, (18) soil in a garden.

In giving the animism examination, each child was taken to a room occupied only by the examiner and the child. The first seven objects lay on the table at which the child and the examiner sat. No example of a living or a dead object was given. Although this had been done in some of the earlier work (21), it was omitted here because this part of the original procedure had been found to be unnecessary (22). After saying "Good morning" or "Good afternoon" to the child and asking him to sit at the table, the examiner began the interview by remarking, "You know what it means to say that something is living, don't you?" If the subject said "Yes," the examiner proceeded as indicated below. If the subject answered in the negative, the examiner first said, "How do you say in Hopi, 'I am living'?" or he said, "If you were talking about a sheep, how would you say in Hopi, 'It is living'?" With the exception of one girl, who refused to answer any questions, the subjects all gave "kata" or "tayta" in response to one of these questions. After being assured in this manner that the child understood the questions, the examiner continued with the remainder of the examination.

The remainder of the procedure was identical with that outlined by Russell and Dennis (21). That is, with reference to each object each subject was asked, "Is the . . . . . living or is it dead?" and after an answer was obtained the child was asked to give a reason by being asked "Why?" or "How do you know?", "Why do you think so?" "How can you tell?"

If the child stated that some of the objects among the first six were living because they could be used and that others were dead because they were broken, it was unnecessary to carry the interview further since the child was obviously in Stage I. On the other hand, if all of the first six objects were said to be dead because they could not move, further questioning was, of course, necessary. This questioning followed the procedure previously described.

The classification of the answers into stages was accomplished in the usual way, except that two Stage IV's were provided: a Stage IV-P (Piaget) and a Stage IV-H (Hopi). If, in the list of twenty test objects, only the dog and the tree were said to be alive, the subject was classified as IV-P. If, in addition, the clouds, moon, spring, fire, and wind were said to be living while all other objects were said to be dead, the subject was assigned to Stage IV-H.

SUBJECTS

The subjects examined comprised all of the Hopi children of First Mesa and Third Mesa between the ages of 12 and 17, inclusive, who were in school when the examinations were conducted, which was between December 16 and December 24, 1941. All Hopi children of First Mesa [5] who were of these ages and who were in the first seven grades were examined at the Polacca Day School on First Mesa. All First Mesa school children who were at a grade level beyond grade seven were attending the Hopi High School at Oraibi and were examined there; all Third Mesa children were, of course, examined on Third Mesa, either at Hotavila or at Oraibi; Second Mesa was omitted from the investigation purely because of lack of time.

In all, 98 subjects, 43 girls and 55 boys, were examined; 44 of these were between 12.0 and 13.9 years; 32 were between 14.0 and 15.9, and 22 were between 16.0 and 17.9.

Subjects below twelve years were not examined because we wished to select subjects who would be certain to comprehend the questions which were asked in English. By twelve years of age most Hopi children have spent six years in school, and hence can be expected to have little difficulty with the language of the examination.

Beyond age 14 not all Hopi children attend school. We have no information on the type of selection which determines which of the older children remain in school, but there is no reason to believe that the duller ones remain. Almost the entire population between age 12 and age 14 was examined and hence we believe we have a representative sample of this age level of Hopi children.

RESULTS OF THE ANIMISM INTERVIEW

Of the 98 subjects, one would not answer at all, one answered only a few questions, and one said, "Don't know," to all questions. Hence 95 usable sets of answers were obtained. Since we do not know whether the three exceptions were merely recalcitrant or whether they were in the "no concept" stage, they will be omitted from our percentages. All three were in the 12.0–13.9 age group. Only one subject, a fourteen-year-old boy, displayed a special

[5] Tewa children of First Mesa were excluded because the treatment of animism categories in the Tewa dialect of First Mesa is unknown to us.

concept. For him things that made themselves were living. This category included, in addition to the dog and tree, lightning and clouds, since he conceived of the clouds as making themselves and of the lightning as coming from the clouds. All other answers were typical of one of the four stages described previously.

Only two subjects were in Stage IV–P; one of these was in the 12.0–13.9 group and one was in the oldest group. More striking still, only two subjects displayed the adult *Hopi* concept of life. These two were distributed in age as were the two mentioned just previously. Furthermore, only seven subjects were in Stage III.

In other words, 83 of the 95 subjects who gave meaningful answers were in Stages I and II. These were approximately equally divided between the two stages (45 in Stage I, 38 in Stage II). The older subjects had a slightly smaller proportion of subjects in Stage II than did the younger, but the difference was not reliable. The results in full are shown in Table 1.

TABLE 1

HOPI CASES IN EACH STAGE AT EACH AGE LEVEL

AGE GROUP	STAGE				
	I	II	III	IV	SC
12.0–13.9	19	18	2	2	0
14.0–15.9	18	10	3	0	1
16.0–17.9	8	10	2	2	0

These results are very different from the results of Russell on white children (18). Russell's study gives data on children in the elementary grades, so that a representative sample was obtained by him only up to age 14. His data, therefore, can be compared with our data only for the age group 12.0–13.9 years. Russell studied three groups, as follows: "F," a Massachusetts urban group; "S," a Virginia suburban group; and, "R," a Virginia rural group. The figures for these groups are compared with the Hopi data in Table 2.

This table shows that, even in comparison with the least-advanced white group, the "S" group, the Hopi twelve- and thirteen-year-olds are considerably retarded. Only 11 per cent of the Hopi are in Stages III and IV, whereas these stages are characteristic of 24 per cent of the "F" group. These differences are highly significant.

The differences between Hopi and white subjects at the high-school level are even greater. The Hopi subjects of advanced ages are not different from the Hopi twelve- and thirteen-year-olds, whereas Russell (20) has found that the majority of white high-school pupils are in Stage IV. (Of the 54 Hopi children between 14.0 and 17.9 years, only two were in Stage IV.)

TABLE 2

PERCENTAGE OF CASES IN EACH STAGE AT AGES 12.0–13.9 YEARS

GROUP	STAGE				
	I	II	III	IV	SC
"F"	24	13	34	27	2
"S"	31	45	11	13	0
"R"	31	30	24	13	2
Hopi	47	40	7	4	1

Discussion of the probable reasons for the retardation of the Hopi subjects will be postponed until data on related concepts have been presented.

ATTRIBUTION OF CONSCIOUSNESS TO THINGS

Since the attribution of life was found to be so widespread among Hopi children, it seemed advisable to attempt to see whether other human qualities were also extended to inanimate objects. This was done by Piaget (14) by determining whether or not children attributed consciousness to various objects. The same procedure in a standardized form has been employed by Russell (19). Both Piaget and Russell found that children frequently conceive as conscious many objects which adults think of not only as lacking in consciousness but also as lacking life.

The preferred procedure in the present instance would have been to employ Russell's standardized technique. However, our time among the Hopi was limited and, since Russell's procedure requires individual examination, its use was out of the question in the time which was available. Consequently, a group test was tried. It was given to grades seven, eight, and nine, at the Hopi High School, comprising a total of 69 subjects distributed as follows: ages 12.0–13.9, 14; ages 14.0–15.9, 42; ages 16.0–17.9, 11. One subject was 11 years of age and one was 18. Each grade was tested separately.

The examiner distributed to each student in the classroom a mimeographed sheet containing the name of each object used in the animism test. A space was provided after each name for the student's response.

The examiner said:

"I want to ask you some more questions like the ones I asked you the other day. But first I want to ask you a question about yourselves. Do you know where you are? Where are you? (The examiner waited for several oral replies, such as "Oraibi," "In school.") Now tell me (the examiner held up the knife used in previous animism interview) does the knife know where it is? Don't tell me aloud, but write down your answer, yes or no, on the first line on your paper, after the word 'knife.' Do not show anybody your answer." The question, "Does the...... know where it is?" was repeated for each object on the list.

We did not believe it was feasible to ask the Hopi subjects to write out a reason for each answer. The only data on the answer sheets, therefore, were a series of "yes" and "no" responses. Stage I answers can be distinguished fairly well in the absence of reasons supplied by the subject, since in Stage I the broken button and the broken dish are said not to know where they are because they are broken or because they are dead, whereas all other objects, with the possible exception of the stone, are said to be aware of their location. Twelve of the 69 papers definitely belonged in Stage I. Stages II and III could not be distinguished, since the answers did not show which objects were considered to move spontaneously. However, 34 of the papers belonged either to Stage II or to Stage III. Fourteen papers exhibited answers which could not be readily classified on the basis of the simple "yes" and "no" responses.

The point most relevant to our results on the animism interview is the fact that only *nine* papers limited "knowing" to the dog alone (the only animal on the list). Thus the widespread animism of Hopi children is corroborated by these questions on the attribution of consciousness to things.

Of the 12.0–13.9 group, three, or 21 per cent, limited consciousness to animals (Stage IV). The only comparable data are Russell's data (19) on Virginia children. In his group, 50 per cent of children aged 12.0–13.9 were in Stage IV, the adult stage. Thus the investigation of the attribution of consciousness to inanimate objects shows an even greater difference between white and Hopi children than was revealed by the animism examination.

MORAL REALISM

The third topic concerning which we questioned Hopi subjects was that of moral realism, and, in particular, immanent punishment. This examination was given to each subject of the animism examination immediately following that examination.

Our procedure was modeled after one used by Piaget (16) and is similar to procedures employed by Lerner (10, 11) and also by Abel (1). Our modifications were in the direction of insuring that the incident described would seem natural in the Hopi environment.

Our procedure consisted in telling the subject the following:

> I am going to tell you a story and then I am going to ask you some questions about it. Some boys went to an orchard and stole some fruit. They ate the fruit and then started home. On the way home they came to a bridge. The bridge broke and the boys fell. Now tell me, why did the bridge break?

Regardless of whether the child gave to this question (question 1) a naturalistic answer or an answer indicating a belief in moral realism, the child was next asked (question 2) "Did the bridge know that the boys had been stealing?"

If the answer to question 1 had been naturalistic, such as "The boys were too heavy," or "The bridge was old," and if the answer to question 2 was "no," then no further questions were asked. Such a record was classified as naturalistic.

If the answer to question 2 was "yes" (*i. e.,* the bridge knew the boys had been stealing) then we asked further, "Is that why the bridge broke?" If the answer to this question was "yes," and if the answer to question 1 had been to the effect that the bridge broke because the boys stole, then no further questions were asked, and the subject was classified as animistic in this examination. (More than animism is involved, but this word is used as a shorthand term for the belief that the bridge knew of the misdemeanor and that the breaking of the bridge was a form of punishment.)

In the few cases in which answers to questions 1 and 3 appeared to contradict each other, the child was asked a final question, "Now tell me, what do you really believe? Why did the bridge break?" These cases were classified on the basis of this last answer. In the 98 sets of responses, there were 25 such papers. In other words, the majority of the children gave consistent clear-cut answers.

As is usual in his work, Piaget in reporting interviews similar to the one described above does not tell the number of cases which he questioned at any age level. However, he does report that one of his collaborators, Mlle. Rambert (16, 251), questioned a total of 167 children between ages 6 and 12. Of the eleven- and twelve-year-olds (numbers not stated) 34 per cent gave answers indicating moral realism.

The chief data on white subjects available for comparison with our Hopi results are those of Lerner (10). Lerner used an analogous but not an identical procedure. His oldest subjects ranged approximately from 10.0 to 12.0 years. Thus they were younger than our youngest subjects. Nevertheless, Hopi subjects aged 12.0 to 13.9 years gave a larger percentage of animistic responses than did Lerner's ten- and eleven-year-old subjects. While the percentage of animistic answers among the youngest Hopi subjects was 64, the percentage of animistic responses among the ten- and eleven-year-olds in Lerner's area A, an underprivileged area, was 31; in his high socio-economic area, area B, it was only 15. The 64-per-cent record of the Hopi twelve- and thirteen-year-olds is almost exactly equivalent to that of Lerner's six- and seven-year-olds from the more favorable environment and is approximately equivalent to that of Piaget's eight-year-olds.

The moral realism of the Hopi subjects decreased markedly with age. Among the fourteen- and fifteen-year-olds it was 47 per cent of the total answers; among the sixteen- and seventeen-year-olds it was only 9 per cent. The numbers of subjects involved in the three Hopi groups were respectively 44, 32, and 22. Only five subjects failed to give classifiable answers, and these five were scattered among all three age groups.

In this connection it is interesting to note that Abel (1) has found a high degree of moral realism among institutionalized feeble-minded girls of ages 15 to 21. Eighty-five per cent of her subjects showed a belief in immanent punishment. The moral realism of these defective subjects was much greater than that of our Hopi subjects of comparable chronological ages.

DISCUSSION

The results presented in this paper show that twelve- and thirteen-year-old Hopi children, in comparison with white children of average intelligence and of the same age level as the Hopi subjects, much more often have concepts characteristic of the first two stages of animism, much more often attribute consciousness to inanimate objects, much more often believe that a bridge may break because of childish misdeeds, and much more often believe that the bridge is conscious of these misdeeds. The comparisons between Hopi and white children of greater age than thirteen years are less complete but are in the same direction. For brevity, we shall refer to these differences as differences in animism, although it is understood that not all of the differences have reference to animism in its strictest sense.

It is known that mental retardation causes animistic ideas, and also moral realism, to persist to advanced chronological ages (1, 8, 9, 17, 23). Therefore, the question must be raised as to whether the greater animism of Hopi children in comparison with white children is due to a native difference in intelligence. This theory is difficult to test, since the Hopi would obviously have an environmental handicap in most mental tests and hence an observed difference could not be attributed to native inferiority. Foreseeing this weakness in most intelligence tests as applied to primitive groups, we chose to test Hopi children by means of the Goodenough Draw-a-man test, believing that this test would place the Hopi at little or no disadvantage. In line with our guess, we found that on this test Hopi children show no inferiority to white norms (5). The Hopi boys, in fact, are superior to white norms. There is no indication of a native inferiority in intelligence on the part of the Hopi, and an explanation of their more extensive animism cannot be given in terms of low intelligence.

The explanation must, therefore, be sought in terms of environment, and no doubt in the cultural environment rather than in terms of the physical environment. The differences in social environment between the Hopi child and the white American child are numerous. Since we cannot vary these social factors one at a time, we cannot find which ones are contributing to the difference in animism. It is very likely that several cultural factors are reinforcing each other. For one thing, the Hopi have a simple material culture, whereas American material culture is the most mechanized in the world. This difference in acquaintance with mechanical artifacts may affect the development of animistic ideas. Furthermore, apart from mechanics, the American culture has a tradition for naturalistic explanation of events, whereas in Hopi culture the naturalistic, the magical, and the supernatural are seldom separated (13). Even the cultivating of corn has animistic as well as naturalistic elements for the Hopi (7). We may mention also the fact that the Hopi subjects were bilingual, while most of the white subjects were monolingual. The effort involved in learning two languages may very well cause the child to be preoccupied with linguistic problems to such an extent as to preclude much attention to natural-science explanations. There is also the pertinent fact that the adult concept itself attributes life very widely, and this fact may make it difficult for the Hopi child to discover his error. These suggestions do not exhaust the possibilities of accounting for the Hopi-white differences which we have observed but merely serve to call attention to the complexity of the problem. At the present time we can see little likelihood of our being able to isolate the various factors which may be involved. It should be noted that at Zuni, which possesses a culture closely related to the Hopi, a high degree of child animism has also been observed (6).

Attention to the differences in the extent of animism between Hopi and white children should not cause us to overlook a fact which is probably more important. This is that the animistic answers, while not equal in frequency in the two societies, were identical in kind. We found practically no answers among the Hopi which are not common among white children. While we did not test very young Hopi children, the facts presented concerning older children indicate that probably Hopi and white children at all ages possess the same types of pre-adult ideas, but that white children give up these childish ideas at a faster rate than do the Hopi.

It is doubtful that the earliest ideas of children differ at all from society to society. The early childhood notions of the sort described by Piaget probably are world-wide. It is likely that they develop out of universal experiences, such as the experiences of self-movement, of visual movement, of frustration and success, of sleeping and waking—experiences which are common to the children of all societies. As we have argued elsewhere (4), it would seem that these ideas are autogenous, *i. e.,* developed by each individual independently of communication with others. Society affects the fate of these ideas, but not their origin.

One piece of research needs to be examined in detail because it seems to contradict the hypothesis just advanced. We refer to the study by Mead (12) which concluded that animism is absent among the Manus children of the Admiralty Islands. Mead therefore proposed that child animism is the outcome of certain kinds of cultural influences.

We cannot accept Mead's finding that animism is absent among Manus children because we believe her methods of attempting to discover it were unsatisfactory. In justice to Mead it should be pointed out that her field work was done in the winter of 1928–29, before the appearance of Piaget's *Child's Conception of the World,* on which the recent research on animism has been based.

Mead presented four types of evidence for the absence of animistic thought among the Manus children. We shall describe each of these and then comment briefly on each. (*a*) Mead found that Manus children did not spontaneously construct animistic explanations of natural phenomena in play and in ordinary life situations. Piaget has not used this method because children's explanations are seldom stated clearly or fully unless they are brought to light by the questioning of the investigator. (*b*) In a large series of drawings, there were no personified natural phenomena or humanized inanimate objects; neither are there in the drawings of Hopi children, who are very animistic. The child has no way of expressing in a drawing the fact that the object pictured is alive. Mead has here confused animism with personification. (*c*) No animistic responses were given to ink-blot tests. It is difficullt to see how animistic ideas could be expressed in this connection. If a child in Stage I says a blot looks like a table, he does not volunteer that the table is alive: to the child that is taken for granted. Questioning is necessary to elicit such information. (*d*) Various tests were used, none of these identical with Piaget's procedures. They were concerned with the following things: (1) the attribution of malicious intent to a canoe which was drifting away; (2) the attribution of communication to Chinese glass chimes; (3) the explanation of the movements of a doll; (4) the attribution of malicious intent to a pencil with which the child had made a poor drawing; (5) the explanation of the action of a typewriter;

(6) the explanation of the opening of Japanese paper flowers placed in water. These tests would seem more appropriate for the investigation of notions of causality (15) than they are for the study of animism. We need not discuss these situations in full. We need only remark that it appears that not once was a child asked the direct question, "Is this living or is it dead?" Since Piaget's methods were not used, there is no evidence that his methods would reveal an absence of animism among Manus children. Mead's results, therefore, do not negate our hypothesis.

SUMMARY

Ninety-eight Hopi children between the ages of twelve and eighteen years were given a standardized interview with respect to animism and also a standardized interview with regard to moral realism, and 69 of them were further questioned with respect to the attribution of consciousness to objects. The Hopi subjects were more animistic and expressed more belief in the consciousness of objects and in moral realism than do white American subjects of the same ages. The concepts of the Hopi children, however, are of the same types as those found among white children.

It is proposed that the differences in the rate at which early ideas are abandoned in Hopi and white communities may be due to a variety of cultural factors which at present cannot be separated.

It is further proposed that the earliest ideas of children are uniform in all societies and are the product of universal child experiences and of mental immaturity. Mead's evidence which is apparently contradictory to this hypothesis has been analyzed and has been shown to be inconclusive, since the evidence was not derived by the use of the methods which have been employed by Piaget and others.

BIBLIOGRAPHY

1. ABEL, T. M. Moral judgments among subnormals. This JOURNAL, 1941, 36, 378–392.
2. BEAGLEHOLE, E., & BEAGLEHOLE, P. Hopi of Second Mesa. *Mem. Amer. anthrop. Ass.*, 1935, 44. Pp. 65.
3. DENNIS, W. *The Hopi child.* New York: Appleton-Century, 1940.
4. DENNIS, W. Piaget's questions applied to a child of known environment. *J. genet. Psychol.*, 1942, 60, 307–320.
5. DENNIS, W. The performance of Hopi children on Goodenough's draw-a-man test. *J. comp. Psychol.* (in press).
6. DENNIS, W., & RUSSELL, R. W. Piaget's questions applied to Zuni children. *Child Develpm.*, 1940, 11, 181–187.
7. FORDE, C. D. Hopi agriculture and land ownership. *J. roy. anthrop. Inst.*, 1931, 61, 357–405.

8. GRANICH, L. A qualitative analysis of concepts in mentally deficient schoolboys. *Arch. Psychol., N. Y.,* 1940, No. 251.
9. LANE, E. B., & KINDER, E. F. Relativism in thinking of subnormal subjects as measured by certain of Piaget's tests. *J. genet. Psychol.,* 1939, **54,** 107–118.
10. LERNER, E. *Constraint areas and the moral judgment of children.* Menasha, Wis.: Banta Publ. Co., 1937.
11. LERNER, E. Observations sur le raisonnement moral de l'enfant. (*Cahiers pédegog. exper. et psychol. de l'enfant,* No. 11.) Geneva: Palia Wilson, 1938.
12. MEAD, M. An investigation of the thought of primitive children with special reference to animism. *J. roy. anthrop. Inst.,* 1932, **62,** 173–190.
13. PARSONS, E. C. *Pueblo Indian religion.* (2 vols.) Chicago: Univ. Chicago Press, 1939.
14. PIAGET, J. *The child's conception of the world.* New York: Harcourt, Brace, 1929.
15. PIAGET, J. *The child's conception of physical causality.* New York: Harcourt, Brace, 1930.
16. PIAGET, J. *The moral judgment of the child.* New York: Harcourt, Brace, 1932.
17. PROTHRO, E. T. Egocentrism and abstraction in children and in adult aments. *Amer. J. Psychol.* (in press).
18. RUSSELL, R. W. Studies in animism: II. The development of animism. *J. genet. Psychol.,* 1940, **56,** 353–366.
19. RUSSELL, R. W. Studies in animism: IV. An investigation of concepts allied to animism. *J. genet. Psychol.,* 1940, **57,** 83–91.
20. RUSSELL, R. W. Studies in animism: V. Animism in older children. *J. genet. Psychol.,* 1942, **60,** 329–335.
21. RUSSELL, R. W., & DENNIS, W. Studies in animism: I. A standardized procedure for the investigation of animism. *J. genet. Psychol.,* 1939, **55,** 389–400.
22. RUSSELL, R. W., & DENNIS, W. Note concerning the procedure employed in investigating child animism. *J. genet. Psychol.,* 1941, **58,** 424–425.
23. RUSSELL, R. W., DENNIS, W., & ASH, F. E. Studies in animism: III. Animism in feeble-minded subjects. *J. genet. Psychol.,* 1940, **57,** 57–63.
24. SIMMONS, L. W. (Ed.) *Sun Chief.* New Haven: Yale Univ. Press, 1942.

THE PERFORMANCE OF HOPI CHILDREN ON THE GOODENOUGH DRAW-A-MAN-TEST[1]

WAYNE DENNIS

Louisiana State University

Received April 17, 1942

INTRODUCTION

With monotonous regularity it has been found that white American subjects make higher average scores on tests devised by American psychologists than do the members of other ethnic groups. We no longer interpret such results as a proof of our own hereditary superiority. Nowadays, in all modesty we take our high scores as an indication only of our cultural and educational superiority. In view of the number of group comparisons which have favored white American subjects, it may be of interest to report that some groups can make better scores than ourselves on one of our own tests. The test is the Goodenough Draw-a-man Test; the people tested are the Hopi Indians, though it is likely that many other Southwestern Pueblo groups can do as well as the Hopi.

The Draw-a-man test suggests itself for use with other cultural groups because the subject to be drawn is universal, the materials needed are few and simple and the instructions are easily comprehended.

We have been interested in examining the performance of Hopi Indian children on the Goodenough test because we feel that Hopi children are under little or no environmental handicap with regard to this test. Practically all Hopi children of between six and ten years of age, the age levels with which we are here concerned, attend government day schools. Pencils and paper are provided by the school, and drawing is one of the favorite activities. For pupils at these age levels there are no special art teachers, although instruction in various arts is offered to higher age groups. For young Hopi children, drawing is a recreational activity, engaged in with little or no comment from the teacher, except that the teacher commonly exhibits in her classroom those pictures which she considers to be the best. The objects most commonly drawn by the lower grade pupils are, we believe, houses and animals rather than human figures.

The general cultural background is probably of more importance to performance in the test than the school situation. The Hopi have engaged in graphic arts for centuries. Their pottery, which is among the finest produced by American Indians, is very skillfully decorated, both naturalistic and symbolic designs being employed. Ceremonial objects, also a part of Hopi culture for centuries, are painted and great care is exercised in the execution of the designs. The preparation of ceremonial masks for use in the native dances is of great

[1] The collection of the data for this study was made possible by a grant-in-aid from the Social Science Research Council. To Mr. Carson Ryan, Principal of the Hopi Schools, and to the teachers of the Hopi Schools, we are indebted for their whole-heated cooperation. Miss Gertrude Marill assisted in the scoring of the tests and in the statistical analysis.

importance. Kachina dolls, carved from cottonwood, are meticulously decorated to indicate the features and the dress of the kachinas or masked dancers. Every child possesses several of these dolls and learns at an early age to recognize the distinctive characteristics of each (3).

Contact with Western civilization, especially within the past twenty-five years, has strengthened rather than weakened the Pueblo interest in art. The handicrafts of the Pueblo peoples have been appreciated by the white man and a widespread interest in Southwestern Indian art has been awakened. This has had a direct economic value to the Pueblos since it has meant better sales for their pottery, weavings, jewelry and other handicraft products. Several Southwestern Indian painters have received national recognition. Among the better-known of the Hopi artists is Fred Kabotie, now an art instructor in the Hopi High School. Several Hopi High School boys are preparing themselves for engaging in professional art work, either on a part-time or a full-time basis.

But graphic art is almost entirely a masculine activity in Hopi culture. Only men may manufacture ceremonial articles and only men may decorate them. Kachina dolls are carved and painted by men only. Even pottery, which is made by women, is decorated primarily by men. This is the traditional division of labor in pottery making and it is adhered to at the present time. There are no women artists, and practically no girls elect to take courses in sketching and painting at the Hopi High School.

SUBJECTS AND PROCEDURE

The Draw-a-man test was given to the entire school attendance of First Mesa and Third Mesa. Time did not permit us to test the children of Second Mesa or of Moenkopi. First Mesa and Third Mesa were selected because the enrollment of these schools is larger than the enrollment of the schools of Second Mesa, and hence time spent in testing brought a larger return. There is no reason to suppose that the schools not tested would yield results different from the schools in which the test was applied.

All Hopi children are required to enter school at six years, and practically all attend until they reach the age of ten years. During the period at which our testing was done, December 15 to December 22, 1941, attendance for these ages was almost perfect. We tested, therefore practically every child on the two mesas mentioned above who was between the ages of six and ten years inclusive. In fact, we tested not only this age range, but the entire school population. However, only those from age six through ten are included in the present analysis, since the Goodenough norms for older ages are of doubtful significance.

Goodenough's procedure was rigidly adhered to in obtaining the drawings. The present writer did the testing. He remained in the room at all times while the drawings were being made in order to insure that the teacher made no suggestions to the children and in order to rule out the possibility that the children might help each other.

The teachers had been informed in advance that the writer wished to give some simple tests to the children, but the nature of the tests was not disclosed.

The writer is convinced that the teachers did not in any way coach or prepare pupils for the test. The Oraibi school was tested on December 15, the Hotavila school on December 19, and the Polacca school on December 22, 1941.

The age of each child was obtained from the school records. The date of birth which appears in these records is derived from the report of a government nurse to whom all births must be reported. The ages, therefore, are highly accurate. Within the age limits of this study, 152 children were tested. These comprised 77 boys and 75 girls.

RESULTS

The entire group yielded an average I.Q. of 108.3, with a standard deviation of 23.3. The range was from 64 to 185.

Analysis of the data reveals a marked difference between the girls and the boys. The girls averaged 99.5 (S.D. 18.9); the boys averaged 116.6 (S.D. 20.1). A difference of 17 points between samples of this size is, of course, highly reliable (C.R. = 5).

The difference between the boys and girls becomes more marked with age. If we divide the subjects of each sex into two convenient age groups (6.0–8.49, 8.5–10.99) we find that the average I.Q of the girls decreases with age, the two averages being 104.2 and 96.5. The I.Q. of the boys, on the other hand, increases with age, being at the two age levels 111.5 and 122.9 respectively. Because of the small numbers involved when the subjects of either sex are divided into two age groups, these age trends are not quite reliable, but we believe they would be maintained if more subjects were tested. Attention is called to the fact that the results for the older Hopi boys are higher than have yet been reported for any white children, even for selected groups.

The explanation of the sex differences in the Hopi subjects is no doubt to be found in cultural factors. As we indicated earlier, the decoration of pottery and the painting of ceremonial objects are masculine occupations among the Hopi. That the sex difference in scores is due to environmental influences seems scarcely to be questioned, since Goodenough (5) has found that among white children the sex difference is much smaller and moreover, it is in the opposite direction, white girls exceeding white boys by approximately four I.Q. points. The difference between the Hopi boys and the corresponding white standards is also probably cultural in origin. If sex differences within a single culture may amount to 17 points, it seems entirely reasonable that a difference between two distinct cultures might be equally large.

The three schools which were tested did not differ significantly. The Polacca school averaged 113.2, the Oraibi school 106.1, and the Hotevila school 105.2. The latter two are the Third Mesa schools, the former enrolls all of the children of First Mesa. The critical ratio of the difference between the combined Third Mesa schools and the Polacca school is 2.

Since there are approximately only 30 Hopi drawings at each of the five age levels, it is difficult to compare Hopi drawings with drawings of other children of the same age. However, with due respect to the inadequacy of the number of cases involved, we have compared the separate age groups of white and Hopi children in a few respects. The white data are those for Goodenough's "normal" groups as shown on pages 24 and 25 of her monograph (5). The percentages of Hopi children of various ages depicting arms, trunk and neck were substantially the same as the percentages of white American children representing these items, and both Hopi and white American children were close to the performance of Partridge's English group as reported by Goodenough (5). The Hopi children, however, exceeded the white subjects in the representation of hair and in employing profile drawings items (8a 18a). The latter comparisons are shown in detail in table 1. The high proportion of Hopi subjects representing hair is understandable in terms of the importance of hair-dressing in Pueblo culture. For the high frequency of profile drawings, however, we have no explanation to suggest. It will be noticed that table 1 also shows that the heel is represented

TABLE 1

Representation of items at various ages

	AGE				
	6	7	8	9	10
Hair					
Hopi subjects	41	75	88	75	86
Goodenough's subjects	16	22	45	45	58
Profile					
Hopi subjects	11	11	35	46	53
Goodenough's subjects	1	2	7	20	28
Heel					
Hopi subjects	15	19	31	33	33
Goodenough's subjects	10	18	37	52	66

somewhat less frequently by the older Hopi children than by the white children. This is probably due to the fact that Hopi shoes do not have an elevated heel; the most common way to represent the heel is to picture the heel of the shoe, and many of the drawings of the older Hopi subjects represent the traditional costume of the Hopi.

We have next to raise the question as to whether or not the Hopi drawings differ from the drawings of white American children in some way not reflected by the standardized scoring procedure. From careful inspection of the drawings we believe that the youngest age group in our sample, the six-year-olds, drew pictures few of which can be distinguished from drawings of six-year-old white American children. The drawings represented only generalized human figures and a few very widespread culture traits. By a culture trait we mean any article of human manufacture and any alteration or adornment of the human body, such as hairdress, piercing of ears, tattooing, etc. Only 9 of the 34 drawings of the six-year-olds represented one or more culture traits. Of these nine drawings, two showed a hat; one represented buttons (but no clothes); one indicated a belt; one portrayed belt plus shoes; one represented belt, buttons and pockets; one included hat and shoes; one depicted hat, belt and spurs; and one hat, belt and shoes. The remaining 25 pictures drawn by the six-year-olds did not represent any clothing, any hair style, or any other culture item.

The older age groups, however, showed a marked increase in the per cent which represented one or more culture traits, as is shown in table 2.

Not only do culture traits increase in frequency with age, but there is an increase in the number of drawings which are recognizable as representations of some fairly specific type of man. This fact is shown in table 3.

TABLE 2

Per cent of drawings in each age group which represented one or more culture traits

AGE GROUP	PER CENT REPRESENTING CULTURE TRAITS
6	26
7	59
8	88
9	92
10	97

TABLE 3

Number of drawings in each age group representing various culture types

AGE GROUP	NUMBER REPRESENTING				TOTAL
	Pueblo Indian	Western	Kachinas	Santa Claus	
6	0	0	0	0	0
7	1	2	0	0	3
8	4	3	0	0	7
9	3	0	1	4	8
10	7	4	1	1	13
Total........	15	9	2	5	31

It will be noted that among the six-year-olds no drawing is a recognizable representation of a member of some particular cultural group, whereas among the drawings of the ten-year-olds 13, or 36 per cent are so recognizable. Of the 31 drawings which portray specific types of men, 15 represent Pueblo Indians. No doubt nearly all of these were intended to represent Hopi Indians, but Hopi hair styles and Hopi dress are so similar to those of several other Pueblos that it would not be correct to label the pictures as peculiarly Hopi. Next to the Pueblo group in frequency were Western figures, chiefly cowboys, cattlemen and gunmen. Only two ceremonial dancers were pictured, probably because in December no dances were taking place. It is our guess that if the drawings had been collected in February and March, when ceremonies are a prominent part of native life, Kachinas would have been commonly chosen as the subjects of drawings. The five drawings of Santa Claus are accounted for by the season of the year and the fact that the teachers had been encouraging the production of such pictures.

DISCUSSION

Goodenough's Draw-a-man Test lends itself to use in an almost universal manner. While it has not been employed as extensively as one might expect in view of its adaptability, nevertheless, it has been applied to a variety of groups, including Eskimos (1), Aleuts (1), and Australian aborigines (11) as well as to diverse groups in the United States (6). Among the latter have been Negroes (6) and some American Indian groups (1, 6, 13).

In Goodenough's comparison of various racial and ethnic populations by means of the Draw-a-man test (6), she found that the California Japanese and California Chinese which she tested equalled the white norms, but that several other groups did not. She found that 69 California Negro children yielded an average only 78.7. Porteus (11) obtained an average I.Q. of 75.4 for 147 aboriginal Australian children.

Anderson and Eells (1) gave the draw-a-man test to 364 Eskimo children, with a resultant average of 89.6. It should be pointed out, however, that the majority of the Eskimo subjects were above the age of ten years. Anderson and Eells do not call attention to the fact that the subjects used by Goodenough for the standardization of the test were between the ages of four and ten years, inclusive. The norms above ten years are hypothetical, and hence many of the scores reported by Anderson and Eells are meaningless. By treating separately the youngest age groups reported by these authors, we find that the average I.Q. of 80 eight-, nine-, and ten-year-old children is 94.8.

Several American Indian groups, tested by means of the drawing test by other investigators, have scored considerably below the white norms. Goodenough (6) obtained for 79 Indian children in the Hoopa Valley (California) Reservation School an average I.Q. of 85.6. For 58 Alaskan Indian children, Anderson and Eells reported an average draw-a-man score of 91.6. Telford (13) gave the Goodenough test to 225 Indian children in North Dakota and found an average I.Q. of 88. Manuel and Hughes (10) testing Mexican children who are chiefly of Indian blood found them below white norms.

It is entirely possible that these groups failed to equal the white norms on the Goodenough because of lack of experience in making pencil drawings and because of their lack of a rich cultural background in pictorial representation of the human figure. The scores need not be taken as an indication of hereditary inferiority.

Although no group previously tested by means of the Goodenough test has scored higher than the white norms, non-white groups have outdone the standardization groups on several other tests. Some of the groups showing a performance better than white American children have been Indian groups. Klineberg (9) found that Indian children on the Yakima reservation equalled white children on the Knox cube test, and on four other tests of the Pintner-Paterson series the Indian children were more accurate, but slower than the whites. Telford (13) found twelve-year-old Indian children of the Indian School at at Wahpeton, North Dakota, (mostly Chippewa and Sioux) to exceed white children of the same age on the Mare and Foal test. The Indian children, in this case, were superior in speed as well as in accuracy. Jamieson and Sandiford (8) tested 41 southern Ontario Indian children with the Pintner-Paterson series and obtained a median I.Q. of 107.5. The same investigators found a median I.Q. of 101.0 for 155 children of the same group on the Pintner non-language test.

On the other hand, there are of course, many studies of Indian children, including the first study by Rowe (12), which reveal poorer test performances on the part of the Indian children than on the part of white children. Haught's study (7) is a recent instance of the same findings. These results should not be surprising in view of the fact that the tests were designed for white American children. Such results no more prove a native inferiority of the Indian than the present results prove a native inferiority of white subjects.

These results should not be interpreted as showing that the Goodenough test is unusually subject to environmental influences. All tests are inevitably subject to environmental influences. Nothing exists in the world which is impervious to its surroundings, and human reactions are no exception to this rule. The Goodenough test is probably less affected by cultural differences between groups than are most tests.

We wish to emphasize again one point previously mentioned in connection with the presentation of the results. We believe that the younger members of two cultural groups will show less differentiation than do the older members, and we believe that children's drawings provide an example of this law of increasing socio-differentiation with age.

SUMMARY

The Goodenough Draw-a-man Test was selected for use with Hopi children because it was felt that Hopi children suffer from no environmental handicaps in drawing performances. The test was administered to practically every child on First Mesa and on Second Mesa who was between the ages of six and ten years inclusive. The number tested was 75 girls and 77 boys, a total of 152.

The girls' average I.Q. was found to be 99.5, the boys' 116.6. The group as a whole averaged 108.3. The difference between the sexes is interpreted as due to the fact that graphic art is traditionally a masculine interest in Hopi culture, and that hence boys develop a greater interest in art and engage in more practice than do the girls. The test indicates no inferiority to white norms, even among the Hopi girls. The superiority of the Hopi boys is given a cultural interpretation. The results indicate that sex differences in social environment within a single group can produce a difference of 17 points on the Goodenough test.

It was found that the majority of the drawings of the six-year-olds showed generalized human figures. Only a few represented culture traits. By ten years of age, however, nearly every child's drawing represented culture traits, and roughly one-third of the subjects drew men whose group affiliation could be recognized. It is proposed that children's drawings show an increase in socio-differentiation with age.

REFERENCES

(1) ANDERSON, H. D., AND EELLS, W. C.: Alaska Natives: A Survey of Their Sociological and Educational Status. Stanford University, Calif.: Stanford University Press, 1935.
(2) DENNIS, W. Does culture appreciably affect patterns of infant behavior? J. Soc. Psychol., 1940, **12**, 305–317.
(3) DENNIS, W.: The Hopi Child. N. Y.: D. Appleton-Century Co., 1940.
(4) FITZGERALD, J. A., AND LUDEMAN, W. W.: The intelligence of Indian children. J. Comp. Psychol., 1926, **6**, 319–328.
(5) GOODENOUGH, F. L.: Measurement of Intelligence by Drawings. N. Y.: World Book Co., 1926.
(6) GOODENOUGH, F. L.: Racial differences in the intelligence of school children. J. Exper. Psychol., 1926, **9**, 388–397.
(7) HAUGHT, B. F.: Mental growth of the southwestern Indian. J. Appl. Psychol., 1934, **18**, 137–142.
(8) JAMIESON, E. AND SANDIFORD, P.: The mental capacity of Southern Ontario Indians. J. Educ. Psychol., 1928, **19**, 313–328, 536–551.
(9) KLINEBERG, O.: Racial differences in speed and accuracy. J. Abn. & Soc. Psychol. 1927, **22**, 273–277.
(10) MANUEL, H. T., AND HUGHES, L. S.: The intelligence and drawing ability of young Mexican children. J. Appl. Psychol., 1932, **16**, 382–387.
(11) PORTEUS, S. D.: The Psychology of a Primitive People. London: Edward Arnold Co., 1931.
(12) ROWE, E. C.: Five hundred forty-seven white and two hundred sixty-eight Indian children tested by the Binet-Simon tests. Ped. Sem., 1914, **21**, 343–368.
(13) TELFORD, C. W.: Test performance of full and mixed-blood North Dakota Indians. J. Comp. Psychol., 1932, **14**, 123–145.

ARE HOPI CHILDREN NONCOMPETITIVE?

WAYNE DENNIS

Brooklyn College

STUDIES of the Pueblo Indian peoples of Arizona and New Mexico uniformly report a minimum of overt displays of rivalry and a comparative lack of aggressiveness and of competition for prestige. The writer has been among those who have noted the relatively small amount of overt competition among one Pueblo group, namely, the Hopi (1). But a low incidence of public manifestations of competitive behavior need not imply the absence of competitive attitudes or of covert expressions of competition. To determine whether competitive behavior among Hopi children might not be elicited in situations in which their responses were not visible to their fellows, certain studies were conducted in the Hopi schools during the month of December, 1941. The two sets of data which were obtained will be called Study I and Study II.

STUDY I

In this study, a task was imposed in which it was possible to improve one's score by cheating. The test consisted of the "coordination tests" used by Hartshorne and May in their *Studies in Deceit* (2). The subject (*S*) is required to traverse printed mazes and to place marks within certain circles. He is asked to do these tasks with his eyes closed, but is not closely monitored so that he may readily open his eyes without apparent danger of detection. The upper limit of honest scores was determined by Hartshorne and May by using blindfolded *S*s. Pupils scoring above this cutting score are recorded as having cheated.

This test was administered at the Hopi high school to all boys and girls of the eighth grade and all boys of the seventh grade. A total of 40 *S*s were tested, using the standard instructions provided by the manual. Each *S* was required to place his name on his test booklet.

From the point of view of our present interest, the most important finding is that 40 per cent of the *S*s earned scores indicative of cheating. The average cheating score for the Hopi was somewhat below the averages presented by Hartshorne and May for three American groups made up of grades 5 to 8. However, the three American norms were exceeded respectively by 10 per cent, 25 per cent, and 33 per cent of the Hopi *S*s.

STUDY II

In this study, the *S*s were asked to indicate a preference for one of two alternatives in each of seven pairs of alternatives. These were:

  1. to be a boy
    or be a girl
  2. to be a man
    or be a woman
  3. to be as young as you are now
    or be grown up
  4. to be the tallest person in your class
    or be like most of the others
  5. to make the best grades in your class
    or make the same grades as most of the others
  6. to earn some money
    or have someone give you some money
  7. to run a race for a prize
    or run a race just for fun

Each student was required to place his name on his paper. While for the sake of completeness all seven questions have been presented above, in the present connection we will be interested primarily in questions 4, 5, and 7, in which one answer seems to imply a desire for prestige or for success in competition and the other does not. These questions were placed before groups of children in mimeographed form, the two alternatives of each question being on separate lines, as they are printed above. In addition, the questions were read aloud by the investigator. The *S*s were asked to indicate their preferences by underlining.

The *S*s consisted of all students attending the Hopi high school and all grade school pupils of First Mesa and Third Mesa in grades 4 through 7. After a few *S*s below ten years of age and a few above age 17 were excluded from the group, data from 180 *S*s (84 boys and 96 girls) remained.

The percentages of *S*s choosing certain answers are indicated below:

Response	Per Cent
to be tallest	
boys	20
girls	10
to make best grade	
boys	60
girls	79
to run for a prize	
boys	72
girls	63

It will be noted that a majority of both boys and girls indicated that they would prefer to make the best grades in their classes rather than make the same grades as the remainder of their class and would prefer to run a race for a prize rather than to run one for fun. Only a minority wished to be tallest.

For comparative purposes the same questions, with the same procedure, were presented to 250 children in comparable grades in a consolidated school in the suburbs of Charlottesville, Va. This group may, of course, not be a representative white American group. However, it is interesting to note that in regard to the questions cited above, fewer white than Hopi children gave the competitive answers cited above. The differences involved are significant at the .01 level.

99

DISCUSSION

In order to interpret findings such as ours, assumptions must be made concerning the motivation of the Ss. One may assume that the child who wishes to be tallest, wishes to make the best grades in his class, and wishes to run for a prize is competitive. Also one may assume that he who cheats on tests does so in order to make good scores in relation to his fellows. Such assumptions must be made both for the Hopi and the white Ss. The necessity for such assumptions seems inherent in all research on competition, if competition is defined in terms of inner attitudes. Such presuppositions are difficult if not impossible to test. However, there was nothing in the behavior of the Indian children to suggest that it should be interpreted differently from the comparable behavior of the white children.

In brief, there seems to be no reason to reject the conclusion that in the tasks which we set for them, the Hopi children behaved competitively, more competitively than some white children. Hopi culture is ordinarily described as cooperative, white American culture as competitive. Our findings may serve to illustrate the principle that one should be wary of interpreting cultural forms as indicators of individual motivation.

SUMMARY

In a study of Hopi children, a considerable proportion of the Ss apparently exhibited competitive behavior. In terms of scores for competition many Hopi Ss exceeded the mean scores of white groups. Although the Hopi traditionally play down overt expressions of competition, it appears that competitive behavior may nevertheless be elicited. The findings illustrate the hazard involved in assuming that traditional patterns of behavior provide a simple clue to the motivation of persons who display these patterns.

REFERENCES

1. DENNIS, W. *The Hopi child*. New York: Appleton-Century, 1940.
2. HARTSHORNE, H. S., & MAY, M. A. *Studies in deceit*. New York: Macmillan, 1928.

Received November 19, 1953.

INDEX